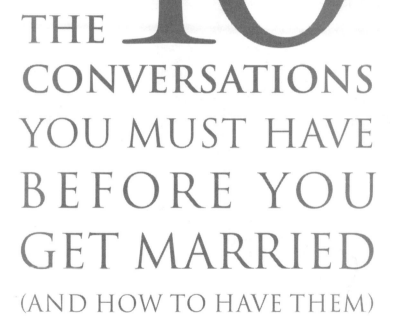

THE **10**

CONVERSATIONS

YOU MUST HAVE

BEFORE YOU

GET MARRIED

(AND HOW TO HAVE THEM)

THE 10 CONVERSATIONS YOU MUST HAVE BEFORE YOU GET MARRIED

(AND HOW TO HAVE THEM)

DR. GUY GRENIER

KEY PORTER BOOKS

Library and Archives Canada Cataloguing in Publication

Grenier, Guy, 1961–
    The 10 conversations you must have before you get married (and how to have them) / Guy Grenier.

ISBN 978-1-55470-067-7

    1. Marriage counselling. 2. Mate selection. 3. Couples. 4. Interpersonal communication.
I. Title. II. Title: The 10 conversations you must have before you get married.

HQ10.G755 2007   646.7'7   C2006-906435-0

ONTARIO ARTS COUNCIL
CONSEIL DES ARTS DE L'ONTARIO

The publisher gratefully acknowledges the support of the Canada Council for the Arts and the Ontario Arts Council for its publishing program. We acknowledge the support of the Government of Ontario through the Ontario Media Development Corporation's Ontario Book Initiative.

We acknowledge the financial support of the Government of Canada through the Book Publishing Industry Development Program (BPIDP) for our publishing activities.

Key Porter Books Limited
Six Adelaide Street East, Tenth Floor
Toronto, Ontario
Canada M5C 1H6

www.keyporter.com

Text design: Martin Gould
Electronic formatting: Jean Lightfoot Peters

Printed and bound in Canada

08 09 10 11 12 5 4 3 2 1

CONTENTS

INTRODUCTION

DESPITE REPORTS TO THE CONTRARY, the institution of marriage is alive and well (and frequently living in the suburbs). Alarming news of escalating divorce rates notwithstanding, research repeatedly shows that the vast majority of people want to be married and eventually get married. Even when marriage fails, the majority of divorced men and women want to get married again and usually do. Human beings are herd animals and social creatures, and we do better when we are coupled. People live longer when they're married. People tend to be happier when they are married. But in spite of these benefits, as a society we don't seem to be *doing marriage* as well as might be expected.

I have spent over two decades studying human behaviour and using what I have learned to help people determine if they have the capacity to be good for and to each other in a long-term, committed relationship. As a psychologist, marital therapist, sex therapist, and educator, I have seen every conceivable combination of couplings, both strong and weak. I am consistently astonished, however, at how many couples are willing to leave to fate, luck, or "relationship momentum" the outcome of their marital choice. I can confidently (and sadly) say that there are couples who have put more time and effort into selecting a car, a home theatre system, or even a cellphone than they ever did into seriously and sincerely looking at the strengths and weakness of their relationship before deciding to tie the knot.

Now, the necessity of learning more about a potential partner before deciding to marry is nothing new. We have the processes and institutions of dating, engagement, and even living together to help figure out if a couple can be good together. However, given the fact that as many as five marriages out of ten end in separation and divorce, we might rightly ask if these processes and institutions are really producing the results we were hoping for. For example, research on cohabiting couples demonstrates that living together does little if anything to ensure that couples are well suited to remain married in the long term: the data indicate that couples who cohabited before getting married are no more likely to stay married than are couples who didn't first live together!

Nobody wants to make a poor choice, and certainly no one willingly chooses the heartache, acrimony, financial setback, and stigma of separation and divorce. So what are we doing wrong? Why, when so many want to be coupled and choose to be coupled, are we seeing as many as half of our couplings fail? One answer might be that we are failing to learn enough about each other from the outset: perhaps we're not asking the right questions, or we're asking only the easy ones.

This book is about taking responsibility—responsibility for your own needs and your own happiness. This book is about convincing you that trusting your life to fate, providence, or good luck is a poor plan. This book is about facing adult realities. Healthy, long-term, sustaining relationships are neither accidents nor quirks of fate. Healthy, long-term, sustaining relationships are real and predictable, and they are something that can be manufactured. And the really good news is that if you know the manufacturing techniques and you start with good basic materials, you can actually produce one for yourself.

INSPIRATION

The initial idea for this book was generated many years ago when I was in graduate school, training to be a clinical psychologist. Interviewing Skills was a required course for anyone with aspirations to clinical practice. On the first day of Interviewing Skills, we, as a group of budding young twenty something psychologists were paired up in twosomes and told to start formally talking to each other. Over the next few months, we would go back and forth, asking and being asked questions. Each week, we would be given a new topic to investigate. Every interview had to be "real"—that is, a genuine topic of human experience—and we were expected to respond to questions in a truthful and sincere way. Only by so doing could our real abilities to extract important information be developed and, of course, evaluated. Videotapes of our interviews were required, and these tapes would be regularly, and often reluctantly, handed in to our instructors.

No one pursues training in clinical psychology because they think they are *poor* communicators. On the contrary, the hubris of youth, combined with perhaps a modicum of talent, led us all to believe that this particular graduate course would be a cakewalk. However, it became clear very quickly that there was a huge gulf between what we thought we knew and what we could actually demonstrate on a videotape. Those of us who fancied ourselves to be far ahead of the curve in terms of expression and listening skills—myself most especially—were alarmed and embarrassed to find that professional critique of our performance revealed we weren't in for the cakewalk that we had presumed. Apparently, we had a lot to learn about clear and efficient communication.

So my first point is this: believing you're a good and effective communicator may not translate into actual skill and expertise. Hardly a week goes by in my office that I don't interview a new couple who claims that they've always been great communicators and that few if any of their problems stem from a failure of expression or listening. Yet almost always, communication errors and missteps begin to emerge in the very first session—often within the first two or three minutes!

The second inspirational seed for this book was also a direct result of this same graduate experience. Interviewing Skills was a second-year course, which meant we, as a group, had already completed one year of clinical training in psychology together and were already pretty familiar with each other. Initially, I was paired up with a fellow student with whom I had become friends during the preceding year, and I felt I already knew quite a lot about my classmate.

I quickly learned how wrong I was. As we went through this series of formal interviews and structured conversations, it was amazing to me how much we didn't know about each other (as well as how much we were able to learn about each other in a short period of time). It was this experience that laid the foundation for my second point: the standard ways in which we get to know each other, while pleasant and elucidating, often fail to reveal much of what there is to know and quite possibly much that is relevant about our potential friends and partners, romantic or otherwise.

Thus, over twenty years ago, I came to realize that we, as a society, may not really be that good at sending and receiving messages, nor do we have our fingers on the pulse of how to get to know each other in a number of important ways. In the intervening years, I have discovered nothing to disabuse me of these notions. In fact, my experience with both patients and students has only reinforced the idea that *learning how to talk to each other* is a wise investment of time and effort. Similarly, *knowing what to talk about*, particularly if you are entertaining the idea of spending a lifetime with someone, is a second skill set that deserves some attention.

These experiences along with my subsequent work with countless individuals and couples have led me to believe that there are ten conversations you must have before you get married. Many of these conversations happen naturally over the course of dating and engagement, but some inevitably get missed, and a few get addressed only in a superficial way. In the following pages, I'm going to outline these ten conversations in sufficient detail and with the necessary checks and balances as to make them truly enlightening and useful in terms of choosing a life-long supporter and partner.

WHO CAN BENEFIT FROM THE 10 CONVERSATIONS?

If you are in a relationship or ever plan to be in one, this book has something for you.

That being said, I have written it primarily for couples who are fast approaching the point of long-term commitment. Few couples, no matter what their stage of commitment, are likely to have had all of these discussions in a formal way. Further, the fifteen rules of good communication outlined in the foundational chapter of this book apply to *all couples*, regardless of how long they've been together. The fifteen rules of good communication are the fundamental tenets of good, productive communication we ought to be teaching primary school children and then nurturing as they move through the educational system. In fact, on a number of occasions, clients have actually told me they benefited so much from learning the communications rules as adults that they immediately started teaching them to their children at home.

In addition, both individuals in a relationship ought to read this book.[1] A common agenda and a shared sense of the rules are

---

[1] I've written this book from a heterosexual perspective. This decision was made entirely to simplify the presentation of issues; it was *not* made to suggest that a heterosexual coupling is the only or correct constellation for adults to demonstrate their love and commitment to one another. The desire to be in a healthy and supportive relationship is entirely independent of sexual orientation and identity. Everything in *The 10 Conversations* applies to emotionally based relationships: if you experience emotion and want to be in a relationship, there is something here for you regardless of whom the subject of your attraction and affection might be.

going to reduce conflict and move things forward in efficient ways. It is also a demonstration of mature commitment to the partnering process. As an analogy, imagine trying to play a game where all the players aren't familiar with the rules or when they're being broken!

We've been taught since kindergarten that knowing and doing are often very different. When it comes to skilled communication and healthy relationships, quality information is good, but practice and experience are better. I'm going to outline for you the ten most important things the two of you need to talk about and how to talk about them. You, however, will have to apply the rules and engage one another.

How to Use *The 10 Conversations*

Completing the ten conversations won't be a chore. Most of what you will be talking about will be important, informative, and even entertaining. But serious and intense issues will also arise. Don't let this scare you. Getting used to dealing with important issues, intense or otherwise, is a part of marriage. And the more you do it, the better and more confident you become.

The purpose of the book is to get the two of you talking, and much of the book is designed to cue you to the issues that you need to talk about. If you follow the steps outlined below, you will maximize the benefits you can get from this book.

1. Agree that both of you are going to read *The 10 Conversations*. Sharing responsibilities for important relationship issues is a cornerstone of lasting, healthy relationships, so setting that tone and expectation right from the start is simply smart planning.

2. Scan the table of contents to get an idea of what we're going to cover and what you're in for.

3. Read "The 15 Rules of Good Communication." Go through it slowly and carefully. Become familiar with what productive rather than destructive communication looks and sounds like. During this process, talk to each other about which rules you are already familiar with, as well as the ones that might be more difficult for the two of you to follow. Talk about the rules by name and become familiar with good communication lingo. Every important pursuit, from medicine to gardening, has its own unique language—this simply aids in understanding and efficiency. Learning how to talk about how to talk to each other is an important pursuit and a skill all by itself. And, like most skills, it has its own words and descriptors.

4. When the two of you are comfortable with the fifteen rules of good communication, it's time to get the ten conversations started. The arrangement of conversations is very specific: some of the earlier ones are designed to help you with some of the later ones. I recommend you each read the conversations in the order I present, and at approximately the same time. You will quickly discover that each of the conversations has been broken down into a number of subissues, each clearly identified by subheadings. Further, almost every conversation has at least one case description adapted from my practice (look for "Realistically Speaking"[2]). These examples are there to highlight an issue, offer you ideas

---

[2] Throughout the book, I describe some of my patients. This humanizes and normalizes the issues we're working with—knowing our problems are similar to those that others have faced helps reduce our anxieties and gives us hope that we can find solutions. That being said, I have to come clean and acknowledge that *no* actual patient of mine is accurately described anywhere in these pages. Although all the presented issues are real, every presentation has been substantially altered and, in some circumstances, descriptions are actually amalgams of several people, couples, or issues. Of course, my purpose has not been to fictionalize or deceive but entirely to maintain the confidentiality my patients have come to expect. I have no doubt my readers fully appreciate this need for descriptive licence.

about how to work through a particularly difficult problem, or help you realize that some topics present challenges to a lot of couples.

After I present and discuss each of these issues, I pose a number of questions for the two of you to answer (look for "The Matter in Question"). These questions are to eliminate any awkwardness that might prevent you from tackling a challenging or delicate issue. They are also there to ensure that important components of a conversation are covered— but don't feel handcuffed by the questions. If there is some additional issue you want to explore within a conversation, knock yourselves out! When you're both finished reading, sit down at an agreed-upon time and place, and use the questions to initiate and fully explore a particular conversation.

The conversation is done when you *both* feel that all the important issues related to that conversation have been covered. This doesn't mean that you necessarily agree on every issue; rather, you are confident that you have a clear understanding of what your potential partner thinks and feels about that particular topic.

I can't make the two of you compatible. I can, however, allow you to determine for yourselves how compatible you are and, through your use of the fifteen rules of good communication, generate confidence that you have at least one mechanism from which you can work through challenging issues.

5. Allocate a few days to complete each conversation. The ten conversations are not intended to be a time-limited test or some kind of challenge to see who can win a debate. Instead, each provides an outline and a mechanism to ensure that you both investigate and negotiate what is important for each of you to build the long-lasting relationship you desire. Spending time thinking about what each of you wants, and returning to a conversation after you have given one another

time to digest what each has heard from the other, is just informed, mature communication practice.[3]

6. Each conversation recommends a movie that highlights some particular aspect of that topic. Use these movies not only as an excuse to have a date night, but also to generate discussion about each of the ten conversations. And you don't have to limit yourself to the question I propose with each recommendation—if there's something else in the movie that feels important, make sure you talk about that as well!

7. Don't forget about the "Troubleshooting" chapter at the end of the book. Like any troubleshooting section, it's there when the going gets tough or when the two of you are having trouble making the progress you want. This means that you don't have to wait until the end of the book to take advantage of it. Similarly, always feel free to return to the rules of communication to tweak your new communication superpowers or to identify and eliminate any poor communication habits that might creep back into your conversations.

I promise that if you complete *The 10 Conversations* as described above, you will know each other better and be more confident about the future the two of you can make. Further, if you apply the fifteen rules of good communication, I promise that your communications will be more efficient, less hurtful, and more focused on the matters that really count in your relationship.

It's a lot easier to establish an expectation for open and honest communication at the beginning of a relationship than it is

---

[3] Even if you think that you've already dealt with the topic of a conversation before reading the ten conversations, *do the chapter anyway!* I can't caution you enough about avoiding those toxic *unspoken expectations*. And if, in fact, you really *have* covered a conversation topic in appropriate detail, when you get to that particular conversation it will simply move along post-haste and you'll be left with the assurance that your instincts were correct. No downside to this!

somewhere farther down the road when the two of you have already developed bad habits. It gets harder and harder to change the quality of a relationship when things like lingering resentments and animosities have built up over weeks, months, and years. For some couples, these animosities are insurmountable. Consequently, it is never too early to learn how to be an effective, honest communicator and never too late to start exploring the issues that affect every couple.

THE 15 RULES OF
GOOD COMMUNICATION

EVERY RELATIONSHIP WILL HAVE ITS share of rough patches and relationship potholes—from time to time almost everyone will suffer an emotional flat tire or relationship bent axle. While we have yet to develop the ideal vehicle to allow the two of you to ride along in perfect comfort and security, we have come up with some pretty effective shock absorbers and safety devices that can smooth out the rough spots and decrease the chances of emotional injury. A clear understanding of the dos and don'ts of relationship communication represents the most robust emotional airbags and relationship bumpers you could ever acquire. What's more, even if you didn't have this equipment installed at the factory, the fifteen rules of good communication are compatible with absolutely every year and model of relationship! And if you'll allow me to stretch this metaphor just a little bit farther, the fifteen rules of good communication never wear out, and they have the potential to dramatically extend the life of your relationship.

But just before we get into the communication rules, let's look briefly at some of the most common communication problems as well as the components of relationship compatibility. See if you hear yourself, your partner, or your relationship in any of the examples below.

Fighting About the Fight

"You spend forever on the phone! I can never get through!"

"You don't know what you're talking about. You're the phone hog!"

"YOU'RE the phone hog, not me!"

"You're insane! I never spend as much time on the phone as you. Nobody can even get close to it because you spend all day sitting on your fat ass, wasting your time with stupid conversations!"

"You're a jerk!"

"You're a bitch!"

...and we're done. Excellent communication skill, lots accomplished, plenty of important information shared, new solutions offered, a greater level of understanding achieved, and both people feeling so much better about themselves and their relationship. For those of you who just heard yourself (or your partner) in this little dialogue, boy, is this chapter for you!

Although the exchange above demonstrates a lot of non-productive strategies, I want to use it to demonstrate "fighting about the fight." Fighting about the fight happens when *the way* something gets said becomes the object of the fight, instead of an actual issue. Time is wasted, feelings are hurt, and sometimes real damage is done to a relationship.

This kind of exchange was doomed to fail literally from the first word. The problem almost always starts when we try to tell someone else what *their* problem is, what it is *they* are doing wrong, or how *they* have caused something negative to happen. Think about this for a moment. How do any of us react when we are told we are wrong, to blame, or in error? We immediately become defensive, don't we? Even if we are actually guilty, being accused without fair trial, so to speak, gets our backs up, and we go into either defence or attack mode, neither of which is truly going to be useful.

If we go back to the above exchange, the problem that needs to be discussed is access to the phone, not who is using it at that particular moment. But the actual issue gets completely lost in insults and accusations. A legitimate issue was presented, but because it was presented badly, what could have been an opportunity for problem solving almost immediately degenerated.

Imagine if the above conversation started instead with a statement like, "I get so frustrated when I need to talk to you on the phone and I can't get through." No blame, no accusations, no fault—simply a statement of feeling followed by a statement of fact.

The point I want to make is that the *way* we say what is important to us is just as important as *what* we have to say. What's more, if we don't say what's important to us clearly and succinctly, we risk losing the opportunity to solve whatever problem we wanted to tackle in the first place.

RELATIONSHIP ICEBERGS

Although my clients have challenged me over the years with all manner of issues, it is the toxic *unspoken expectation* within a relationship that most commonly causes damage and heartache. By *unspoken expectation* I mean an idea or belief that seems almost blatantly obvious to one partner, yet remains unacknowledged, unrecognized, or minimized by the other. Over the years I have heard about thousands of unspoken expectations, and they run the gamut from the mundane to the bizarre. Examples of unspoken expectations include the idea *of course* she will want to stay home to look after the kids, *of course* he knows there will be a lot of travel in my career, *of course* she knows having sex twice a day is what I will always want, *of course* he knows my leisure activities are very expensive and will have to be budgeted for, etc. None of these expectations are unreasonable on their own. Nor is it a problem to have expectations of your partner. The relationship killer, however, is when these, or any other expectation, remain unsaid and unnegotiated. It's not that we might have expectations of those that we love, but rather that we presume, particularly when we are in love, that our partner automatically shares these expectations.

Unspoken expectations are to relationships what icebergs were to the Titanic: while there might be only a glimpse of them on the horizon, their power to destroy is hidden beneath the surface, is immense and unquestionable, and can puncture and sink what was thought to be impervious. The fifteen rules of good communication, and in fact the totality of this book, are specifically designed to help reveal these relationship-threatening icebergs long before they have an opportunity to breach the hull of what the two of you have together.

CONFLICT AS A FACT OF LIFE

Most people are *conflict avoidant*; that is, most of us prefer to avoid or minimize conflict with others. This is a natural, healthy, and expected way to be. Conflict is unpleasant, threatening, and stressful. Even litigators and others who argue for a living don't like being in conflict and take steps to avoid it whenever practical. Being conflict avoidant is a reasonable state and is actually a trait psychologists encourage.

That being said, we also have to face the reality that there will be times in our lives when conflict is going to be necessary. It borders on the irrational to believe that as we move through all the relationships and events of our lives, we will never be in conflict with anyone. If we accept the inevitability of interpersonal conflict, we could also rationally conclude that having the tools to move through conflict as expeditiously as possible would be a good thing. Please note, I'm *not* saying that avoiding conflict is going to be the right answer, but, rather, being able to move through conflict quickly and respectfully is the best plan. When we are willing to avoid conflict at all cost, we move from the rational *conflict avoidant* to the irrational *conflict intolerant*. Being unable to tolerate conflict means that a host of bad things happen, including swallowing personal feelings, needs, and desires, and this brings with it the highly toxic *lingering resentment*.

My discussion about conflict is here to make the point that *learning to deal with conflict* is going to be a much better strategy than allowing conflict intolerance to reach a point where your needs don't get recognized or accommodated. We don't have to like or encourage conflict to recognize the desirability of having good conflict-management tools. In a similar way, we keep a box of Band-Aids in the medicine cabinet, not because we hope to get hurt or because we are actively seeking opportunities to get hurt, but rather as a reasonable acknowledgement that sometimes accidents happen and it's better to be prepared.

Determining Compatibility

When it comes to enduring and satisfying marital relationships, everyone talks about "compatibility," but what does this really mean? Is there any way to quantify or break down this nebulous concept in a way that might provide direction or evaluation? Many marital theorists have taken a kick at this particular can, myself included. I'll contend that compatibility—how well two potential marital partners fit with each other—can be evaluated along three different dimensions: (1) love, (2) similarity, and (3) a healthy approach to conflict management.

Love
Regarding love, I'm a scientist, not a poet. Defining love is typically left to lyricists and romance writers, and perhaps rightly so. However, science does have a comment or two to offer on love. In fact, there is actual scientific research about how people experience love, the chemical changes that happen when someone is in love, the kinds of decisions people will make as a function of their love for someone else, and a host of other issues. For our purposes here, I want to draw your attention only to a couple of the general scientific findings about love and coupling.

There are good data to show that passionate love—the fireworks kind of love, the I'm-so-hot-for-you-I-have-to-be-with-you-or-I-think-I'm-going-to-die kind of love—typically has a shelf life. Now, we didn't really need science to tell us this. We all know this intense, head over heels, irrational flavour of love seldom lasts forever. Although many hope that passionate love of this type would last a lifetime, data from a variety of sources suggest that most couples can expect to feel this kind of love for each other for something like six to thirty months.

This little love factoid actually leads us to an important conclusion, at least as far as *The 10 Conversations* is concerned. It suggests that making lifetime commitments somewhere within this time frame might not be in everyone's best interests. Think of it as being akin to deciding to buy a house with a twenty-five-year mortgage when you're drunk. It doesn't mean you won't love the house and feel great about your choice in the future, but it does mean that all the important issues that could have been considered might not have been or, at best, were substantially distorted.

So science informs us that passionate love doesn't last forever, and we can surmise for ourselves that making important choices when we're experiencing that kind of love, while by no means fatal, might not always be in our best interests.

Here's the second thing science tells us about love. We have lots of data that show that when things go well in a relationship, the passionate love we were just talking about morphs into a more mature, less irrational, more stable, lasting love. If passionate love is about heat, mature love is about warmth. It is the warmth you feel for someone you can count on, for someone you feel you can trust, for someone who feels predictable to you and who shares your view of the world and the good and bad you both find there. Compatible couples will be those who both feel their love for each other evolve in this way. Having a realistic understanding of both the irrational qualities of early love and how this love changes over time will increase the chances that the two of you fall into the non-distressed couples category as opposed to the distressed couples category. Distressed couples far more frequently have unrealistic views of what love is and how love changes over time.

If I could, I would tell you how to determine if you love one another. Unfortunately, all I can realistically offer is a description of two of the most important flavours of love. Beyond that, all I can do is send you back to the poets and lyricists to see if what you are feeling for each other matches the myriad poetic descriptions of what love is about.

If, however, we take as a given that those reading this book have found someone they love and are willing to exercise appropriate caution when making lifelong commitments by taking into consideration how much their relationship has evolved, we can move to the next issue that warrants consideration from a compatibility perspective.

SIMILARITY

The second factor as far as compatibility goes is straightforward: *similarity*. Happily, I can give far more direction when it comes to evaluating this aspect of compatibility.

In assessing similarity, essentially we can ask if two people who love each other also think the same way, like the same things, share the same goals, and want the same things from life. It is this second quality of compatibility that ten of the twelve chapters of this book cover. Following this introduction and a discussion of the rules of communication, the two of you can begin to explore the ten most important issues any couple needs to examine as far as similarity in fundamental wants and needs is concerned.

PRODUCTIVE CONFLICT MANAGEMENT

The final component of compatibility is a *mutually beneficial conflict-management process*. No matter how similar a couple might see themselves as being, they won't agree on everything. To the extent that there is a well-understood, effective, fair, and mutually benefiting process in place that allows them to work through their differences, we have the final component of compatibility. The absence of this element, however, means that a couple will fear conflict because it seldom gets resolved in productive ways. When you fear conflict, you avoid it, but this leads to people swallowing their disquiet and anger, which then has the tendency to become a ticking time bomb in the relationship.

What is required is the skill and ability to talk—and potentially to fight—in a productive, meaningful way. Productive, meaningful conversations (or arguments) are ones that stay on track, focus on the important issues at hand, and ensure that both parties feel heard and understood at the conclusion of the process. And this is exactly what the fifteen rules of good communication are designed to do: allow two people to exchange information, even contentious information, in efficient, respectful, succinct, and accurate ways, and by so doing keep the focus on resolving a conflict rather than see it exacerbated by inefficient, disrespectful, rambling, and inaccurate discourse.

How to Use the 15 Rules of Good Communication

The communication strategies that follow are broken down into four basic categories:

1. Productive communication strategies

2. Destructive communication strategies

3. Anger-management strategies

4. Long-term relationship-management strategies

The rules are first presented on the next page as a basic list. They are also available in an abbreviated, printable version at www.drguy.ca/15rules. Ideally, you will post the rules in some visible and easily accessible place. This is done for three specific reasons:

1. Displaying the rules is an explicit commitment to the process of improved communication.

2. Displaying the rules acts as a reminder that you are both interested and willing to improve the way you share information with each other.

3. Displaying the rules makes them accessible, and thus they can be referred to easily.

Both of you ought to read over the rules and discuss them. In so doing, you will probably talk about which rules will be easy to follow and which ones may pose a particular challenge. This is a good strategy, as forewarned is forearmed. It also sets the stage for a good-faith commitment to good communicating. Learning to communicate well isn't that easy. It takes concentration, patience, and practice to develop this new skill, and these requirements are typically hard to come by, particularly when there is an inflammatory issue on the table. The entire purpose of the rules is to reduce how long an issue stays inflammatory. The more you use the rules, the more quickly you get to resolving problems and sharing feelings, which of course are two of the most important reasons for any communication.

Another part of this good-faith commitment involves the two of you learning to tolerate feedback from each other in terms of how well (or poorly) the rules are being followed. Again, this can be a serious challenge, particularly when things have become heated. But if you're interested in learning to do anything well, you will have to learn to tolerate feedback. This is true of learning a new job, learning to drive, or learning how to be a good communicator. So when your partner notices that you have been using "you" language or slipped in a couple of inappropriate superlatives, he or she calls you on these rule violations, and being able to hear this as constructive criticism and not as attack will be absolutely essential.

Being committed to the rules is not as important as being committed to each other and learning how to build a sustaining relationship together. Therefore you don't follow the rules because they are rules. You follow the rules because you are committed to the idea of improving communication with your partner.

In the next section, titled "The 15 Rules of Good Communication (Extended Version)," each rule is expanded upon to give detailed explanations on the tools for clear, effective, and productive communication. These tools are necessary for any couple to learn before having the ten conversations that follow, so I strongly suggest that you read the extended version carefully.

The rules are arranged in an order that increases the chances that the most common problems of communication are dealt with as early as possible. However, to be an effective communicator, ALL the rules must be assiduously applied. Through the application of these rules, exasperations like fighting about the fight, as well as a host of other communication blunders, can become a thing of the past, and the two of you can get on with building a happy and productive life together.

THE 15 RULES OF GOOD COMMUNICATION

Productive Communication Strategies

1. *Focus on feelings, not facts.*
2. *Sending messages: stick to what you know ("I" versus "you" language).*[4]
3. *Receiving messages: paraphrase or explain what you just heard.*
4. *Table the issues, but don't kitchen-sink (don't try to solve every problem in one conversation).*
5. *Use "the power of the Post-it," or remember to take turns.*
6. *Pick a good time to talk.*
7. *Use good body language.*

Destructive Communication Strategies

8. *Using absolutes (i.e., never, always, must, should, etc.).*
9. *Yelling.*
10. *Insults.*
11. *Mind reading.*

Anger-Control Strategies

12. *Keep anger on the clock (the 30-minute rule)*
13. *Take a time out: the 24-hour rule.*

Long-Term Relationship Maintenance Strategies

14. *Regularly indulge in w(h)ine time: connect with your partner for at least twenty minutes a day.*
15. *"How we doin'?" Ask your partner this question every couple of months for the rest of your lives.*

---

[4] The concepts of "I" language, paraphrasing, and kitchen-sinking have been around for many years and are not unique to this book. Anyone schooled in communication technique will be familiar with these concepts and their effectiveness.

THE 15 RULES OF GOOD COMMUNICATION (EXTENDED VERSION)

PRODUCTIVE COMMUNICATION STRATEGIES

We start with the seven "dos" of communication and then move to the four "don'ts." Some of the productive communication rules are easy to put in place (e.g., picking a good time to talk), while others are more challenging and typically require a degree of discipline (e.g., using "I" language and paraphrasing). And still others may demand a complete shift in mindset. In fact, we begin with just such a rule.

1. Focus on Feelings, Not Facts

The first of the fifteen rules of good communication sets the tone for *all important* discussions with your partner. For some, this rule seems counterintuitive. "Why would you want to focus on *feelings* rather than *facts*," they ask? "Facts are facts," they say. Facts are indisputable, empirical, rational, measurable, and testable. Facts make the world go round; facts get things done; facts are what you can count on. If you want to make an argument, if you want to set a standard, if you want to build a case, you build it on facts. Feelings don't have the kind of clout that facts have. Feelings come and go; feelings are different from one person to the next; feelings change with the wind; feelings are wishy-washy. You don't win an argument with feelings—you win it with facts.

No question, facts have it over feelings in a lot of different ways. In the physical, the legal, and the business world, facts *are* what's important. Start talking about feelings in the science lab, the boardroom, the construction site, and you'll get laughed out the door. In these arenas, feelings are not only less valuable than facts, but also a liability. Make emotional rather than rational choices, and you're not doing good science, good business, or good leadership. Let your feelings get in the way and you risk clouded judgement.

If all this is true—*and it is*—why do I take the position I do? How can I advocate feelings before facts?

Context is everything
Let's go back to first principles. While all I've said disparaging feelings and trumpeting facts is true, the truth of the superiority of facts over feelings applies only in certain contexts. For example, facts *are* what it's all about in science and business. An intimate trusting relationship however is a different world, a different context, a different part of our daily existence. Along with the worlds of science, business, and academics, there is also a social world, an intimate world.

We create the social world primarily because we are social creatures. We are herd animals. We like the company of others, we seek them out, and this isn't just about safety or food production or defence or some other empirically grounded issue. We simply prefer, and in fact we *feel better* in the company of others, and this is a very important reality. When we're with others, we feel safe, whether we actually are safe or not. When we're afraid, we seek the company of others, whether that removes the source of our fear or not. What's more, this *feeling reality* is not a weakness or detriment. The fact that we have feelings about others, and they have feelings about us, allows us to move through adversity with greater confidence and to take joy from individual and communal experiences. What we might save in costs isn't why we seek out a long-term relationship. We seek out a long-term relationship because of how it makes us feel and how we feel about the person we are in love with. The facts of a relationship and the facts of the person we are in love with play a role, but in terms of importance, they come somewhere after the feelings we have.

From this perspective, we could conclude that social relationships are more about feelings than they are about facts. We choose to be with people because we *like* it that way, not because people are *correct*. We choose to be with a particular person because of the way they make us feel, not because they're the right height or they have the appropriate eye colour (these facts, however, may have an influence on what we like). As a corollary, do you select a piece of music or hang a work of art on your wall because of its facts? Do you listen to the song because it has the right number of notes? Do you look at the painting because it contains the correct shade of blue? Unlikely. More probably, you enjoy the music and the painting because of the feelings they evoke. And how absurd would it be to argue about whether a particular song or painting was *correct?*

So, fundamentally, we choose to be with each other far more because of feelings than facts. It's not illogical to conclude that important conversations about being a couple also ought to be focused on feelings rather than facts. Of course, facts don't get left out of the process; they just aren't prioritized the way feelings are. We will be using facts to support feelings, to offer examples, and to strengthen a position we are trying to take. Remember, the rule is not to leave facts out of the communication process, but rather to demote them from being the most or only important thing there is to talk about. The reality is that when you're having an important conversation with your partner, your motivation will most often come from how you feel about an issue, not the facts of the issue.

Okay, at least within an intimate relationship, feelings are important, maybe more important than facts, but how do you *focus* on feelings when you're talking? What does a "feelings-focused communication" even sound like?

How to focus on feelings
Focusing on feelings isn't hard to do, though it doesn't come naturally to some. I'm reminded of a business executive I saw years ago. In our first session, he sat down and told me about a troubling family issue he was trying to deal with, and after his description of the circumstances, I asked him how he felt. He looked a little puzzled, but then shrugged and explained that his elbow was a bit sore, but aside from that, he was feeling fine. It took two more queries and an explanation of the role of emotions in dealing with

family members before I finally made it clear to him that I was interested in knowing about his emotions, his feelings about the family difficulty, not his physical health! As I said, talking about feelings doesn't necessarily come naturally to everyone.[5]

The easiest way to make any particular conversation a feeling-focused experience is for both parties to start every statement they make with an "I feel...[insert emotional label here]" statement. I know, I know, it sounds stupid, and there have been countless times when clients have mocked me when I have made this suggestion in session. On the other hand, you don't argue with success. Starting any important conversation or statement with an "I feel..." comment sets the tone for the rest of the conversation and reminds both parties that thinking about expressing their feelings on the issue is going to be at least as important as a mustering of facts. As silly as it may sound, using the "I feel..." technique really works.

There are, of course, the clever people out there who look for the loopholes and exceptions. Perhaps the most obvious misuse of a feeling-focused communication and the "I feel..." statement is the very clever, "Well, I feel...you're an idiot!" If this appeals to you, let me remind you about the good-faith aspect of learning to communicate well. As with any set of rules or laws, there is both a spirit and a letter of the law. Feel free (sorry!) to stick to the letter of the communication rules if it allows you to feel superior and clever and whatever else your ego needs. However, if you're interested in reducing tension and learning to communicate well, getting pedantic about the communication rules is not going to get you where you want to go.[6]

---

[5] Once our miscommunication about the meaning of feeling was cleared up, we made excellent progress. However, this client loved to kid me, and at the beginning of many of our subsequent sessions he would start with a description of all the aches and pains he was "feeling."

[6] And just so you know, the "I feel you're an idiot" statement is a violation of Rule 2, so actually it's not even that clever.

To quickly review, facts are important, but in intimate relationships, you need to be talking about feelings. You do this by ensuring every important thing you have to say starts with an "I feel..." statement, which might sound dumb but really works when you give it a try. And finding clever ways around using the rules is really just a waste of time.

Feelings are important, but...
Now that I've made the case for feelings and their importance, let me add a cautionary note: *while you always attend to feelings, you can never be too impressed by them.* There is no question that feelings are important, particularly when we're talking about intimate relationships, but feelings don't represent unchanging, immutable truths. Feelings change over time, change as a function of new experiences, and change as we mature. Feelings are the brain's descriptive statistics: they're the summary of previous experiences along with thoughts and abstractions. This makes them very valuable, *but* this doesn't make them truths. Feelings are important, but they are not sacred. This is why the rule is, *focus* on feeling rather than fact. To be clear, the rule isn't, focus *only* on feelings and *ignore* facts.

2. Sending Messages: Stick to What You Know ("I" versus "You" Language)[7]

Without doubt, this is the most useful of all the communication rules. No other single rule does more to improve how couples communicate. In fact, if you apply only one of the fifteen communication rules, let this be it.

Stick to what you know!
Any of you who have had any formal training in communication will already know about *"I" language*, as its benefits have been espoused by psychologists, mediators, and communication specialists for decades. Using "I" language essentially means three

---

[7] The mnemonic for this rule is IOU: I over you.

things: you stick to what you know, you take responsibility for what you say, and you do these first two things by actually using the word "I" at the beginning of your statements to indicate a personal position and personal truth. Essentially, using "I" language means you start any important statement with words like "I think..." or "I believe..." or "I feel..." (You can even get fancy if you want to and try statements like, "It is my contention that..." or "For me, the course of action would be...")

In essence, the use of "I" language means that when you have something important to say, you're not saying it as though it were an obvious truth or some proven scientific fact. Rather, you are tempering what you have to say and acknowledging that there might be other ways to think, feel, or believe but, at the same time, making a clear statement about your own thoughts and feelings. Who knew so much could be accomplished with such a simple technique?!

Let me offer a quick example. Consider the statement, "That was the wrong way to do that." While some might hear this as relatively innocuous, it will also be heard as definitive and absolute. There doesn't seem to be much room for negotiation or any other opinion, does there? Imagine that you are the person receiving the statement. In all likelihood, your first thoughts are going to be defensive rather than contemplative. From a communication point of view, how much goodwill do you imagine will be generated by absolute statements that leave little room for negotiation and make others feel defensive?

How to use "I" language
Now let's take the same statement and simply tack an "I" statement onto the front of the sentence. We get one of the following: "*I think* that was the wrong way to do that," or "*I believe* that was the wrong way to do that," or "*I feel* that was the wrong way to do that." Notice that a change in tone is immediately evident. What's more, the latter statements are all *more accurate* than the first, non-"I" language statement.

Until any of us are imbued with omniscient knowledge and we actually and truly know *everything there is to know in the universe*, anything that comes out of our mouths is, strictly speaking, just an opinion, regardless of how true we believe it to be. This is a particularly important point for those who pride themselves on their ability to speak rationally and objectively. If you have been using or continue to use anything other than "I" language, you have been overstating your case. When you stick to "I" language, however, what you have to say is essentially bulletproof. As the keeper of your thoughts and feelings, no one is in a better position to describe what you think and feel than you are, and no one can challenge you, with any kind of authority or veracity, on what you are saying.

Of course, if you want to, you can undermine productive communication by using "I" language in bad faith. Remember, "I" language is about taking ownership of what you have to say and sticking to what you *know*. This means focusing on your own thoughts, needs, desires, etc., rather than vindictively finding fault or purposely trying to insult, offend, or hurt someone else. While "I think only a moron could make such an idiotic statement"[8] is clearly an "I" statement, it's probably going to be less productive than saying, "I think there are flaws with that argument." Even really good rules will have exceptions. Rules like "Always use 'I' language" work far better within a general context of a good-faith commitment to improved communication, not a pedantic adherence to the letter rather than the spirit of the rule.

When you use the word "you," you're wrong...
The antithesis of "I" language is *"you" language*. There is so much wrong with "you" language I barely know where to start. "You" language happens when you use the word "you" and make an unequivocal statement about what you think someone else is

[8] Take a look at Rule 10 if your instincts frequently take you in this direction.

thinking, feeling, or believing, such as, "You think we should do it this way," or "You said this was the wrong way to do it," or "You always want to control me."

While "I" language leaves room for negotiation, "you" language is definitive and judging. While "I" language means taking ownership for what you have to say, "you" language is about dodging responsibility. But worst of all, while "I" language means you stick to what you know, "you" language is about leaving reality and entering the world of idle speculation, and it means you are talking about something you don't know. You don't *know* what someone else is thinking, feeling, or believing. If and when you use "you" language, you are wrong! Regardless of how long you've known them, how deep your connection may be, or how many profoundly moving experiences you have had with a person, you don't *know* what is going on in someone else's head. You might have a good idea; you might be able to take an educated guess; you might have a ton of past experience to go on—but when it comes right down to the reality of the situation, you *never know* what someone else is thinking, feeling, or believing! Until there is a physical data cable that connects your brain with someone else's, any "you" statement you make will be at best speculation and at worst completely off the mark.

In almost every circumstance, a "you" statement can be translated into a more accurate and productive "I" statement. For example, "You are always trying to control me!" is better stated as "I often feel controlled." The "you" statement "You don't understand me!" is better stated as "I don't feel well understood." The "you" statement "You're ugly and your mother dresses you funny" is better stated as "I need a drink and a time out." With some thought and patience, refocusing on what you are thinking and feeling rather than trying to guess at what you think someone else is thinking, feeling, or believing is going to be a better approach to communication, problem solving, and conflict management.

...except when used as a question

There are exceptions to even the best rules, and so it is with the "never use 'you' language" rule. In one particular circumstance, using the word "you" *is* entirely appropriate.

You get to use the word "you" when you want to ask a question. In the service of achieving clarity, clearing up misunderstandings, or paraphrasing (see Rule 3), asking the person you're talking to to restate their position or to help you understand what they think, feel, or believe is completely appropriate. For example, rather than saying, "You always think that way," you could *ask*, "What do you think?" Rather than saying, "You said the other day..." you could *ask*, "Tell me again what you said the other day." Rather than saying, "You're not making any sense," you could *say*, "I don't understand," and you could *ask*, "Could you tell me again what is important to you?"

Learning to talk in "I" language and to banish "you" language is difficult and takes practice. No one I have ever taught has got it right quickly or easily. The mental gymnastics of translating anything you want to say that has the word "you" in it into a modified statement that contains "I" means stopping and thinking about much of what you have to say, at least when you're first learning to do it. This leads to tremendous frustration, as people often feel they're not able to say what they want. Although this is entirely perception instead of reality, it doesn't change the feelings of frustration that people may have at the time. But the benefits of both of you learning to talk in "I" language far outweigh the difficulty of learning how to do it. It isn't an exaggeration to say that learning to talk in "I" language and to banish "you" language is the single most curative change a couple can make to improve their ability to communicate with each other.

3. Receiving Messages: Paraphrase or Explain What You Just Heard

If "I" language is the most important rule, *paraphrasing* is the most difficult. However, with this difficulty comes a guarantee: when couples assiduously use paraphrasing, it is impossible for a discussion or even a fight to get off track! Quite a bold statement, I know, but it is nevertheless true.

Paraphrasing means that you repeat aloud what your partner said to you *before* you provide your input, rejoinder, or point of view. The purpose of this technique is to ensure that the two of you are talking about the same thing. For example, he says, "I really hated going out for dinner last night." As a paraphrase, she says, "So you didn't feel like going out last night?" perhaps imagining that he was too tired or stressed to enjoy the meal.

While this is an excellent paraphrase, it turns out that it didn't actually capture what he was trying to say. What he was actually trying to say was that he resented feeling that they often go to restaurants that she chooses rather than the ones he might prefer. Obviously, this was not clearly expressed in his first statement, and the fact that she paraphrased means that he can clarify the real intent of his original message. He might respond, "No, I meant that I didn't like that restaurant and would have preferred we go somewhere else." By using paraphrasing, she showed him what she heard in his initial message but also allowed him to offer a clarifying statement that more closely resembled his feelings.

And this is the power and beauty of paraphrasing. Paraphrasing ensures that messages are clearly understood by both parties so little or no time is wasted fighting about misunderstandings.

When you paraphrase, you don't repeat what the other person said word for word or even at the same length; you put it in your own words and, ideally, as briefly as possible. Paraphrasing isn't a memory test—you restate as succinctly as possible the main point of what you just heard, not every single detail. However, there is no limit to the number of paraphrases that might be required for any particular point. When couples first start using paraphrasing, two, three, or more "back and forths" might be needed before it is clear that both people are on the same track, that the message has been clearly sent and understood.[9] If the rule concerning "I" language and "you" language is about sending messages, the rule concerning paraphrasing is about receiving them. And with these two rules we have represented both aspects of good communication: the need to send messages clearly and the need to receive—hear— them just as clearly.

Listening and thinking

Paraphrasing keeps things on track in two different ways: it requires that you *listen very carefully* to what is being said and, by demanding that you restate things in your own words, requires that you *think about and try to understand* what was said. There's really no downside to these two requirements, and it would be fair to wonder, with these two obvious benefits, why everyone doesn't paraphrase all the time.

The problem is that paraphrasing has the tendency to really slow down a communication with its demand to check (and potentially recheck) that both people are on the same page. This slowdown is experienced by many as frustrating in and of itself. And it can be particularly annoying when issues have become heated, and self-control and discipline are being sorely tested. Unfortunately, there is no quick remedy to this shortcoming of paraphrasing. But, as the old saying goes, anything worth doing is worth doing well. Remember, the long-term payoffs of paraphrasing are a dramatic decrease in anger and acrimony, and far fewer misunderstandings.

If you embrace the concept of paraphrasing, you learn to listen and, by definition, you learn to listen *well*. Remember, fifty percent of communication is listening. If you fail to listen, you're

---

[9] Using paraphrasing as an opportunity for mocking or mimicking the person who is talking is counterproductive, insensitive, and potentially damaging. Making fun of the way somebody said something or hiding behind paraphrasing to correct someone's usage or grammar has nothing to do with improving understanding and would simply be another example of bad-faith communication.

missing half of what is going on and you significantly increase the risk that *you're* the one singing "Empty Chairs."[10]

4. *Table the Issues, But Don't Kitchen-Sink*

We have talked about the most counterintuitive rule (1), the most useful rule (2), and the hardest rule (3). If Rule 4 has a distinction—beyond sounding like some arcane food preparation suggestion—it would be that it is the *scariest* of the communication rules. Rule 4 is about the most important yet challenging demand of good communication: honesty.

Being honest . . .
Tabling the issues means being honest. If you feel something, think something, or believe something, being honest about it is going to be the most useful direction to take. We could use other expressions to define this rule—such as "No pussyfooting around," "Get down to brass tacks," "Discus the bottom line," "Come clean on an issue," or a variety of other commonly used phrases—and if one of these works better for you, by all means use it, as they all essentially mean the same thing. The point here is that a focus on honesty is going to be required for anything that approaches good communication.

That honesty is the best policy is nothing new, and we're not going to beat this one to death. Suffice it to say that you're never going to make a life together if you operate under the assumption that you will always agree about everything, always feel the same way and with the same intensity about everything, and always have the same needs. Learning to deal with these differences is in fact one of the greatest challenges of building a healthy relationship.

Unfortunately, at least in some circles, there seems to be a growing list of things that we are *not* supposed to be honest

---

[10] Check out Don McLean's website for the lyrics to this song. (Don McLean is the guy who wrote and sang "American Pie.") His song "Empty Chairs" drives home the point of what can come of failing to listen to an intimate partner.

about. According to the politically correct, telling your partner that you find someone else sexually attractive is inappropriate. Expressing any thoughts, feelings, or needs that have a genderist quality is also a no-no, according to the politically correct. And don't even think about telling a partner that you think they've put on weight!

It seems to me that if you're interested in learning what you need to know about a partner so you can make an informed choice that will hopefully last a lifetime, you'd better be learning about what they *really* think and feel, and, conversely, they'd better be learning what you *really* think and feel. The idea that you remain honest in an important relationship *only up to the point* where it might hurt someone's feelings and then you back off is naïve. If it's important to you, you talk about it. If you think your partner drinks too much, you tell them. If you think they have a body odour problem, you tell them. Not telling them means being dishonest, potentially swallowing important feelings, and nurturing lingering resentments.

Of course, using "But I'm just being honest" to cover the fact that you're really interested only in hurting someone's feelings or winning an argument is another example of insensitivity and ego satisfaction, and is no different than using insults (see Rule 10). Equating honesty with a licence to hurt or insult is immature. If you find yourself in a relationship with someone who is an avid user of this communication technique, it's best simply to wait till this person grows up to have a conversation with them. In the interim, walk away.

. . . in measured doses

The second part of Rule 4, no "kitchen-sinking," is about limiting not *what* you talk about but *how much* you talk about. In important conversations, particularly those that have the potential to be volatile or intense it's best to limit that particular conversation to that *one particular issue*. Trying to solve more than one important problem at a time dramatically reduces the chances that anything productive will be accomplished. Better to limit the scope of any particular important conversation to one topic and stick to it. The term "kitchen-sinking" comes from some people's tendency to bring up every important issue they can think of and throw it into the mix—metaphorically, they throw in everything, including the kitchen sink.

Special note on Rule 4: Kitchen-sinking as "bait and switch"
Kitchen-sinking not only is a common mistake couples make, but also a strategy that some people use when they feel they are losing or might lose a particular argument. When it looks like they're losing ground or might not be able to defend their position any longer, the purposeful kitchen-sinker brings up some other issue (or insult), not so much because they honestly feel that headway can be made in resolving that issue as well, but because they need to derail the current conversation or argument. At best this is an immature strategy, but at worst it belies a need to win that is greater than a desire to work out a problem.

Being honest with each other while at the same time reining in thoughts and feelings so that a focus on a single important issue can be maintained is not a small challenge. Few communication rules epitomize better the idea that courage and discipline are two critical requirements of good communication.

5. Use "The Power of the Post-it," or Remember to Take Turns

Interrupting is perhaps the most common bad fighting habit, and that's saying something, given how common and how many bad fighting habits there are! We interrupt when we disagree, when we can't control our temper, when we don't think we're getting our fair share of air time, and when we're not paying attention. We interrupt when we don't respect the other person, or at least when we don't respect what they have to say. Interrupting happens when listening stops and self-indulgence steps in.

41

On a personal basis, you can effectively deal with interrupting by choosing to simply stop doing it. Bite your tongue (literally, if you have to), take a breath, focus your attention on what is being said, and wait your turn. How simple is that?

Of course, one of the small flaws with the above plan is the "wait your turn" part. Sometimes we, or the person we're fighting with, forget what should have been learned on the playground. In these circumstances, I like to invoke "the power of the Post-it":

1. Only the person holding the Post-it may speak.

2. You hold the Post-it for no more than three minutes, after which time it MUST be passed to the other person.

3. If you want to talk longer, you can ask to hold on to the Post-it, but only for three minutes at a time and only if the other person agrees.

This is a relatively easy rule since it simply represents a visual way of taking turns when you talk. Whoever holds the Post-it note has the right to speak. Because it seems a little childish, some couples feel they can skip this rule. Unfortunately, forgetting about taking turns (and using the power of the Post-it) means that when things get more emotionally heated, the opportunity to keep the conversation in the productive zone has been lost. (Office supplies as communication therapy—who knew?!)

6. Pick a Good Time to Talk

When you've got something important to talk about, give the issue the respect it deserves and set some time aside to talk about it. Trying to talk to your partner about something important when someone is watching TV, when someone needs to relax after a hard day, when the kids are running around, or when you have company over for an evening's entertainment are all examples of failing to pick a good time to talk.

The right time and place

Ideally, couple communication is a two-way street, with both participants engaged in the process. This means you are both *prepared* to have the important conversation. If both participants are going to bring their best and most considered thoughts and feelings to the table, both also had to have an expectation beforehand that this important conversation was going to take place.

"Putting your partner on notice" is an excellent communication technique. It means that when there is something important you want to talk about, rather than just ambushing your partner with your already-thought-out ideas, you let them know that there is an important issue you want to discuss and ask if they'd give that issue some consideration. You also ask them when they would be willing to have this important discussion. Putting them on notice might require a little bit of patience and discipline on your part, but this self-control will be well worth it.

Similarly, if you want to increase the chances that progress will be made when discussing an important issue, you also give thought to the environment in which the two of you are trying to talk. Trying to have an important conversation with the stereo blaring, when your desired degree of privacy may be compromised, or when your surroundings are full of distractions will likely lead to frustration. Structuring your environment or selecting a quiet place to talk goes hand in hand with putting your partner on notice.

Don't muddy the water

Don't try to have an important conversation when either or both of you have been drinking, smoking up, using 'shrooms, or indulging in any other mind-altering substance or procedure. Important conversations present sufficient challenge in and of themselves, and we don't need to contaminate the field with mood alterations or cognitive distortion. Alcohol has never, in my experience, improved the resolution of an important issue, so don't stack the deck against yourselves in this manner. If you find that by happenstance, however, you've wandered into an important discussion when you have been drinking (or smoking or whatever), call a spade a spade and explain that because you've been drinking (or smoking or whatever) what you might think or say is not necessarily going to be the best representation of what you really want or believe. If you want, you can even invoke the 24-rule (see Rule 13) if necessary. If you are in the United States when this happens, you could also plead the Fifth.

7. Use Good Body Language

Using good body language is a pretty obvious technique of good communication, but like so many of the above rules, it tends to get ignored over time.

We can all recall times when we have felt put out because we knew someone wasn't listening to us. We knew this not because of what they said, but because of how they held their body. Crossing your arms; looking away; listening to the radio, TV, or iPod; continuing to read a paper, magazine, book, recipe, instruction manual, etc.; rolling your eyes; huffing; grunting; and smirking are all examples of body language that is designed to send negative, disrespectful messages.

While body language can very effectively send a message, it is often an *indirect way* of sending a message. If you and your partner are going to be good communicators, you will want to use direct and clear ways of exchanging information, not techniques that are prone to misinterpretation or ones that allow someone to dodge responsibility for a message or feeling.

Good body language means looking at the person you're talking to. Good body language means orienting your frame toward the person you're talking to. Good body language means nodding your head to show you understand and are listening. Good body language means you express your negative feelings with words and explanations rather than just crossing your arms, rolling your eyes, or turning away.

Women are more on target than men

Although I'm not a big fan of explanations based in gender differences (primarily because the more we investigate these differences, the more we find they don't actually exist), there does seem to be some consistent research that indicates that women are better than are men at accurately reading body language. Rather than taking this as the truth, however, why not make it the subject of a discussion between the two of you? Describe to one another what you think you know about each other's body language and listen carefully to the conclusions each of you draws.

Being physically threatening is another form of body language. If you are with someone who tries to use this tactic, leave them until they grow up. If you are a person who uses physical threats to try to get your point across, get professional help to deal with your lack of maturity and your anger-management failures. Physical threats are a form of abuse and need never be tolerated.

DESTRUCTIVE COMMUNICATION STRATEGIES

These are the "don'ts" of communication. Unlike the seven rules described above, you want to do fewer and eventually none of the things described below. For good communication to happen, both the dos and the don'ts need to be attended to simultaneously. Think of it like driving a car: while you need the gas pedal to get somewhere, you also need the brakes to stay in control.

8. "Never" Use Absolutes (i.e., Never, Always, Must, Should, etc.)

Contradictions in the title aside, if you want to instantly lose an argument or immediately undermine the importance of what it is you are trying to say, use an absolute or superlative. Tell your partner they "always" do something, or that they "never" listen to you. Tell them what they "should" be doing, thinking, or feeling. Tell them what "everyone" "must" do, and the things that they do but "nobody else" "ever" does.

You lose when you use absolutes and superlatives because the person you're talking to simply has to come up with a single exception to your blanket statement, and now you're wrong. With one simple example of a time when they *were* listening or they *didn't* interrupt, you have lost your credibility. It's the same phenomenon so often portrayed in the TV legal dramas where the litigator finds one error or misrepresentation in what a witness has to say, and in so doing calls into question the totality of their testimony.

But let's be clear. It's not so much about credibility, or at least it shouldn't be, when you're talking to your partner; rather, it's about losing your focus on how to have a productive rather than a destructive discussion. Remember, for important conversations, you want to be focused on feelings rather than facts (Rule #1). Using absolutes or superlatives opens the door to a fact-focused, adversarial exchange rather than one that is feeling focused and cooperative. You'll find yourself "fighting about the fight" almost instantly when you use absolute statements ("You *always* say that!" "No, I don't!" "Yes, you do," and so on). As soon as a discussion descends into this territory, you might as well roll the videotape to find out exactly who said what, and then one of you can prove that the other was wrong. Excellent way to make progress, don't you think?

You want to replace any absolutes or superlatives you're tempted to use with "I"-based, feeling statements. Instead of saying, "You *always* interrupt me," which also breaks Rule 2, you could say, "I've been interrupted again, and that really frustrates me!" Instead of saying, "You *never* listen to me," try, "I'm not feeling heard," or even, "I get so angry when it feels like what I have to say gets minimized!" When you avoid absolutes, you dramatically increase the chances that the two of you will stay on track.

Special note on Rule 8: Don't should *on yourself and don't* should
on your partner
I think we ought to seriously consider having the word *should* banished from the English language. *Should* is a dumb concept.

Should is about guilt; *should* is about shame; *should* is about recrimination. *Should* makes us feel inadequate, stupid, and immature. *Should* is about superiority, judgement, arrogance, and condescension.

Should makes sense only if we have perfect data; that is, if we know everything there was and is to know. With perfect data, *should* starts to make sense, but in any other reality, including the one most of us live in, *should* is more likely to get us fighting about the fight than solving a problem. When we all have unlimited resources and time machines, we can all be held to the standard that *should* demands. Until that day, we might just have to muddle through with speculation and feelings.

Don't *should* on yourself. Try replacing *should* with statements like, "Next time, I'll try..." or "I choose to..." instead of "I should have done this or that." Don't *should* on your partner either. Replace "You should have done it this way," with statements like, "Perhaps if it had been done differently, maybe..." or "I would have preferred that..." *Shoulding* on anyone is really a waste of time and stinks up the process of good communication.

9. Yelling Doesn't Make It So

Everyone knows that yelling is bad, right? Well, maybe not so much. I'm going to try to make the case that, from a good communication perspective, yelling, while definitely not ideal, is not quite as bad as you might think and can actually be useful in some circumstances. Further, I'm going to try to convince you that the simplistic idea that yelling is always bad metaphorically paints some people into a communication corner where they end up feeling helpless and trapped. And after I've done all this and demonstrated that yelling is not the demon it's been made out to be, I'm going to suggest that if you do all the *other things* I've described in this chapter, the chances that you will actually need to yell will diminish over time anyway, so in the end very little if any yelling is necessary.

The bully yells

Let's start with "You shouldn't yell." Not a bad rule. Yelling is typically about bullying or trying to scare someone—and neither of those could be considered positive communication skills. If you really want to win someone's heart and mind, do you honestly think you're going to accomplish this by scaring them into adopting your point of view? Now, if you're interested only in doing the bully thing, or if you don't think your position can be sustained in any other way, go ahead and do the yelling thing. Just don't fool yourself into believing the person you've been yelling at really supports you. But if you're not looking for the support and understanding of the person you want to be in a long-term relationship with, why bother to communicate at all?

The insecure yells

Sometimes yelling is about winning. This is the "yelling makes it true" ideology. Nobody likes to lose, and sometimes a win at the cost of yelling feels better than a loss without the raised voice. But remember when mom or dad yelled at you? Remember how the louder they got, the more you believed them? Next.

The manipulative yells

Yelling might also be used to embarrass someone in a public place. This is just an immature, cheap shot. If you're interested in scoring points rather than solving a problem, keep this one up.

The excited yells

Occasionally, yelling is about getting too excited. Here, the problem is really about self-monitoring rather than bullying or winning at any cost. We can all be forgiven for getting too excited every now and then. Better self-monitoring is called for in these circumstances, however, because you're probably still not accomplishing what you think you are when you yell. Yelling in this circumstance is perhaps more forgivable but still ineffective.

An appropriate context for yelling?
Okay, so yelling is often a poor communication strategy, but is it *always* bad? Are there no circumstances where yelling might be okay or even, perish the thought, useful?

What about yelling in frustration or anger? This can't be good—or can it? We've all heard the message that we need to control our anger (and we do) and that we shouldn't let our anger "get the better of us" (and we ought not to). However, I'm going to make the case throughout this book that we ought to feel our feelings and that we ought to focus on feelings rather than facts. Frustration and anger are feelings, so shouldn't we be feeling and expressing them? I'll contend that this is where issues become a little less black and white and we might cut ourselves and our partners a bit of slack—not a lot, mind you, but maybe a little.

Perhaps if we thought of yelling as an exclamation point at the end of the sentence, we could find the utility in yelling. Imagine if you wanted to write an important story, a story that you felt strongly about, a story that really meant something to you, maybe even a story that, if it didn't get told, would leave you feeling helpless, ignored, and minimized. Imagine this story told only in monotone. How much impact do you think it would have? Without the occasional exclamation point, do you think, as a reader, you would really be getting the emotional tone the author wanted to impart to you? In this context, the occasional exclamation point would not only be useful but also even be expected, might provide the colour and intensity the author wanted to convey, might even draw attention to the most critical aspects of what the story was about!

But, to extend the metaphor a bit, imagine you put exclamation points at the end of every sentence! What if you felt everything you said was critically important! Every observation was vital! Every conclusion was insightful! Nothing you wrote could be ignored! All your thoughts needed to be attended to! How long would it be before the reader stopped taking you seriously! Your exclamation points would lose their meaning! Worse, there would be no way to

49

distinguish the crucial from the less so! It wouldn't be long before readers stopped taking the entire story seriously! They might also start to reconsider how much respect they had for the author!

My point is that yelling to get someone's attention, yelling to let someone know how bad things may have become, yelling to tell someone how upset you are, can actually be a very useful communication tool! However, once you've got the person's attention, once you've let them know there is something really important that you need to say, your yelling has probably accomplished all that it can and it typically has no further utility. In fact, further yelling will just start to undermine your message. Like a cymbal in an orchestra, it is there to drive home a musical point and is never used as the only instrument to carry the tune.

A cymbal of good communication?

I have seen many couples who, from the beginning of their relationship, either by accident or design, set up the rule that there was *never* to be *any* yelling. When couples like this walk into my office, they have arrived with their own special Catch-22: they are upset about something but are not allowed to express how upset they are. I have seen couples who have made life-altering choices like *moving to another country* or *adopting a child* in large part because they had no mechanism within their relationship to express strong feelings. Lots of people prefer to avoid conflict, but this is conflict avoidance morphed into conflict intolerance.[11]

It is extremely unlikely that you will go through your life having to deal only with people exactly like you, who think and feel exactly the way you do, and have the same needs and desires at the same time. In the absence of these conditions, it seems unlikely that you will be able to avoid all conflict.

And it isn't the presence or absence of conflict that creates problems in a relationship: *healthy, non-distressed relationships will*

---

[11] Jump back to the "Conflict as a Fact of Life" section (page 20) if the distinction between conflict avoidance and conflict intolerance is unclear.

have conflict. The more critical issue is whether the members of the relationship are either so conflict-averse that they can't deal with conflict effectively and thus get mired down in fight after fight, or so conflict intolerant that they pretend the conflict doesn't exist at all, and negative feelings and lingering animosities grow and fester over time?

If we demand that communication situations, particularly those that centre on important issues or emotionally intense circumstances, be conducted without showing emotions, we back people into a corner. Essentially we are saying that, yes, this is an intense topic, but you're not allowed to show it. Not such a good idea from my perspective.

Worse, hiding feelings leads to what we call *incongruence*, which is a fancy way of saying you are showing one feeling but experiencing another. Typically, incongruence shows up when someone smiles when they're talking about something that is upsetting to them. Incongruence really messes up good communication because it confuses issues with inconsistent messages, and in fact actually gives the message receiver the option of *completely ignoring* what is being said. The "I think I'd prefer to simply ignore what is being said" logic goes something like this:

Even though she is saying something that sounds serious and upsetting, she is actually smiling and occasionally even offering a "gee whiz" kind of laugh. While she might be doing this to try to reduce tension, I'm just as entitled to interpret this as meaning that the entire issue is not that serious and since this is the far easier course of action to take on this particular problem, I'm going to choose to ignore, or at the very least minimize, the importance of what she is trying to say. Boy, was that an easier way to handle this situation: bullet dodged!

Women seem to be more prone to this communication problem than are men, although both do it frequently. But both genders are just as entitled to ignore incongruent messages, and in so doing contribute to miscommunications and breakdowns in understanding.

My final shout-out on yelling
Now that I've made the case that even though yelling is not necessarily such a bad thing even though it gives rise to aversion, let me make a final point. To the extent that people learn and apply all fifteen of the communication rules, the tendency—in fact the need—for a communication to have moments of yelling automatically starts to dissipate over time, primarily because the degree of understanding between the two of you substantially increases. As the two of you improve your communication technique, you at the same time learn more about each other's needs, wants, and desires. Future conflicts will remain a possibility, but doubts about your ability to deal with them will decrease.

10. Insults Are a Waste of Time
Unlike yelling, insults are always a waste of everyone's time. Insults aren't designed to improve a communication; they are there only to hurt each other's feelings. There are fewer faster ways to destroy a communication opportunity or eliminate something positive coming from an important conversation than resorting to insults.

Insults are a failure of intellect and self-control. They are a failure of intellect because, no matter how clever you think your insult may be, the mental gymnastics you went through to generate the put-down would have been put to better use working out the problem rather than exacerbating it. Insults are a failure of self-control because you're more interested in feeling good about yourself in the moment, and at the expense of someone else, than you are in figuring out how to have your needs met in a more enduring and constructive way.

And don't kid yourself that you can insult someone and then apologize later, with no damage done. Caustic words are wounding, and relationships can die the death of a thousand cuts.

Relationships end every day where there hasn't been some major crisis or violation of trust, but rather a series of repeated jabs and put-downs that have had a cumulative destructive effect. The same thing goes for claiming that an insult was "just a joke." If it's funny to hurt your partner's feelings, you need a better hobby.

Occasional slip-ups aside, if you're "into" insulting your partner, grow up or face the real possibility of losing the pleasure of your partner's company. If your partner is into insults, leave and find someone better: it won't be hard. Insults are the antithesis of respect.

Special note on Rule 10: Insults as pet names
Some couples use insults or caustic phrases as pet names for each other. Rather than being an insult, words like *jerk*, *ass*, or *bitch* are actually terms of endearment for these couples, or at least are meant to bring humour to a circumstance or to diffuse a tense situation. (One of the more memorable examples of this from my practice was the couple whom, when I asked how the past week had gone, sheepishly looked at each other, and then she replied, "Well, things have gone pretty well, primarily because he has been *less of an enormous prick*.")

My clinical experience suggests that this is a dangerous route. Over the lifespan of a relationship, inevitably there will be moments when the meaning of such a pet name is called into question and ends up inflaming a situation rather than calming things down. As innocent as it might seem, careful consideration and even editing of pet names is good policy when it comes to long-term relationship building.

11. No Mind Reading

"If I have to tell him what I want, it doesn't count. He should just know!" Great philosophy in some idealized, *Harry Potter* world, but a lousy way to run a relationship in the one we've got. Maybe at some point in the future we'll have that data cable built into the backs of our heads and we can download all that we hope and desire to our partner. Until then, we're stuck with talking.

If you want something, believe something, feel something, need something, or are afraid of something, tell your partner about it—don't expect them to figure it out on their own. When you have been together for twenty-five years, have experienced all of what life has to offer, and endured the thrills and sorrows of life's many paths, sure, at that point maybe you could expect your partner to have a degree of insight into the dimensions of your inner world. But until you've put this kind of time in, don't start sabotaging your newly minted relationship by having unrealistic expectations as to how "connected" the two of you are.

If you resent the idea that you're going to have to explain your wants, desires, and preferences to your partner, keep in mind that they get to resent you and hold you to the same standard as well. Rather than setting each other up for a test of empathy or telepathic ability, it will be far more useful to create a culture in which no important want, desire, need, thought, or feeling is taken for granted by either of you. This entire book is about helping the two of you identify the most important thoughts and feelings you have about the most important marital issues, and communicate them to each other. In all of the ten conversations, I make the point that one of the surest ways to feel disconnected from your partner is to fail to let them know what you think or feel about an important issue. The unspoken hope or the silent expectation for change in a partner are among the most toxic qualities a person can bring to a relationship.

No assumptions, either!
Just because you believe something to be true, doesn't mean (a) it *is* true or (b) your partner *believes it to be true.* We could also substitute *obvious* or *common knowledge* for *true.* The way you see the world counts, absolutely. But don't kid yourself that because you see things a certain way, everyone else does as well, including your partner.

Each of the ten conversations is about revealing implicit and explicit assumptions both of you may have about important issues. As comprehensive as the book is, a complete list of these assumptions would be impossible to generate. Don't miss an opportunity to confer with your partner about what you think or believe by operating under the belief that "everyone knows that" or "that's so obvious it doesn't need to be talked about." If you're right, confirm it by checking things out with your partner. Why risk having things go off the rails? The power of paraphrasing (Rule 3) quickly helps reveal differences in beliefs and attitudes, and in so doing helps eliminate assumptions that might have the two of you talking in circles.

And, to be clear on the distinction, the bad habit of *mind reading* is about the mistaken belief that your partner should "just know" what you think or feel, while the bad habit of *assumption* is about the mistaken belief that your summation of facts and data will be exactly the same as your partner's summation of the facts and data. You have led different lives, and what seems like an obvious truth to you *may or may not* be so obvious to your partner.

Special note on Rule 11: Entitlement disorder
Even when the toxic quality of mind reading and assumption is revealed, some people refuse to give them up. Despite coaching and practice, they still expect their partner to *simply know* what they're thinking and to automatically believe all that they believe.

Although not an official diagnostic label, some of my colleagues and I have come call this phenomenon *entitlement disorder*. People with entitlement disorder[12] appear to operate under the general assumption that others have an *obligation* to solve their problems. The entitlement disordered have the *expectation* that others see the world the way they do. The entitlement disordered firmly believe their needs and desires are *obvious* for

---

[12] It would have been less cumbersome to abbreviate entitlement disorder to ED. However, in psychology and most other circles, ED has come to mean erectile disorder and we already have enough to deal with without that kind of confusion!

all to see, and should be prioritized accordingly. At their very best (or perhaps their most florid), the entitlement disordered will take the time to calmly explain to you what you have obviously been missing, but then, following their cogent and charitable explanation, now fully expect you to mobilize your heart, mind, and soul to the great and grand purpose of getting down to business and giving them what they so richly deserve. The entitlement disordered don't become so much righteously indignant as hurt when others, surprisingly to them, fail to rally to the cause. Further, from the perspective of the entitlement disordered, after having offered a *description* of their needs (an *explanation* of their needs would be superfluous), they are mystified as to why any further description would be required—once should be enough! And it is the entitlement disordered who have a very difficult time giving up on the idea that others are supposed to automatically know what they want and need (i.e., read their minds) and to operate under the same assumptions as they do.

This affliction seems to manifest most frequently in younger adults, although in rare cases it can persist into old age. I say in rare cases because, as a general rule, life has a way of correcting entitlement disorder. Repeated experience of the world just not caring tends to have a curative effect.

If you are among the entitled, good luck with that. And if your partner is among the entitled, think long and hard about how long you want to wait for them to reconsider their ill-informed position. You might also want to jump to the "Troubleshooting" chapter at the end of the book for tips, techniques, and observations about how to handle situations where one person steadfastly refuses to consistently operate in good faith and follow the rules of good communication.

Anger–Control Strategies

12. Keep Anger on the Clock (the 30-Minute Rule)[13]

We all get angry. Anger tells us we are frightened, insulted, frustrated, insecure, put upon, etc. These are all important feelings, and important feelings are better acknowledged than ignored. It seems unlikely that we will be able to move through our lives without having to experience anger, and while this is unfortunate, it remains a truth. Planning to always escape anger is probably a low-probability plan. Left with the reality that we will likely have to experience anger, we then move to the next-best plan: dealing with anger in an efficient way, and hopefully one that minimizes our experience of this unpleasant state. Once we know something has gone wrong or has made us feel threatened, it's time to move to coping and eventually to solving the problem.

Forgiveness is dumb

Forgiveness has never made any sense to me. How can it be rational to acknowledge that someone has done something wrong to you, *but then take a position that this is okay?* Why would we ever say, "Don't worry about it," or "It's no big deal," when something has hurt us or made us angry? How does this fit with any mature respect for feelings, particularly one's own?

Trying to manage anger from a forgiveness perspective is a poor strategy. However, please note that I'm not saying there aren't good reasons to *manage and reduce* anger. All I'm saying is that trying to get there through forgiveness is just another way of saying your feelings don't count, and this doesn't do anyone any good. Similarly, there is absolutely no utility in forgetting aversive

---

[13] Please note this is offered as a *rule of communication*, not a general psychological principle. Those who have suffered trauma or other great injury or insult will require this *and other* strategies to move past the pain and anger they feel.

experiences (that is, the "forget" part of the seriously flawed "forgive and forget" perspective), as this simply leaves you vulnerable to their happening again. Instead of forgive and forget, why not consider "reconcile and reframe?" You get the same alliterative effect, as well as processes that might actually prove to be of some worth!

Deciding to move past something, however, is not such a bad strategy. Deciding that odious things can hurt or insult us but don't have to define our lives is a type of anger management that, to my mind, makes some sense. Operating within this model means that once anger has served its purpose, it is no longer necessary. This is of course a good thing, because anger is pretty unpleasant to have to endure. What's more, prolonged anger prevents us from moving forward with our lives, and failing to deal with it means that we risk continuing to feel victimized by whatever the hurt was. Accepting the idea that lousy experiences are going to happen, while at the same time rejecting the idea that lousy experiences must define who we are, is what reconciliation is all about, and for my money makes a lot more sense than forgiveness. Consequently, we have the "30 minutes of anger" rule.

Everyone is entitled to be angry when they've been hurt or insulted, but this is different from saying they must remain angry for the rest of their lives, or even for the rest of the day. Feel your feelings and let others know you've been hurt, insulted, minimized, or whatever. But once this has happened and you've honoured the way you feel about something, once you've had your thirty minutes, it's time to get back to solving problems. Nurturing your righteous indignation for hours, days, or even longer simply takes you out of the game. It also allows some to avoid responsibility.

13. Take a Time Out: The 24-Hour Rule

The 24-hour rule has similarities to the "time outs" we give children. But don't let this similarity cause you to dismiss it. The 24-hour rule is used when tensions are running high, when there is too much yelling, or when insults start to fly. It can also be used when someone feels bullied, or if it just seems that the time is not right for an important conversation.

Step 1: Stop talking

There are two steps to using the 24-hour rule, and the first step is simply to say, "I'm calling the 24-hour rule!" When this happens, the conversation or argument stops, NO QUESTIONS ASKED. To the extent that someone keeps talking or arguing, they are saying they are not interested in improving the level of communication within the couple; they are saying they don't want to try to make things better. Not respecting the 24-hour rule (or any of the fifteen communication rules) can be viewed as acting in bad faith and represents a choice to not respect the overall attempt to communicate in better ways.

Step 2: Start talking again

When the 24-hour rule is used, it is important to understand that *the conversation or argument is not over.* This is where the second part of the 24-hour rule comes into play. The person who invoked the 24-hour rule now has to take responsibility for *restarting the same discussion,* sometime in the next 24 hours. This could be in five minutes, in a couple of hours, later that evening, or even the next morning, but it MUST happen within the next 24 hours. Thus, using the 24-hour rule doesn't stop a conversation; it simply provides a mechanism to better prepare both parties for that conversation or to dial down tensions if feelings were getting so heated that they were interfering with the discussion proceeding in a productive rather than a destructive direction.

The 24-hour rule accomplishes a number of desirable goals in addition to reducing tension. For example, people quickly learn that the 24-hour rule is an exercise in patience. Being able to control intense feelings while communicating is a skill *all* adults ought to have. And to the extent that this skill has already been developed, a couple may find their need for the 24-hour rule will not be that great. For other couples, the idea of gaining control over intense feelings so they don't derail an opportunity for constructive communication may be new and difficult to learn. Some couples may never have to invoke the 24-hour rule, while others may find that, in the beginning at least, they are using it frequently.

The 24-hour rule also improves equality between two people. It demonstrates that no one person's thoughts or feelings are more important than another's. Just because one person is angry or upset doesn't mean that everything has to stop so those intense feelings get addressed immediately, at that particular moment (for example, recall the entitlement disordered described above).

Good faith and the 24-hour rule

Good faith has to be applied to the use of the 24-hour rule. Over the years, I've come across a number of people who have come up with very clever ways to abide by the *letter* of the 24-hour rule but not its *spirit*. For example, one man called the 24-hour rule when, upon returning from work, his wife started talking about having children (an issue he had no interested in exploring). Because he never wanted to have this discussion, after invoking the 24-hour rule that evening, he woke his wife up at 3:00 in the morning, claiming he was now ready to have the kids discussion.

In another couple, she invoked the 24-rule over three consecutive days every time he wanted to talk about arranging their vacation. She knew (and he didn't) that the deadline to buy tickets at an affordable price would pass in three days, so she used the 24-hour rule in a passive-aggressive way to eliminate his most desired vacation option.

Other misuses of the 24-hour rule have included invoking it when someone knows they or their partner will be unavailable to restart a conversation because they have other important commitments, using the 24-hour rule out of laziness or apathy, or consistently calling for 24 hours when a particular topic is brought up.

In yet another couple, he used the 24-hour rule whenever she started to cry. His declared intent was to allow her to calm down, even though she consistently stated that she didn't need time to calm down. In therapy, he eventually revealed that he had no tolerance for crying because his mother had used this when he was a teenager to make him feel guilty and beholden. Rather than reveal these feelings and this baggage from his past, he hid behind the 24-hour rule and did not take responsibility for his feelings of anger and frustration.

In these examples—and there are plenty more—people chose to use a communication rule to manipulate their partner or the situation rather than communicate in a productive manner. This is what I mean by operating in bad faith. While these manipulative approaches may work well in a courtroom or in business negotiations, where the nature of the relationship is adversarial, it's a lousy way to treat your partner. The purpose of being with someone is to enhance your life through the pleasure of your partner's company, not to score points or manoeuvre and control them. However, and let's be frank here, if this is what brings you pleasure, it's time to rethink some important issues, such as what your partner means to you, what your relationship needs might be, or what intimate relationships mean to you in general.

With the good-faith use of the 24-hour rule, no one has to endure inappropriate yelling or being intimidated. In fact, both parties learn very quickly that getting "all big and bad" is pretty ineffective and will simply lead to frustration because the partner on the receiving end will simply end the communication by calling the 24-hour rule. As the saying goes, "Saying it loud doesn't make it so," and the 24-hour rule is one way to formalize this.

Essentially, the good-faith use of the 24-hour rule forces both parties to be civil to each other if they want to continue talking about a particular issue. Further, if you are the type of person who can't let an issue go, your partner's invoking of the 24-hour rule will help you learn the discipline required to forgo the immediate gratification you feel you must have.

Long-Term Relationship Maintenance Strategies

14. Regularly Indulge in W(h)ine Time

The w(h)ine-time rule is about keeping the two of you connected. This rule also makes the point that good relationships don't just happen; they are created and nurtured by putting in time and effort.

W(h)ine time means that five days a week, for the rest of your lives, the two of you sit down, pour yourselves a pleasant beverage, and share the events of your day. This happens Monday to Friday for at least twenty minutes, with each of you getting ten minutes. If you want to talk longer, fine, but no less. If you want to do w(h)ine time on the weekends, feel free, but keep in mind that weekends don't tend to be as regimented as weekdays, so trying to establish a regular w(h)ine time on Saturday and Sunday can be more challenging.

W(h)ine time is not something the two of you do while you're cooking dinner, helping the kids with homework, or watching TV. If you want to talk then too, great. Just don't fool yourself into believing that you are having a w(h)ine-time conversation. W(h)ine time means the computer is put to sleep, the phone is taken off the hook, and the TV and radio are powered down. W(h)ine time means cellphones, Blackberrys, iPods, and pagers are turned off. W(h)ine time means the kids are told that mommy and daddy are having grown-up time and they are not to be disturbed unless it is an emergency. Put w(h)ine time in the same category as having your first cup of coffee or brushing your teeth before leaving the house: you want to make it an essential and expected part of your day. Essentially, w(h)ine time is *protected and respected time* meant entirely for the two of you to connect.

Relationship glue

As the name implies, the conversational content of w(h)ine time can be about upsetting, worrying issues or pleasant, relaxed ones. You can talk about either or both. Actually, the balance of the issues you talk about is not the critically important component. What is critical is the opportunity to explore what I refer to as *relationship glue*. Relationship glue consists of the mundane issues, the inside jokes, the little cares and concerns that each of you has. In fact, over time, it will be these things that make your relationship unique.

You can talk about the highlights of your day, the major events, with just about anyone: getting transferred, having a fight with a co-worker, or starting a new project is the kind of material you would share with most people, maybe even with strangers! This material is not the stuff of intimacy. The magic of w(h)ine time is that you don't necessarily focus on these more "important" topics, but rather the little, seemingly meaningless details of your daily life: the little annoyances, victories, or observations in which few others would truly be interested. The "big issues," while important, don't really represent relationship glue because they aren't particularly personal or idiosyncratic. Rather than a headline, relationship glue is the short special-interest piece buried deep inside the newspaper of conversation. And w(h)ine time is the opportunity to read and consider those special little bits of news that are of interest to only a select few.

15. How We Doin'?

You've probably heard that changing the oil in your car is the single most useful thing you can do to maintain your vehicle. Every five thousand miles or ten thousand kilometres, you're supposed to do this basic, standard maintenance. Depending on how much you drive, this typically means an oil change every three or four months. Metaphorically, this type of regular maintenance is what you want to be doing with your relationship as well. And to extend the metaphor a bit, in the same sage way that a regular oil change is perhaps the best thing you can do for your car, checking in with your partner as to the ongoing status of the relationship may also be the best possible approach to long-term relationship maintenance you can take.

You "hit the highlights" in the "How we doin'?" conversations—sex, parenting, money, vacations, family interactions, etc. Actually, you can use the topics of "The 10 Conversations" as a content guide for "How we doin'?" conversations.

Ideally, at the beginning of the year, when you get your new calendar or daytimer, the two of you sit down and mark in when (and potentially where) you will be having your "How we doin'?" discussions. Two important relationship-management activities happen here. First, you both participate in committing to keep the process of relationship examination and management active and current. Second, you eliminate the possibility that there will be misunderstandings about when these important conversations will be taking place.

An ounce of prevention

"How we doin'?" conversations prevent lingering resentments from coming to full flower by ensuring that there are regular opportunities to deal with upsetting issues. They demand a culture of problem solving in the relationship and dramatically reduce the possibility of issue avoidance and the use of passive-aggressive strategies. Essentially, "How we doin'?" conversations make being frank and candid with each other a regular and expected event rather than one that's exceptional. Finally, as long as there's honesty, "How we doin'?" conversations mean that no one gets blindsided if they're told the relationship is failing to meet their partner's needs. The potential need for a greater level of relationship maintenance or assistance (i.e., marital therapy) is seldom missed if the two of you are regularly engaging in "How we doin'?" conversations.

Because the answer to the "How we doin'?" question might be "Not so well!", regular "How we doin'?" conversations are easy to put off or avoid. However, as will be the message throughout this book, successful marriages are not accidents; they are made, and one of the prime building materials in constructing a happy and healthy relationship is the liberal application of courage and discipline.

FINAL THOUGHTS ON THE COMMUNICATION RULES

Think of the fifteen rules of good communication in the same way you think of the rules of driving. Most people follow most of the driving rules most of the time, and most of the time, most people get where they want to go without a problem. Few people follow all the rules all the time, and a case could be made that, in a lot of driving situations, strict adherence to each and every one of the rules of the road is not really necessary. (Who actually comes to a full and complete stop at every stop sign they come across?) But when traffic is heavy or is moving fast, when there are a lot of people on the road, or when road conditions are less than ideal, the more closely we all adhere to the rules, the safer we all will be.

It's the same deal with the communication rules. Being casual about using the rules is probably not that dangerous when the issues you're talking about are relatively mundane. But when you have something important to talk about, when a subject is complex, or when feelings about a topic are intense, the closer the two of you stick to the rules, the safer you'll both be.

CONVERSATION 1:
Having Kids

THE QUESTION OF WHETHER to have or not to have children is the first of the ten conversations that must happen before a couple decides to marry. This conversation is perhaps the most obvious of the ten, but because having it is a bit of a no-brainer, many think they have actually had the Having Kids conversation and settled the issue when in fact a number of important issues remain to be discussed. You can imagine, for example, a young couple discovering they both love spending time with kids and agreeing that they both want to have children together. It's only later that they discover that her idea of having children means having two kids after they've been married for a couple of years, while his idea of having children is having five, starting the night of the honeymoon!

So what are the components of the Having Kids conversation? Although you might reasonably think it simply starts off with the standard "Do you want to have kids?" the first of the ten conversations actually needs to begin a couple of steps before this.

CHANGE IS COMING

First of all, having kids will *change your life forever*. Let me say this again: having kids will *change your life forever*.

I stress this for two reasons. First, because it's true, so you should give it more than just passing consideration. Second, because unfortunately it's become a cliché, and when anything becomes a cliché, its importance gets minimized and lost. Don't believe me? Well, remember when your mom told you to "be careful" when you were playing? How long was it before "You be careful, now!" got mentally coded simply as "something mom says" rather than, "Oh, perhaps I should stop for a moment and consider any potential risks that I might incur should I continue to conduct myself in a careless and cavalier fashion?" Okay, if you actually ever did think like this, you probably got beaten up a lot, but that doesn't change my point. Mom was right and so am I.

So, as we get started with the first of the ten conversations, let's be clear about a key theme that will run through this and all of the subsequent conversations. The actual words we use when we talk about substantive issues potentially have more importance than we might realize. For example, "I love kids," may mean, "I want to have kids," but it might also mean, "I think kids are hilarious to watch on the playground, but I haven't really given any thought to the idea of becoming a parent myself," or even, "I love kids because thus far in my life, most of my experience with them has been to give them back to their parents when I quickly became bored or exhausted with them!"

To the extent that we make presumptions about what someone means, particularly when we are talking about very important issues, we set ourselves up for disappointment—or worse. The strategy, then, is to both state positions clearly and to listen to positions *critically*. By *critically* I don't mean to look for a way to start a fight or to try to find flaws in what the other person is saying. By *critically* I mean that each of us has to constantly question whether we truly understand what the other person is saying. Therefore, being critical means critically questioning *ourselves* on the meaning of what someone is saying. We are all prone to "hearing what we want to hear," particularly when it comes to deep and heartfelt issues, and in no context is this more dangerous than in determining how compatible we are with a potential lifelong partner. It's easy to be blinded by love in these circumstances, but this only increases the danger of miscommunication.

So, in this, and in all of the ten conversations, *being clear about what you say and critical of what you hear* will henceforth be a standing order. Nothing someone says *ever* gets taken for granted, and when there is even a hint of a glimmer of a smidgen of a chance that someone might be taking something for granted, checking in with the other person to ensure that there is a common understanding as to what is being said *is a must!* The technique of paraphrasing described in the communication rules is a very effective way to ensure that nothing gets taken for granted. I encourage everyone to review this rule (and all the other rules as well) as we move through each of the conversation chapters in the book.

Now that I've gotten that out of the way, let's return to the idea that having children will change your life forever.

THE "IF" PART OF HAVING KIDS

After a couple gets married, and sometimes even before, the question "So when are you planning on having children?" can be expected with the regularity of gas prices dropping after you've filled the tank. In some circles, many people continue to believe that *the* reason to get married is to make babies. The "married equals babies" belief has a long and noble history, and is well represented in almost every culture. In fact, there have been places and times in history where the inability to have children was considered justification for terminating a marriage (or worse). A very clear message has been passed from generation to generation that if you weren't planning on making babies when you got married, your dedication to your society was in question, as was your understanding of what marriage was about.

This somewhat strident set of attitudes is thankfully less common today. Further, we no longer live in a world where the ability to produce children is the primary factor in the viability of a society or a marriage. With the world's population growing exponentially, there are places where continued growth in population actually *threatens* the existence of a society rather than strengthens it. Consequently, the societal imperative for continued reproduction can quite legitimately be questioned. Perhaps more than at any other time, parenthood can and should be seen as a *choice* rather than as a cultural or marital necessity.

That being said, there continues to be pressure for couples to have children. For many, failing to have kids is failing to have a family. The absence of children in one's relationship means that what is denoted in phrases like *family get-together, family car, family vacation,* or *starting a family* are apparently things that will never be experienced. Without children, it is widely held that you never created a "family of your own." It's pretty clear that in North America, the absence of children implies the absence of family. However, many others would dispute this and contend that "family" isn't so rigid a concept and that a couple choosing to spend their lives together quite adequately represents all that is good as far as "family" is concerned.

PRONATALISM

Pronatalism is the fancy-shmancy word that describes the set of policies and attitudes that encourage and expect parenthood for all couples. *Pronatal attitudes* are extremely common in North America, and particularly so in some religious circles. In fact, failing to reproduce is actually thought of as "sinful" in some spiritual systems. Of course, there are many systems of belief, and not every religious system supports the idea that everyone must make babies. But it's important in this, the first of the ten conversations, to keep in mind that the ubiquity of a belief doesn't make it correct. A hundred, a thousand, or even ten million people believing something still doesn't *make* that something true. As an example, hundreds of years ago, all the people in the world believing the Earth was flat didn't make it so. So too with pronatalism. All the belief systems in the world can't determine the "correct" reproductive choice for any particular individual or couple. The facts are that not everyone *can* reproduce, not everyone *wants* to reproduce, and not everyone has the *time, patience,* or *inclination* to provide a loving, healthy environment for a child, and this won't be changed by all the dogma in the world!

Let me be crystal clear, then, about where I think the Having Kids conversation ought to go. I'm *not* suggesting that deciding to forgo having children is the right or most informed choice. *Nor* am I saying that having children is the correct, informed choice. What I am suggesting is that there is no de facto *correct* set of feelings or attitudes one should have about having children. Unfortunately, and all too frequently, our North American society does not take quite so balanced an approach, and so it also needs to be made clear that there are a set of pre-existing pronatalistic expectations in our society that serve to make people feel guilty, selfish, immature, or ill informed if they feel that remaining child free is a good and correct choice for them. The pressure these pronatal attitudes can bring to bear is not inconsiderable and can lead to ill-conceived parenting obligations (pun intended).

Anecdotally, allow me to confess that I have been just as guilty as the next person of uncritically harbouring pronatalistic beliefs. From my graduate days, I can vividly recall learning that a colleague was planning to remain child free. My initial and overriding thoughts were simply that she was ill informed and was being immature. Of course, I thought, she will eventually come around and see that she, as a bright and informed person, will be happier having children. When she realizes that she might end up alone in her old age, of course she will change her mind. And of course this thinking was simply a projection of my own priorities and fears.

Prior to this, I had thought that being child free was something to be tolerated only if biology conspired to leave a person or couple incapable of having children. Voluntary childlessness was out of the question for the truly informed, or so I thought. And my attitudes were not in any way informed by spiritual or religious thinking. It was simply inconceivable (sorry, did it again) to me that a smart, healthy person could choose childlessness as an informed option. I even remember my plans to gently confront my colleague and help her see what I felt were the obvious errors and omissions in her thinking. Essentially, I was heavily invested in propagating the propaganda of pronatalism.

Of course that's not what happened. In talking to my colleague about how she could arrive at such an erroneous conclusion, it was I who learned the error of my ways. The concept of pronatalism, let alone its ubiquity and profound influence, had never crossed my mind before, and this after having completing an undergraduate degree that in large part focused on psychological concepts and social forces. In truly listening to my colleague, I came to recognize the assumptions *I* was making about couplehood, the meaning of family, the conditions of happiness, and—forgive me for getting philosophical here—the meaning of life.

Although I had never given it any thought before, I came to realize that there were more than a few reasons why someone might choose to not include children in her or his life plan. At the personal level, dedicating a life to career, artistic, or spiritual development might preclude having children. Feeling emotionally strained with personal problems or desiring maximum personal freedom might also be important reasons to remain child free. A concern about the ever-increasing demands on our environment or feeling uncertain about the safety of the world and the future could also number among the reasons someone might have second thoughts about becoming a parent.

Given the diversity of personal experience and feeling, a list of all the potential reasons that someone might choose to remain infant unencumbered would be impossible to generate, and it is not necessary for our purposes here. What is important is taking the opportunity to seriously consider one's personal strengths, weaknesses, hopes, and desires, and in so doing chart a personal life course that maximizes the chances that those hopes and desires are realized. To do this, being aware of the subtle and not-so-subtle influences on our thinking and decision making is a must. Recognizing the pronatal bias of our society does not necessarily mean rejecting it! It simply means being aware it is there and factoring this into the process of making a personal choice about having children.

So now you're aware of potential pronatal influences on how and why you might be thinking about having kids. What exactly do you do about those influences, or perhaps more to the point, how does this awareness help you with the first of the ten conversations?

A number of years ago, an American group called the National Alliance for Optional Parenthood (NAOP) constructed a terrific list of questions everyone should consider when the question of "Do you want to have kids?" comes up. What was great about their questions was that they were non-judgemental, came with little or no pronatal bias, and truly encouraged people to think about important issues related to becoming a parent. For years, when discussing fertility, pregnancy, and childbirth with students in my human sexuality classes, I have used the NAOP questions to encourage students to consider their options.

Building upon the questions first posed by the NAOP, here is a list of questions focused on the choice of whether or not to have kids. Any of these questions could be used to get the Having Kids conversation started, and all of them should be addressed in the Having Kids discussions.[14]

---

[14] This format will be used throughout *The 10 Conversations*. After an issue or important point has been identified, I'm going to offer one or more specific questions that the two of you can use as conversation starters. See, you don't even have to worry about how to start a particular conversation or broach a particular issue. I'll give you the tools you need to ensure that you cover all the highlights.

The Matter in Question: Having Kids

KIDS Q1. Am I, and are we, willing to dedicate twenty years or more to the care and development of another person?

KIDS Q2. Do I, and do we, enjoy the kinds of things that are involved in bringing up a child? Do we like to play, show affection to others, be patient, be creative, etc., all of which are substantial requirements of parenthood? From an emotional perspective, are we capable of understanding some-one else's feelings and helping them deal with intense emotions?

KIDS Q3. When it comes to important choices, do I have a history of making up my own mind and choosing a course for myself, or am I strongly influenced by social trends or the opinions and choices of others?

KIDS Q4. Have I, and have we, considered how having a child could positively and negatively affect our careers, plans for the future, privacy, social and recreational interests, etc.?

KIDS Q5. Have I, and have we, seriously thought about our ability to provide the resources a child needs to flourish? For example, have we thought about how we will find enough money and time to meet the considerable needs of a child? In allocating these resources, what do we think we might feel: joy, resignation, resentment, or some other feeling?

KIDS Q6. If I were to discover that my partner's feelings about having children were substantially different from my own, would I avoid expressing my feelings to avoid conflict?

KIDS Q7. How would I feel if my child's goals, values, beliefs, or identity were substantially different from mine? For example, what if my child held different political or religious beliefs? How would I feel if my child had a different sexual orientation from mine?

KIDS Q8. If I, and we, decide not to have children, have we thought about the long-term implications of this choice? For example, have we thought about how we might like to spend our holidays or what our retirement might be like in the absence of children?

KIDS Q9. If we were to determine that as of now we don't want to have children, how certain are we that this is the lifelong choice we want to make? Are we ready to consider permanent forms of birth control like vasectomy and/or tubal ligation?

KIDS Q10. Is there an expectation on either of our parts that a child might help resolve personal or relationship problems? Is the thought of having a child primarily about compensating for feeling unloved, rejected, hurt, disrespected, or other related needs? How much of my potential desire to have children is about wielding power, being an authority, or simply being in charge?

Underlying many of the above questions, and touched on in Kids Q10, is, "How stable and committed is our relationship, and could it withstand the stress and strain of bringing a child into the world?" Although I doubt that this really needs to be said, allow me to state for the record that having a child will NOT improve an already troubled relationship. As described below, having children is a tremendous challenge, and strained relationships seldom stand up to the additional demands a baby and child brings. However, since this entire book is about helping you determine exactly how stable and committed your relationship is, let's set that particularly large and complex issue aside until more of the ten conversations have taken place.

THE "WHEN" PART OF HAVING KIDS: TIMING AND STRESS

Let's suppose that in response to the "if" part of the having kids issue, you and your partner determine that rug rats are in fact something you want in your future. If so, the "when" part of the issue remains, so let's look at some of the basic facts about making babies so the two of you get to *choose* when you enter parenthood rather than having it thrust upon you. Essentially, let's address the "planned" part of planned parenthood. For those of you who have considered pronatalism and such issues and determined that having kids is not what you want, feel free to skip the rest of this conversation and move on to Careers, as the remainder of this conversation deals with follow-up issues related to having kids.

Having kids can be stressful, time consuming, and scary as hell. Even given the joyful moments, the experiences of profound love and affection, and the wonder that children bring to our lives, it's still scary as hell. It can also be hilarious, deeply moving, life affirming, and profoundly rewarding. Having kids reminds us of the miracle of life, the excitement of learning, and the intensity of a bond we may never have experienced before. Having kids is also scary as hell. So just to be clear, if you want to go down this path, having kids is great but also—and say it with me now—SCARY AS HELL.

Now, believe it or not, I'm NOT trying to frighten you. (But did I mention that having kids is scary as hell?) Actually, what I'm trying to do is paint a realistic picture of what having kids is like. While there are irreproducible moments of joy, there is also a profound commitment to bringing another life into the world, and the reality of this needs to be faced head-on. Knowing what you're getting into is a far better plan than relying on some ill-informed, fantasy model of child- or parenthood.

The Matter in Question: Having Kids

KIDS Q11. **What, if anything, scares *you* about the thought of having a child or children of your own? What scares *your partner*?**

GOOD TIMING

One you've decided you want to have kids, you have to start thinking about when to have them, and this brings us back to the "scary as hell" concept. From a timing perspective, it's critically important to understand that, in all likelihood, having a child will be, among other things, a stressful and difficult time.

Now, I'm not going to bore you with a description of the profound fatigue and loss of sleep that goes along with having a newborn. Neither am I going to pontificate on the loss of spare time or the total elimination of any sense of privacy you may have enjoyed before bringing your own children into the world. And because it would be nothing more than a juvenile, self-serving ploy, I'm not going to *even mention* things like vomit on your shirt, pee in your car, food ground into the carpet, poo under your fingernails, or the smell of the diaper bucket and sour milk pervading your home.

What I *am* going to point out is that, because having kids is hard, it's a really good idea to try to control or limit the stress from other areas of your life. From a very practical perspective, this means that it's a good idea to try to have a child at times other than the ones when you're going to be under substantial stress in other areas of your life. For example, bad times to have children would include when you're moving to the other side of the country with little or no social support, when you're entering the most difficult part of professional training, or when you're working four jobs at once just to make ends meet. There is no nobility in needless suffering, and adding insult to injury from a stress perspective is just bad planning. Looking ahead in your life and making choices that minimize predictable sources of stress is both good personal and relationship management. There will be plenty of times when stresses build up in unexpected and unpredictable ways. Making choices to reduce stress when possible is simply smart life planning.

A PERFECT TIME SELDOM HAPPENS

Now I want to make an important distinction. When I talk about choosing a lower-stress time in your life to start having a family, I'm not suggesting that people have to wait until everything is perfectly organized in their lives before they start trying to make babies. Perfection seldom happens in anyone's life, and waiting for it means a whole lot of living gets passed by. Historically, if people had waited for perfect parenting conditions before making babies, it is doubtful we would even be here as a species. It must also be recognized that we no longer live in a world where the survival of our species or even of our culture is solely dependent upon our individual ability to reproduce. The rush to reproduce in past societies can reasonably be replaced with a more pedestrian pace to parenthood. More than any other time in our history, there are more, and more varied, forms of birth control to allow couples to select the most opportune times to get pregnant.

WHEN THE TIME ISN'T QUITE RIGHT

Unplanned pregnancies aren't the end of the world. They are, however, extremely stressful and have ended relationships that might have survived had they been given more time to grow, mature, and amass resources and social supports. With our ability to choose when we want to become parents, why take chances?

One of the subtopics of the Having Kids conversation ought to be about how the two of you are going to avoid having kids until you have decided you're ready. For example, while the birth control pill is extremely reliable, the burden of contraception rests entirely on the shoulders of the woman. Does this feel reasonable to the two of you? Are there alternatives that you two should explore? Planning on using condoms as a long-term birth control option is perfectly reasonable, but have the two of you talked about how this might affect other aspects of lovemaking, such as spontaneity and sensual satisfaction for him? (Sex is a huge issue all on its own and needs to be looked at in detail. Given how much there is to cover, we're only touching on contraceptive issues right now and leaving many of the remaining issues for the Sex conversation.)

The Matter in Question: Having Kids

KIDS Q12.   How much do the two of you know about your contraceptive options? Where could you collect more information should it be required?

KIDS Q13.   What form(s) of birth control—e.g., the pill, condoms (male, female, or both), the rhythm (basal body temperature) method, hormone injections, implants, cervical cap, contraceptive sponge, etc.—is (are) acceptable to *your partner*?

KIDS Q14. What is *your* preferred method of birth control?

KIDS Q15. Have the two of you talked about what each might feel if a birth control failure occurred? What options are acceptable to each of you?

KIDS Q16. What thoughts and feelings do the two of you have regarding more permanent forms of birth control like vasectomy and tubal ligation?

FERTILITY AND TIMING

And speaking of deciding when you're ready, let's quickly look at some basic facts about marriage and fertility.

Couples increasingly have been delaying both getting married and having children. More and more people are getting married in their mid to late twenties rather than their late teens and early twenties. This trend has been developing over the past few decades. A number of speculations for this have been posited, but I suspect the strongest social force at work here is the fact that more and more people aren't waiting until after they're married to have their first sexual experiences. There's no question that a few decades ago, the desire to have sex, often for the first time, was a major motivating factor in the decision to get married, but this is far less the case in today's society. Personally, I think this is an excellent development—learning about your sexual likes and dislikes BEFORE making a lifetime commitment to a single partner seems an overwhelmingly more logical choice than knowing little about your own and your partner's sexual interests and just hoping that the two of you are sexually compatible. By the way, I'll talk a lot more about how to assess sexual compatibility in the Sex conversation.

There is, however, one very serious consequence that doesn't seem to get the attention I believe it deserves, and that is the consequence that delaying marriage has on fertility. Few couples seem to realize how precipitously a woman's fertility decreases as she moves from her twenties to her thirties. The optimum age for women to conceive is actually between the ages of twenty-two and twenty-six, when the chances of conceiving during any particular monthly cycle are about twenty to twenty-five percent. But these days, most women aren't married by that age.

As a woman enters her thirties, these chances start to drop considerably. When a woman reaches the end of her third decade, her chances of conceiving in any particular cycle have fallen from one in four to one in twenty, or about a five percent probability per menstrual cycle. In one of nature's great gender inequities, men's fertility doesn't decrease with anything like this rapidity, and it is quite possible for a man to father a child well into his retirement years.

In addition, the chances of miscarrying also increase with a woman's age. In her twenties and early thirties, the chance of miscarriage is about one in ten. But after the age of thirty-five, the chance of miscarrying doubles to one in five, and by the time a woman is in her forties, it has increased to one in three.

This is relevant to the Having Kids conversation for two very important reasons. First, it helps you know your chances of conceiving, and this helps you assess the potential risks you might be taking by putting off having kids. Second, it's important to know these numbers if you suspect either you or your partner might have a fertility problem.

Running Out of Time

Problems conceiving are more common than many realize—it is estimated that one out of ten couples will experience some type of fertility problem. So let's take a quick look at the implications of either you or your partner having a fertility problem.

Say you follow the current averages: you both wait till you're about twenty-nine or thirty to get married. As is often the case, couples typically wait a couple of years after they marry before they start trying to have children. For the unfortunate one out of ten, they have trouble conceiving, which is most often defined as failure to conceive naturally after trying for a year. Sticking with these numbers, you would both now be about thirty-two years old. As the female partner, your fertility has already started to naturally decline (in addition to whatever is preventing you from conceiving), and your chances of miscarrying are also starting to increase. Deciding that you want to seek the advice of a fertility expert, you call to book an appointment but find that the high demand means you'll have to wait for a few months, which in my experience of working with couples is quite common. When the two of you are finally seen at the fertility clinic, you are informed that an extensive battery of tests will need to be done to determine if whatever is preventing you from conceiving can be ameliorated. (Incidentally, about forty percent of the time the fertility problem has something to do with the woman, and forty percent of the time it has something to do with the man. In the other twenty percent, it either has to do with both or there is no identifiable reason why a couple is having a problem. On the other hand, for slightly more than half of the couples seeking treatment, they are able to conceive naturally within their second year of trying, so for some couples it just takes a little longer.)

In the above example, you two are now in your thirty-fourth year and, using common estimates of reproductive viability, have only about a six-year window left within which you get to use much that modern technology has to offer in terms of baby making, assuming you have the time and resources needed to engage in fertility interventions. As of this writing, a single attempt at in vitro fertilization (IVF) costs close to C$5,000, but can be more or less depending on the procedures required. At the most optimistic, there are about seventy-two menstrual cycles left for you to try to have your first baby, which might seem like a lot. But let's say it takes two to five IVF cycles, which some might consider optimistic, before there are positive signs of a pregnancy (approximately sixty-five cycles left). The chances of miscarriage have continued to increase each year; unfortunately, you're the unlucky one out of five in this age range and the pregnancy fails. Following the miscarriage, you try again, but this doesn't occur for about six months (approximately sixty cycles left), and you are now in your thirty-fifth year. Having a child at this point is not impossible, not at all hopeless, but it is decreasingly likely, while conception attempts are increasingly more expensive; what's more, you've been given a season's pass for the emotional roller coaster of repeated fertility attempts.

My point? Only to remind you that there aren't endless tomorrows as far as making babies is concerned. The stories in the media about this forty-year-old female executive or that forty-five-year-old female rock star having her first child misrepresent the more common reality and lead people to believe they have more time than they really do. Using more realistic data to inform your Having Kids conversation will unquestionably allow you to make more informed choices.

As with the "if" of the Having Kids conversation, here are some "when" questions you and your partner could use to help continue this, the first of the ten conversations.

The Matter in Question: Having Kids

KIDS Q17. What is the age range we want to fall in when we have our first child? Have we thought about the kinds of things we might like to do with our child, and have we considered how likely or

unlikely these activities might be as a function of our age as parents?

KIDS Q18. Where do we hope to be in our professional or career development when we start having children? What conflicts might exist between our professional or career development and our preferred timing for starting a family? Are there any other life goals either or both of us have that might conflict with starting a family?

KIDS Q19. If we want to have more than one child, have we worked backward in time to figure out when we should get things started? What about the spacing of our children's ages? Do we want them to be close together or farther apart, or do neither of us have preferences in this regard?

KIDS Q20. What are our thoughts about the number of children we would like to have? What seems reasonable to each of us? Do either or both of us have clearly defined ideas as to what we think the "size" of our future family will be? Are we willing to negotiate should there be a substantial discrepancy between our desires?

KIDS Q21. Would either of us want to "keep trying" until we had the little boy or girl that we might so desire? How far might either of us want to go in this regard?

KIDS Q22. If we were confronted with a fertility problem, what are our thoughts about dealing with this?[15] How far does either of us feel we would want to go in pursuing fertility treatments (i.e., time, number of attempts, amount of money, etc.)? Would either of us consider options like fostering or adopting a child?

PARENTING

The last major topic to be covered in this chapter is a quick exploration of issues related to parenting. Of course it's not necessary or even reasonable to think that you must have all possible parenting issues worked out this early in the game. Much of what parenting is about can't be known until you're in the thick of things. At this stage, we're still just talking about the possibility of making babies and becoming a parent. However, our experiences of childhood and thoughts about our own parents will have a substantial influence on what we feel about becoming parents ourselves. So the purpose of this part of the Having Kids conver-

---

[15] Until anyone is actually confronted with this kind of circumstance, it's not really possible to know with certainty what the resulting feelings will be. However, there is much about marriage that is going to be uncertain. We don't have to have all the answers at any particular time, but having a mechanism in place, such as good standards of communication, is a terrific way to build confidence that when uncertainties arise, there will be ways to work through them. Think of this question and others like it as practice in communication and problem solving. Creating a culture within your relationship of having the important discussions, and having these discussions in a productive rather than a destructive way, is of critical importance and can't be stressed enough. The inability to have important discussions, in a constructive manner, is a strong indicator that a relationship isn't durable and potentially lacks the respect required to manage the inevitable marital ups and downs that await.

sation—the "potential to parent" part—is not to task you with exploring every potential parenting possibility. Rather, the purpose is to start you both thinking about the importance of approaching the parenting part of having kids from an informed perspective, rather than one that is characterized by the simple hope that it will all just work out.

SORRY, BUT I HAVE TO GO ALL PSYCHOLOGIST ON YOU FOR A MOMENT . . .

Our personal experiences of childhood will have a strong influence on what we think growing up ought to be about. Those with happy childhoods will want to see the events and experiences of their childhoods reproduced for their own kids, while those whose memories of childhood are not as positive will want to take steps to ensure things go differently. Differences in expectations can be as benign as whether a child should take piano or guitar lessons, or how old they should be when they start learning to swim, or more impactful like when or if a child should be sent to a summer camp or away to a boarding school. The intensity, both positive and negative, of our personal experiences will inform us as to what we feel comfortable offering our own children. It will also have a profound influence on the basic question of whether or not we even want to have children.

Negative and traumatic experiences in childhood can have far-reaching consequences, but not everyone who was traumatized in childhood will continue to be influenced by these events on a daily basis. Many people have had horrible childhood experiences and have still grown up to be happy and healthy individuals, partners, members of society, and parents. It is also true that some have been unable to escape the ghosts of their pasts and continue to experience the aftereffects of negative childhood experiences. It is therefore extremely important to understand this particular point: psychologically speaking, history IS NOT destiny! We are NOT destined to continually suffer from the events of our past. Nor are we destined to become our parents. If this were true, if we were incapable of growing and learning, of making different choices or of taking different paths, as a species we would never have left the trees! Some who have suffered abuse or neglect at the hands of caregivers end up psychologically damaged, and with reason. For a small group of these individuals, parenting *is* a bad choice, primarily because they continue to deal with their own compromised sense of self. However, and for the vast majority of people who have suffered unfortunate circumstances, this is not the case and they are perfectly capable of becoming a more loving and caring parent than they themselves had. Contrary to some pop psychology thinking, people are quite capable of becoming more and better than what they were offered as children!

Realistically Speaking: Leo and Sandra

Unspoken assumptions, the misuse of communication superpowers, and unresolved family baggage contributed to Leo and Sandra coming to my office. Leo and Sandra had been married only a year, but sexual and mood problems were beginning to damage their relationship. Sandra had initially come to my office on her own, worried that her anger and its negative influence on her libido were taking the couple down a road of continued marital conflict. It quickly became clear, however, that a babymaking discrepancy was far more at the root of their conflict than was any mood or sexual desire disorder.

Leo was a very pleasant person to spend time with. He was well spoken, intelligent, and had a real flair for telling a story. Unfortunately, his skills as a raconteur were actually contributing to the marital discord he and Sandra were experiencing. As a seasonal politician, Leo commanded attention and had the ability to steer a conversation in whatever direction suited him. And when it came to making a baby, Leo felt neither the topic nor the role of father were well suited for him. Whenever Sandra would bring up the issue, he would deftly change the topic, tell a story about world overpopulation, or elaborate on the latest news in the media of a parent in conflict with their teenager. All this served to stifle serious discussion of ever having a child of their own. Leo was essentially using his well-developed communication skills to control what did and didn't get talked about. What's more, as it turned out in therapy, Leo *really* didn't want to talk about having a child because of unspoken doubts about being a dad that stemmed from trauma he had experienced growing up as a foster child and had never told Sandra.

Although Sandra had always wanted and planned to have children, she never really put this issue on the table when they talked about getting married. Believing, as many do, our society's pronatal dogma, she was sure that Leo would simply come around to wanting to have children and thus never really pressed the issue in the early months and years of their relationship. Now, however, she was unable to penetrate Leo's ability to avoid the issue and was feeling unheard, angry, helpless, and depressed about their future.

A combination of individual and joint sessions with Sandra and Leo helped reveal what was really going on in their relationship and why Sandra was withdrawing from Leo both emotionally and sexually. Relationship repair was achieved when we were able to increase Sandra's assertiveness, decrease Leo's control of the communication process, and then have both reveal what they really wanted and feared as far as having children was concerned. When both felt their needs and doubts were actually heard and appreciated by the other, they agreed to start trying to have a child.

CUTTING OFF YOUR NOSE TO SPITE YOUR FACE

Over the years, I have had a number of clients who, as a function of horrific experiences in childhood, were bound and determined to never themselves reproduce. In some of these cases, the primary motivation was a "fuck you" to their own parents. By denying their parents the experience of grandchildren, these people hoped they would both communicate how profoundly angry they were with their parents and at the same time deny them the

87

pleasure of a future generation. Sometimes this is done in a very obvious and overt manner, as characterized by statements like, "Because of the way you treated me, I'm never going to have children!" More often it is done covertly. In the latter case, rationales and off-the-mark explanations are offered to anyone who questions why these people have chosen not to have children. In this passive–aggressive style, anger and hostility are expressed in subtle, nondirect ways, with the hope of avoiding direct conflict while at the same time creating hurt and damage. Sometimes the message gets across and sometimes it doesn't. My quarrel, however, isn't so much with the method (although as far as methods go, we could do much better) as with the result.

Denying yourself the opportunity to be a parent to spite someone else is the proverbial cutting off your nose to spite your face. In an attempt to punish someone else, you punish yourself. Unfortunately, there is a circular, twisted logic to this course of action that feels consistent with the injured sense of self created in that childhood of abuse or neglect. This circular, twisted logic goes something like this:

> Because I don't feel worthy, it's unlikely I have anything worthy to offer as a parent. I'm angry, hurt, scared, etc., by the person (people) who did this to me and would like nothing more than to get back at them. However, despite being a grown-up now, I still feel helpless to do anything directly about what happened, though this powerlessness also makes me tremendously angry. If I don't let those who hurt me have grandkids, I get to deny *them* the experience, which in a small way helps deal with my anger. Also, in a subtle way, I get to announce to the world what they did to me. I get to show how damaged they have made me feel, and the overriding result of their damage to me is that I don't feel worthy as a person. Because I don't feel worthy...

In circumstances like these, I vigorously suggest that, before any long-term course of action is settled on, some time be spent talking with a psychologist who is familiar with these kind of issues. Now, I won't be constantly recommending that people go see a psychologist to work out every issue that comes along. But in these particular circumstances—that is, when we are talking about the long-term influence of child abuse or neglect—the issues can be deep, complicated, scary, and undefined, and getting help from a professional experienced in dealing with this type of trauma is more about efficiency than anything else. A complete description of all the possible crimes of parenting that might come to light in these circumstances is far beyond the scope of this book, but not beyond this book's general theme, which is about constructing a happy, sustaining, long-term relationship. Ignoring deep and important issues and failing to seek the necessary help (independent of a choice to have or not to have children) is without question a poor strategy both for the individual and a relationship. Psychological storage space, so to speak, is far too valuable a commodity, and skeletons are far better dusted off and removed, rather than allowed to take up valuable room in some mental closet.

The Matter in Question: Having Kids

KIDS Q23. **If possible, find the courage to describe for your partner one of your more unpleasant memories from childhood. How, if at all, has that experience influenced your thoughts about becoming a parent yourself?**

THE SEMANTICS OF MAKING A BABY

Setting aside issues arising from childhood trauma for now, are there other discussions that could be part of the Having Kids conversation? Specifically, what might be some of the other issues that ought to be tackled from the perspective of potentially becoming a parent?

In common usage, *parenting* has become a verb rather than a noun. This reflects the evolution of our thinking about the importance of being a parent. That is, you don't become "a parent" just as a function of making a baby; you are presented with an opportunity to demonstrate your ability "to parent" by learning and doing all those good-parent things. More and more, it is recognized that *becoming a parent* takes only a moment but *learning to parent* takes a lifetime of dedication, love, and sacrifice. As I've said before, there is no way you can have all this figured out before having your own kids. However, there are a number of things the two of you can do to see how well suited you are to work together as a parenting team.

To begin, look at how you and your partner have interacted with other people's children, perhaps nieces or nephews, or the kids of a neighbour or friend. This is an opportunity to start to develop the "potential to parent" part of the Having Kids conversation.

The Matter in Question: Having Kids

KIDS Q24. Have you noticed differences in how each of you handled parenting-like tasks when dealing with nieces, nephews, or any other children you might have taken care of? Are there things that rubbed you the wrong way in how your partner may have reacted or spoken to a child? What about your partner's feelings about how you conducted yourself? Are there things that your partner has done that you admire or feel you could not have done as well?

90

KIDS Q25. Describe for each other a positive situation from your childhood that has had a lasting impact on you. Describe what your parents did or how they reacted. Describe what in their reaction worked or didn't work for you. Describe any lasting impact(s) their response(s) may have had. What feelings and thoughts arise from hearing each other's stories? Can either of you imagine what you might have done or not done had you been the parent in the situations described?

There are plenty of books and magazines out there about the rewards and trials of parenting. There are also plenty of real-live parents out there already, including your own, who have walked the walk and talked the talk, and may have thoughts and ideas about what it is to bring a new life into the world. Read everything you can get your hands on and talk to everyone you think has something useful to say. As we say in psychology, "data good," meaning that collecting important information to help make choices is almost always a productive strategy.

MINOR CHALLENGES

Let's try moving the conversation in a somewhat different direction. Give some consideration and discussion to what the two of you might do, or at least what you think you might do, if a child of yours turned out to be less than physically or mentally perfect. Issues like "when?" and "how many?" quickly lose their simplicity when more serious and long-lasting issues are brought to the surface. And because I know a few of you out there are thinking this, let me say for the record that thinking and talking about what might go wrong in terms of having kids *will not* jinx, curse, or lay some other type of voodoo or evil eye on you! Superstitious thinking of this sort will prevent you from facing and discussing important issues. It would be like being afraid to remind your kid to put on her seatbelt because this might "bring on" a car accident—just plain dumb! Tough and scary issues need to be tackled head-on with maturity and a set of reasonable and adult sensibilities, not with superstitious thinking that's a throwback to our cultural past, when the ways of the physical world where poorly understood.

The Matter in Question: Having Kids

KIDS Q26. Speculate about how you might react if you found out that your child had a serious birth defect. Do you want to have tests like amniocentesis or genetic screening to determine if a birth defect might exist? What would you do if you learned that your child would have Down syndrome or a serious learning or physical disability?

First-Time Parents and the Care and Feeding of Relationships

First-time parents tend to be overprotective of their new bundle of joy. This is all about fear and protectiveness. We've all heard the jokes about the couple who covered everything in the house with pillows and relocated every electrical outlet three feet above the floor when their first child started walking, yet allowed the second child to juggle knives. As we learn about protecting children by being parents, we become in equal parts more confident in our abilities to look after a child and more relaxed about our need to protect the child. Essentially, as we learn more about parenting, we are less prone to catastrophize about every little thing that might go wrong.

My purpose here is to try to accelerate this learning process and offer a little advice, all within the context of wrapping up the first of the ten conversations.

Some first-time parents are hesitant to bring in a babysitter. They haven't developed the confidence that things will be okay, nor have they been able to sufficiently dial down their worries about what might happen to Junior. This combination of factors makes them unwilling to trust their pride and joy to the care of others.

While the sentiment is admirable, maybe even cute, the result tends to be more toxic than many couples realize. Child care, especially when we're talking about a first-born, and everything is new and sometimes scary, *can be exhausting!* It's both physically and psychologically draining. From a stress-management point of view, circumstances that generate high levels of stress and physical fatigue like the first-time responsibilities for child care typically demand time off. This of course brings us back to bringing in a babysitter. Unfortunately, in some couples, one or both party has so many anxieties, so many fears for the safety of the child, and such high needs to maintain their level of protectiveness that it is impossible to even imagine leaving their child in the care of someone else. This is particularly true for couples who do not have extended family nearby and thus can't bring in a trusted relative to help watch the child (this issue dovetails with those discussed in the upcoming Location conversation).

My advice is to take the demands of care and feeding very seriously, but not just in regard to Junior. Your relationship needs nurturing and nutrients as well, and on a regular basis. Over the years, I have helped couples deal with a wide variety of marital problems, and perhaps one of the most surprising results has been how effective access to a good and trusted babysitter can be in reducing marital discord and repairing relationship damage. The need for a babysitter boils down to the idea that your relationship with your partner needs love and attention just as the child does. It's easy to forget this reality when there are diapers to change, doctors' appointments to keep, and late-night feedings to attend to. The inability to temporarily escape the ever-present demands of a child (or children) can end up leaving one or both of you feeling trapped. Feeling trapped creates helplessness and anxiety, these feelings turn into resentment and anger, and then guess where all these negative feelings get directed?

The Matter in Question: Having Kids

KIDS Q27. **Although this is a bit of a challenge, ask each other how you might feel about someone babysitting your child. (I understand this is a bit of a stretch, but I'm only looking to encourage you to get the process started.)**

KIDS Q28. **In a similar vein, what might you think about having your child in daycare?**

KIDS Q29. **Watch the movie *Parenthood* (1989, Steve Martin, Mary Steenburgen). Which of the many parenting styles depicted comes closest to how each of you thinks you might parent?**

Exploring future issues, particularly ones that have proven to be challenges for other couples, is just good strategic relationship management, and this particular issue is ideally suited for this type of practice.

FINAL THOUGHTS ON THE HAVING KIDS CONVERSATION

As I said in the introduction, the Having Kids conversation is the first of the ten conversations because many think they have already had it, but in my experience most couples have not tackled a number of very important issues related to the idea of having children. Few of the ideas or issues I've brought up here are particularly novel or startling, but that wasn't really the point. Reviewing and talking about each idea and issue in a systematic way is the real challenge.

If there is one overriding message that you can take away from the Having Kids conversation, it's that making babies and doing the parenthood thing ought never be a life course that is chosen lightly. No one should ever be drafted into service when it comes to joining the ranks of mom and dad. Entering service should be voluntary and not due to a sense of social obligation or a failure to properly plan. Think critically about what you and your partner want from life, and from your life together, free of assumption and baggage.

Finally, with this and all of the subsequent conversations, once you've got the discussion process started, give each other some time to think about what each of you has brought to the table. We're going to be talking about big, important issues within each conversation, and ideas and attitudes about topics like these are likely to evolve with time and consideration. Take a stand when necessary, but not before there has been a lot of talking, listening, and consideration. When you give yourselves and each other the opportunity to think broadly about each of these issues, you never really know what you might *find*.

CONVERSATION 2:
Careers

THE SECOND CONVERSATION IS about how you will go about earning a living and how this can and will influence your marriage. Essentially, the two of you need to explore, first on your own and then together, what it is you each want to be when you grow up.

Why do you need to have a serious talk about jobs and potential careers before you tie the knot? Well, consider any of the following facts:

- Work injuries can be life altering and high levels of work stress can be fatal.

- Commitments to and expectations for job performance can leave little or no time for other important marital, parenting, and life events.

- The people we work with often become a primary source of social support, entertainment, and recreation.

- Most affairs start on the job.

- The type of job or career we pursue is directly related to the lifestyle we can afford, which will influence everything from where we live to the degree of security we might hope to have in old age.

I'm of the mind that any one of these factoids is probably worth at least a few minutes of your consideration and a brief mention to the person who you hope will be your lifelong partner.

As with all of the ten conversations, the Careers conversation might also be influenced by hidden assumptions or social expectations that will need to be ferreted out and examined from a somewhat more rational perspective.

What am I talking about? Well, remember in "Having Kids" how I talked about how pronatalism can create a kind of unseen social momentum that has some people believing that they are *supposed* to have kids even if they don't feel that this is a good choice for them? In the Careers conversation, there's another social force—another ism—we're going to have to face head-on.

GENDERISM

Despite the odd protest to the contrary, we still live in a world where male needs often get priority over female needs. This shouldn't come as a surprise, as men still rule the world. Protests that we live in an egalitarian society will be made only by the naïve and the politically correct. In reality, women still earn less than men (in many cases even when doing exactly the same job) and still do a disproportionate amount of child care and work around the home. While things have moved in a more egalitarian direction in the past few decades, we are nowhere near the ideal of men and women having parity in Western culture.

However, gender politics is not what this book is about. As much as a more gender-equal world is what I believe most of us would like, we have a long way to go. The current world is what it is, and failing to recognize unpalatable realities like gender inequity is like closing your eyes when you cross the street.

That being said, crossing the street doesn't have to be terrifying or even frightening as long as we take a long and considered look at what dangers might be present before we attempt to cross. While gender inequity unquestionably exists, we don't have to be endangered by it, at least in our primary relationship, as long as we take a long and considered look at how it might adversely influence the choices and assumptions that shape our thinking, and by natural course make egalitarian choices as we create a marriage. But just like pronatalism, the disguised social momentum of genderism is going to be another force that has to be clearly examined as the two of you construct your life together.

The Matter in Question: Careers

CAREER Q1. See if you can tease out the answers to these two riddles:

1. As she comes up the front steps, a wife hears her husband shout, "John, don't shoot!" followed by a gunshot. She runs in and finds her husband clutching his wounded arm, a pistol on the floor, and a trucker, a soldier, and a blacksmith all standing there. Although she has never met these people, she immediately walks up to the trucker, slaps him in the face, and says, "How could you?!" How did she know who the guilty party was?

> 2. A father rushes his son to the hospital, and the child is immediately swept off to the operating room. The on-call surgeon steps up to the operating table, but upon seeing the patient exclaims, "I can't operate on this person—he's my son!" How is this possible?[16]

One of the most obvious places where genderism rears its ugly head is when we start talking money, making a living, and careers. Therefore, and for the record, let's be clear: gender doesn't make one person's—typically the guy's—job or career more important than someone else's—typically the gal's. Gender doesn't give you a leg up (or a leg down) as to who's more entitled to pursue what they want to be when they grow up. Men's jobs or careers are not more important than women's, despite the fact that this has been a social assumption for pretty much the entire history of Western culture. While it would be nice if this didn't need to be categorically stated, the fact remains that many mistakenly believe that men's jobs are more important than women's simply because it is what men, as opposed to women, do.

For some, this little discussion of genderism may seem at best unnecessary and at worst insulting. What is really interesting, however, is the fact that some will be insulted because the idea of genderism influencing how a marriage is constructed will be so obvious that it seems a waste of ink and paper to even describe it. But, for others, the insult will be my assertion that genderism continues to even exist in this day and age, and thus consideration of its influence is entirely unnecessary.

In response to the indignation of both camps, allow me to say that no slight is intended and that if you have constructed

---

[16] Of the three people standing around the husband, only the trucker is *male*, and the surgeon is the boy's *mother*. Did genderism get in the way of your figuring these out?

a relationship where genderism has had nothing but a benign influence, carry on. But let's return to those two riddles I used at the start of this section. For those who didn't immediately come to the conclusion that the trucker was the only man among the three witnesses or that the surgeon was a woman, be warned.

Try some of these questions on for size, both as something for the two of you to talk about and as a way to assess how genderism may or may not be influencing your thoughts about employment and career.

The Matter in Question: Careers

CAREER Q2. If she ends up with a more lucrative job than he does, how would that make you feel? Would it violate any of your expectations?

CAREER Q3. You get a call that your partner is bringing the boss home for dinner. Who's doing the cooking?

CAREER Q4. You sit beside a guy on a plane, and during casual conversation you learn he's a nurse. How long before you ask him why he didn't become a doctor? Would you ask the same question if you were sitting beside a female nurse?

CAREER Q5. The school calls, your daughter is sick, and somebody has to leave work and get medical attention for her. Any *assumptions* as to which of the two of you will be leaving work?

> **CAREER Q6.** You're going to have a baby. Who will be taking parental leave and for how long? Again, any *assumptions* that you might want to share with your partner?

Genderist assumptions and beliefs have the potential to destroy relationships, and as such need to be identified early and confronted. Drawing conclusions about others based on their talents and skills makes perfect sense. However, concluding you truly know or understand someone simply based on their gender is to be dangerously misinformed. If you can't give up genderist beliefs, finding someone who shares your prejudice might seem a good answer, but don't kid yourself. It will be only a matter of time before the underlying inequity you presume and espouse comes back to sabotage what you thought you knew and had.

For the purposes of the Career conversation, now that the existence of genderism has been revealed, we can move on to other important career issues. We will be revisiting gender as an ongoing issue throughout *The 10 Conversations* (for example, just wait till we get to the Sex and the Division of Labour conversations). But for now, let's look at a few of the other critical components of what both of you need to think and talk about when it comes to how your work will influence your marriage.

JOB OR CAREER: THE SEMANTICS OF MAKING A LIVING

Ideally, from a life satisfaction point of view, we find a form of employment we really love. Far more often, this idealized situation is not fully realized and we end up liking our work, or at least finding aspects of it enjoyable. Sometimes, in less than desirable circumstances, the highest expectation we can have is to tolerate the work we do. And, tragically, sometimes we hate what we do for a living and, even worse, feel we have few alternatives for how to bring money home and make ends meet.

You probably don't need a psychologist to explain that how you feel about what you do for a living will influence your relationship. Hating your job can end up being a relationship killer, and with good reason. Feeling angry, resentful, disrespected, threatened, harassed, under the gun, minimized, stifled, cheated, overlooked, or unsuccessful for eight or more hours a day is not going to have a neutral influence on the emotions someone brings home with them at the end of the day.

Thinking seriously about what you want to do from an employment perspective not only influences the kind of life you lead and can afford, but also has a profound influence on the nature and stability of your long-term intimate relationship. A case can even be made that how you feel about your work affects how long you live. A large body of research has indicated that people living in high-stress situations (like the ones that exist when you hate your job and feel powerless to change what you do) end up dying years before those who don't experience similar levels of stress. Thus, making good educational, training, and vocational choices is critically important for a lot of reasons, not the least of which is the health and success of the most important relationship you will ever have as an adult.

In an attempt to assist in making good employment choices, I'm going to contend that a clear distinction needs to be made between a "job" and a "career." While *jobs* are important, far more often it is a *career* that brings us happiness, both individually and as couples.

A job is something that covers the bills. A job gets you paid for your time and your labour. Essentially, a job is about the money. A career, on the other hand, is about what you want to do with your life. A career makes you feel good about yourself; a career makes you feel like you're making a contribution; a career is about meeting your needs, not just an employer's.

Careers are about figuring out "what you want to be when you grow up" and then doing something about it. Careers represent long-held dreams, plans for the future, self-fulfillment, self-actualization, and a whole bunch of other fancy psychology-sounding terms. Essentially, careers are in large part about how we define ourselves. Typically, jobs have none of these higher qualities. If jobs are about money, careers are about feelings. A job may or may not make you feel good about yourself, but the primary purpose of a career is to do just that.

While it might appear that I've just made the case for pursuing a career instead of a job, let me offer a caveat: while working on a career substantially increases the chances you're going to enjoy your workday, not everyone sets about having a career, nor does having a career represent some higher calling. That is, not everyone has to be "about" what they do for a living. For some, what they do to make money is simply that: a means to an end. For these people, the most important part of their lives is *not* about how they earn the money they need to survive, but rather about family, hobbies, sports, artistic expression, or any of a number of other pursuits. Don't let me leave you with the impression that having a job rather than a career represents some kind of failure.

But getting back to premarital issues, *the distinction between a job and a career can be critical in identifying important issues that the two of you need to talk about.* For example, imagine that only one of you has career aspirations and has taken steps in this regard to plan out things like training, school, financial planning, whatever. Important differences now exist between what the two of you want. These differences themselves aren't necessarily going to be a problem, but the failure or inability to recognize and talk about them will be.

Understanding the job/career distinction means that the two of you now have very important issues to discuss and explore together. These issues centre on what each of you wants and what might be required to achieve those goals. These issues potentially touch on a wide range of future relationship issues, such as where you might need to get training, time you might have to spend apart, where you might end up living, and the lifestyle that you will be able to afford.

Realistically Speaking: Sarah

Sarah had recently been transferred to London, Ontario, by the office supply company that employed her. She initially came to see me to help resolve some mood and past relationship issues. Just after she started therapy however, her company informed her that she was going to be transferred again, this time to a city on the other side of the province. Once again, she was going to have to start all over, learn a new territory, and establish new sales contacts. Not surprisingly, she was pretty upset. She was just beginning to settle into London: she was getting to know her way around, she was making new friends, she had joined a health club and hired a trainer, she was learning where the most popular bars and restaurants were, she had started giving some consideration to which neighbourhoods she preferred from the perspective of potentially buying a house, and, in general, she was beginning to feel like she was establishing a home for herself.

I asked Sarah to tell me about her work, and specifically what her work meant to her. She liked it all right, she told me, but it had never been something that got her excited. She explained that a school friend with connections in the company had found her this job, and as she had just finished school and was looking to start paying off her student debt, she happily took it. This work was never something she had imagined herself doing, nor was it something that made her feel particularly proud or satisfied. She was good at her work, as testified by the fact that they kept moving her from one location to another to improve sales.

I asked Sarah to consider the job/career distinction. I wondered aloud if perhaps the "job" she was in was worth, or *ever could* be worth, giving up the stability she had recently established and valued. We talked about different things she might like to do, not just from an employment perspective, but things that might meet other needs besides paying the rent and reducing her student debt. We talked about why she went to school and if what she was doing was tapping into the academic skills she had cultivated.

As a result of these discussions, Sarah came to the realization that while she had been successful at her current *job*, it was never going to meet her *career* aspirations. Her job was never going to allow her to explore and grow the talents she most loved about herself, nor was it ever going to provide her with an enduring sense of satisfaction with what she was doing for eight to twelve hours a day. Moving yet again to keep this type of job felt like too much of a sacrifice. In short order, not only did Sarah refuse the transfer, but she tendered her resignation. At the same time, she started reviewing the calendar for the local university and made the firm decision to pursue a career in human relations. In no time at all, she added to her academic credentials and has since been ecstatic about her new position as an HR director for a large local company.

Realistically Speaking: Ming-Lee and Tom

Ming-Lee and Tom came to see me for what seemed like a sexual problem. They were experiencing what we call a "desire discrepancy," with Tom wanting sex far more frequently than Ming-Lee. Upon investigation, however, it became clear that Ming-Lee's lack of interest in lovemaking was far more about feeling minimized and losing her self-identity than it was anything to do with sex.

Ming-Lee had been living in Vancouver for many years, and, building on her understanding of the East Asian markets and her ability to speak Mandarin, she had established a very satisfying and lucrative career in the import/export business. She and Tom met while skiing in Whistler and eventually fell in love. Following only minimal discussion and planning, they decided that she would move to London so they could be together and potentially start having children. Now, as much as I love London, it can't really be thought of as a hotbed of international trade and is certainly far removed from the East Asian marketplace. The choice that Tom and Ming-Lee made to have her relocate was based primarily on the fact that Tom was a successful businessman in his own right and his entire operation was based in this city.

Neither Tom nor Ming-Lee had given much consideration to the job/career distinction, and not unjustifiably saw Ming-Lee as a highly skilled and very employable person. So while there was no real challenge in Ming-Lee finding a job, it quickly became clear that she was never going to have the kind of *career* she'd once had if she continued to live in London, Ontario. Some discussion and consideration at the "front end" of their growing relationship about the meaning of jobs and careers might have served them better. Neither understood how important Ming-Lee's career was to her self-esteem, her independence, or her identity.

It's also important to point out that neither Tom nor Ming-Lee had a history of making capricious decisions, and both had a track record of dealing with important issues in a frank and candid manner. But when it came to any type of career conversation, the only issue of substance they had really tackled had to do with income levels and protecting the assets that each of them had brought into the relationship.

After much talk and tears, they decided to end their relationship and Ming-Lee returned to the West Coast.

Sarah's case demonstrates how you need to give some thought to your own career needs, while Tom and Ming-Lee show how competing career needs are best identified and addressed as early as possible. Use the questions below to start thinking about your employment options, the job/career distinction, and if and how your choices and your partner's might coincide or conflict.

The Matter in Question: Careers

CAREER Q7. What do you want to be when you grow up? How focused on *job* or *career* do you think you will be?

CAREER Q8. How much do you know about the position or profession you might like to pursue? What type of education, training, and experience might be required to be successful in this position? Have you thought about the time and resources that will be required to acquire that education, training, or experience? Have you shared the answers to these questions with your partner? What do you know about your partner's answers to each of these questions?

As a final comment on the job/career distinction, let me acknowledge that we aren't all born into the same circumstances, and consequently the choices that can be explored are not the same for everyone. This impediment to pursuing a career, however, is less about privilege or disadvantage and more about granting ourselves the opportunity to *think* about our options. We all experience options and limitations. Focusing on the latter rather than the former becomes a personal failure, not one dictated by circumstances. As any psychologist will tell you, the way we think about things plays a huge role in how we see the world and its opportunities. Choosing to focus on the opportunities we can create is a far more successful strategy for personal and relationship success than is a fully realized description and list of all the limitations we might have to endure.

The Matter in Question: Careers

CAREER Q9. Watch the movie *Disclosure* (1994, Michael Douglas, Demi Moore) together. Discuss how traditional gender roles were switched back and forth and how important professional *ambition* was in both of the main characters' lives (see below as to why the two of you need to be talking about ambition as part of the Careers conversation).

CEOs[17] AND HOW THEY DESTROY THEIR MARRIAGES

Okay, with the above issues taken care of, we're making great progress in covering a wide range of important topics the two of you need to talk about in regard to employment and exploring how job or career choices might influence what each of you think your future together might look like. Although it might seem like I'm going to backtrack, I now want to return to genderism, or at least an issue that has a strong suggestion of it.

As I started my work as a psychologist and marital therapist, I began to see people in relationships plagued by a wide variety of problems. However, I quickly identified a common thread that characterized the problems many of them were having. Let me use Eric and Diane as an example.

Realistically Speaking: Eric and Diane

Eric and Diane had been together for eight years before they came to see me, and their relationship was pretty much over

---

[17] CEO is the abbreviation for chief executive officer, who is typically the person who runs a large company. However, within the current context, a CEO can actually represent *any* type of executive, businessperson, or career-driven individual.

when they first walked through my door. Eric was the owner of several financially successful companies and epitomized the concept of a self-made man—a businessman through and through who had learned that hard work and self-confidence were key ingredients to business success. He had learned to be a leader, to be decisive, and to control fear, knowing that fear was a sign of weakness in the business world. Eric was solution focused and had the ability to size up a situation in short order. He could confidently choose a course of action or offer a way to correct a problem that quickly resolved the situation to his advantage. Eric knew what he wanted, and seldom if ever settled for anything less.

With this background, you can imagine Eric's surprise when things became troubled and then intolerable at home. In the past, he had been a success in school, in sports, and in business, and he was completely unaccustomed to failure. To have the situation at home fall apart was inconceivable.

His wife, Diane, had become more and more distant from him over the years. Eric was puzzled and angered by Diane's gradual withdrawal and believed that as he achieved greater success in business, their sense of connectedness lessened. He speculated that Diane was actually jealous of his business success, and this angered him.

He thought it started when she insisted they take separate vacations. After that, their social schedules became increasingly independent. In short order, they were sleeping in separate beds. Eric reported that he wouldn't have been surprised if he learned that Diane was having an affair, given their lack of contact, sexual and otherwise, but also felt that this was not part of her character. Given her withdrawal, he felt entitled to have an affair himself, but had done nothing to pursue this. Before what he saw as Diane's withdrawal from him, sex had been good, and he continued to find her sexually attractive. As neither had thought themselves good parenting material before they were married, as a couple they had decided to remain child free, so the distance between them had nothing to do with parenting or child-care conflicts.

When they were in my office together, Eric did most of the talking while Diane typically just stared past him. When I specifically asked questions of Diane, she had no trouble expressing herself—that is, until Eric jumped in, which he did with considerable frequency. When Eric didn't agree with something Diane said, he would quickly offer a counter-explanation and Diane would immediately fall silent. He wasn't rude or verbally abusive, and neither Eric nor Diane retreated to name calling or insults, but Eric was a verbal bully, always getting in the last word. Eric's frustration at the relationship discord was also much greater than Diane's, and he complained bitterly about how she would no longer even consider the potential relationship remedies he thought were appropriate and reasonable. Eric was certain that if she had participated in the activities he had planned for them, there would have been ample opportunity for the two of them to remain connected and important to each other. But her withdrawal and his anger were bringing their relationship to an end.

Diane's view of things was a little bit different. She too had a successful career, though not in business. She was a respected health-care professional and held a senior position in her community. She contrasted how she felt when she was at work with how she felt at home and was no longer able to reconcile the two. At work she felt respected, influential, and independent, but at home she felt taken for granted, second class, and weak. At home her opinions were influential only when they were the same as Eric's. She felt she had little power in their relationship and had become relegated to following Eric's lead. She no longer sought to have her needs in the relationship met because they were so often minimized or dismissed.

Diane discovered early in their relationship that she didn't like dealing with Eric's adversarial and competitive nature. She didn't like fighting and in fact thought fighting indicated that there was something wrong with a relationship.[18] Rather than remaining

[18] Recalling the "Conflict as a Fact of Life" section from page 20 would be a really good idea just now.

resolute in her opinions or needs, she found she was more comfortable capitulating to Eric. She saw herself as constantly having
to choose between two poor alternatives: stand up for what she
wanted and cause relationship-damaging conflicts or deny her
own needs, give in to the things Eric wanted, and avoid fights and
discord. As she saw herself as emotionally strong, she felt that
she could handle the self-denial that the latter choice required.
What's more, Diane also held on to traditional gender beliefs that
included the idea that women are supposed to be more attentive
to men's needs than are men to women's. Since it was the "job"
of the woman in the relationship to be the peacemaker, she was
following tradition in denying her own needs and letting Eric manage and shape the relationship. However, years of applying this
strategy had left her wondering why she was spending her life in
a relationship that wasn't meeting any of her needs.

Neither Eric nor Diane appreciated what had really happened
in their relationship. With the benefit of hindsight, it was clear
that both had colluded with the other to allow Eric to run the marriage as if it were one of his companies. Essentially, Eric was
CEOing his relationship. He was bringing into their marriage the
skills and talents for which he had been richly rewarded in the
business world. If nothing else, Eric was a leader and a decision
maker, and this had made him successful. Quite rationally, he felt
that being a leader and decision maker in his relationship would
also be a successful strategy and applied this skill set whenever
he felt it was needed. He didn't need to consult or question when
it came to making business choices, so why would he do this at
home? He knew that fear and doubt were signs of weakness in
the business world, and he certainly wasn't going to appear fearful or doubtful in front of his wife! In fact, Eric was of the mind
that much of what he was in the business world was what he
was supposed to be at home. Like Diane, Eric also bought into
traditional gender roles and believed that men should be "large
and in charge" at home, and a failure to do so meant he wasn't
being a "man."

When Eric saw things going badly in his marriage, he did what he did best and became decisive and solution focused, *independently* coming up with action plans that were going to fix things. He gave the situation some thought and then *told* Diane what was wrong with the relationship and what the solutions *were going to be*. In doing this, he fully expected that she would be as willing as he to implement his solutions. The irony was that in trying to fix things between the two of them, he was actually making things worse. Eric was used to being a leader, to taking charge, to being listened to, to independently coming up with solutions, and to being fearless in the face of adversity. Even though he was at home, Eric was doing great business. Unfortunately, he was also doing lousy relationship.

MARRIAGES ARE ABOUT FEELINGS, NOT PRODUCTION

Marriages are about partnerships, not hierarchical corporate structure. Marriages are about shared decision making, not top-down management. Marriages are about using your feelings to inform your choices, not hiding or minimizing your feelings and making choices based *only* on logic. (How many music CDs would you own or how much art would you have on your walls if you could choose only the "correct" or "logical" piece?) Marriages are about consulting, not dictating. Marriages are about feelings, not production. You are not with someone because their hair colour is exactly the right shade or their résumé meets expectations. You are with someone because of how they make you feel. Much of what our lives together ought to be about is sharing feelings, not leading or following.

Both Eric and Diane had missed this understanding of marriage and created for themselves marital roles that were more consistent with corporate structure where he led and she followed, rather than a partnership where equality and walking beside each other were the expectations. Eric was a great CEO, but in treating his wife like a corporate subordinate, he had destroyed his marriage. She was culpable too in that she allowed her feelings to go unexpressed and was now past the point of caring.

I mentioned genderism earlier in this section, and in part the troubles that Eric and Diane were experiencing were related to their adherence to traditional gender roles. Often men are the ones who assume the reins of power in a relationship, as are women the ones who choose to be led rather than become leaders themselves. However, I could have chosen any of a number of other couples whose problems were essentially the same as Eric and Diane's, but for these other couples, it was *she* who was CEOing the marriage rather than *he*. Men do not exclusively own the poor relationship strategy of treating their marriage like a business, and women do not exclusively own the poor relationship strategy of failing to express their needs consistently and assertively.

> ### The Matter in Question: Careers
>
> **CAREER Q10. Is there a clear leader and a follower in *your* relationship? If yes, how did these roles come about? Are you both happy with your position? What similarities and differences do you see between your relationship and that of Eric and Diane?**

SHARED EXPECTATIONS AND JOB- OR CAREER-SPECIFIC STRESSES

It's a simple truth that many marriages can survive when there's little to stress them. Only when there are challenges is the true mettle of a marriage tested. This is true of us as individuals as well. Each of us is best measured when we are faced with limitations rather than limitless resources. We are who we are when our resources are stretched to the limit, rather than when, at least metaphorically, things are "turning in well-oiled grooves" and we're fat and happy. We can all be generous and caring, if only for a moment, when we risk nothing to be so.

These observations about stress are not offered to be cynical but as a cautionary tale. To continue the Careers conversation, let's narrow our focus to specific careers and acknowledge how they might bring with them unique stresses that will, as a matter of course, strain a marriage.

Every job or career will bring with it a unique set of challenges. Working on a production line will test someone in different ways than would working in sales, writing a book, serving in the military, speaking as a public figure, etc. However, that stress and challenge exist is not necessarily the greatest threat to a marriage. In the category of "forewarned is forearmed," it is the unknown or unanticipated stresses that may pose the greatest risks to our relationship stability. When we know about something, when we can anticipate a problem or a stress, we have a greater opportunity to do something about it. I've described how CEOs, or more accurately those enmeshed in the business world, often mistakenly apply the right set of rules in the wrong circumstances. That discussion could simply be seen as a fleshed-out example of how a stress unique to being a businessperson could adversely affect a marriage. Take some time with the questions below to see if you and your partner can flesh out how other jobs and careers could stress a relationship.

The Matter in Question: Careers

CAREER Q11. As a warm–up exercise, imagine what the unique stressors would be in each of the following professions. Further, imagine what the stressors might be if you were *married* to a person in each profession. In most instances, you will be able to imagine more than one strain or challenge. I have provided one or two examples of the stresses that might be associated with each particular vocation, but these obviously are not the only possible ones. When you're done, compare your thoughts with your partner's to learn what each of you think of as the major specific job- or career-related stresses.

a. Seasonal farm worker (e.g., time away from home, hard physical labour, etc.)

b. Firefighter (e.g., life-threatening work conditions, etc.)

c. Politician (e.g., public scrutiny and criticism, etc.)

d. Physician (e.g., on-call work, strains of life-and-death decision making, etc.)

e. Chef (e.g., regularly working late, long hours, etc.)

f. Store clerk (e.g., work that may fail to challenge, seasonal increase in workload, etc.)

g. Mortician (e.g., an unconventional career, constant exposure to death and grieving, etc.)

h. Professional athlete (e.g., physical injury, short career timeline, etc.)

i. Small-business owner (e.g., sole responsibility for success or failure, etc.)

j. Bank executive (e.g., demands to predict future trends, etc.)

k. Research scientist (e.g., being immersed in competitive "publish or perish" environment, etc.)

l. Salesperson on commission (e.g., vagaries in trends and cash flow, etc.)

m. Middle manager (e.g., the often contradictory demands of underlings and supervisors, etc.)

n. Social worker (e.g., vicarious exposure to trauma, etc.)

o. Entertainer (e.g., fickleness of public demands, pressure to constantly develop new material, performance anxiety, etc.)

p. Working in a family business (e.g., complications arising as function of business versus family needs, family conflict, etc.)

q. Working in your partner's family business (e.g., feeling like an outsider, etc.)

(By the way, a measure of success for this question is not that you think the same way, but rather that you've given one another some idea of what is frightening, stressful, or challenging to you. The ability to talk about and share fear is an important measure of relationship intimacy.)

CAREER Q12.   Now go back to Career Q7 and discuss all the stresses and strains you each think might be associated with what each of you want to be. Again, discuss the strains from both perspectives; that is, from the perspective of being in the position and of being *married* to a person in that position.

Ambition

We should not only be looking at what each of you want to be when you grow up and the particular stresses that might come with a specific job or career, but also asking *how much* of something you want to be. For example, is working for a large company enough for you, or is it your plan to be running that company by the time you retire? Does operating your own store represent your heart's desire, or would you feel like a failure if at the time of retirement you weren't running an international franchise? To meet your own needs, do you want to be a teacher, a principal, or the director of the board of education? Everyone says they want to make a million dollars. Are you actually serious? Do you have a plan? Have you thought about the sacrifices and decisions that this might entail? And how might you feel if you don't actually accomplish this goal? Essentially, what are your ambitions, what might you need to do to accomplish them, and, most importantly, have you shared your thoughts and vision with your partner?

As the two of you are addressing the above issues, it is critical to keep in mind that while ambition is a good thing, it's not for everyone. There isn't a "correct" amount of it to have. Ambition is like artistic talent: it's something that can be developed with attention and practice, but some are simply born with more of it than others.

As will be true with almost every topic we cover in *The 10 Conversations*, *unspoken assumptions* about ambition (or any issue significant to you) can be profoundly damaging. Imagine if she assumes that he wants to climb the corporate ladder in the same way she intends, yet he is truly happy staying where he is. Alternatively, imagine that he expects her income to continue to increase as her career develops over the years of their marriage, but she has aspirations of becoming an artist with a limited income or to attend to the needs of children and home. Or yet again imagine that he feels he has to keep progressing at work, while she is frustrated that she sees less and less of him at home.

The Matter in Question: Careers

CAREER Q13. If it wasn't part of your Career Q7 conversation, tell each other about the ambitions you have about your job or career. In so doing, have you uncovered any unspoken assumptions?

CAREER Q14. What messages, if any, did the two of you get from your parents about ambition, work ethic, and how self-esteem may or may not be related to what a person does for a living?

FINAL THOUGHTS ON THE CAREERS CONVERSATION

The entire purpose of this book is to help the two of you make good decisions about what your futures will look like. If the Careers conversation has gone well, a very special and powerful thing will have begun to happen, and this very special thing represents one of the most important qualities the two of you could ever build into your relationship. By giving serious consideration to topics covered in the Careers conversation, you come to not only a better understanding of things like gender expectations, the meaning of work, and the role of ambition, but also potentially an understanding of how important it is to *look after your own needs even while you are thinking about how to strengthen your relationship.* Essentially, the very special quality that I'm talking about is the recognition that you actually may not need each other.

On countless occasions, I have seen individuals who, as a function of taking their relationship for granted, were devastated when it surprisingly came to an end. They were not only emotionally devastated, but also found themselves in a desperate position from a practical standpoint. In taking their relationship for granted, they had also failed to consider how they themselves might make ends meet, where they might live, how they might finish their education, and so on, if their partner were ever to leave.

Accepting responsibility for our own personal welfare is a critically important part of maturing and successfully assuming adult responsibilities. This applies to practical needs as well as emotional ones. Balancing our sense of connectedness with our partner against our own sense of autonomy is a vitally important personal and relationship task. Downloading this responsibility to someone else is just dangerous and immature. Every relationship is a risk, and thinking that you are immune to this reality is to live in a world of magic and dragons. Smart and informed self-management means accepting responsibility for your own success and happiness at *all* times in your life.

The greatest benefit of spending time thinking about and discussing what it is you want to be when you grow up will be getting the point that each of you has the opportunity to be independent of the other. That is, when you think about and plan a career path or an employment objective, you dramatically increase the chances of reducing your dependence on someone else to make ends meet. If you're aware that each can survive without the other, neither of you will be under the mistaken belief that the other has to stay in the relationship for practical reasons. To put things very simply, having spent time working to develop a career means that no one is forced to stay in a relationship strictly for financial or stability reasons. You want to be in a relationship because it works for you, not because you need the results of the work. It is the pleasure of the relationship that keeps you there, not purse strings.

As I have said, we still live in a genderist society, and in my opinion this is a message more young women than young men need to hear. All claims to the contrary, women are less often expected to develop their job and career interests than are men, and this is dangerous.

Let me also be clear that financial dependence is not a gender-specific problem. I have seen many men who, when their wives chose to end their relationship, found themselves financially destitute, not because of child-support or alimony payments but because they had simply assumed they would always be able to count on their wives' income and as a consequence never really looked to fully develop their own careers or earning potential.

So the Careers conversation can have the double-edged quality of bringing you closer together while clarifying how the two of you can, at least from an employment and financial perspective, choose to go your separate ways. Of course, this isn't meant to frighten you; it's meant to ensure that you both understand the reality of the world you are planning to enter.

Further, this duality underlies another critically important message that is present throughout *The 10 Conversations*: good choices are made when you have good information, and good information is sometimes a challenge to accept. But if we're interested in facing the challenge of a creating a happy and sustaining relationship, we'll willingly accept the burden of learning to communicate in frank and candid ways about *any* important issue that comes along. A head-in-the-sand approach is never tenable, and we're left with the reality that if we honestly want to learn what we need to know, we have to put in the time with our partner to talk it *out*.

CONVERSATION

Money and Financial Styles

COUPLES FIGHT MORE ABOUT MONEY than about any other issue. Little speculation is required to understand why: money represents a very concentrated form of resources. In one small, easy-to-handle package, money represents time, effort, opportunity, material stuff, status, freedom, safety, affirmation, problem solving, success, rescue, failure, responsibility, leisure, connection, conflict, and the list goes on. Few other things in our society carry with them such an extensive catalogue of attributes. What's more, we all sample from this lengthy list of connotations differently: what money means to one person is not necessarily what it means to another. For some, money can be all about success and status; for others, lifestyle and leisure; and for others still, freedom and affirmation.

If the love of money represents the "root of all evil," it also represents the root of all "good" and all "neutral," since it can be used for all purposes—good, bad, and indifferent. At its most basic, money can mean only what we decide it means. "A penny saved is a penny earned," right? But what about "Penny wise, pound foolish?" How do we reconcile "A fool and his money are soon parted" with "Fortune favours the bold" and "No one ever got rich without taking a risk"? Do we adhere to the idea that "you only live once," or should we build our lives around the story of the ant and the grasshopper? When perception, platitude, p psychology collide in such vigorous fashion, is it any der that we as individuals and couples have conflicting and eep-seated differences as to how the chameleon that is money ought to be managed?

It's a safe bet that there will be conflicting feelings on money's meaning and its allocation in most nascent relationships. Given the topic's complexity, we can fairly ask if there were ever one better suited to learning to talk in a productive rather than a destructive manner. For the purposes of this book, let's give the concept that money talks a somewhat more literal meaning and identify useful ways to reveal what both of you think and feel about money.

WE ALL NEED MONEY

Plain and simple, in our modern world, money is a must. While the idea that money makes the world go around may be obvious to some and distressing to others, the reality remains: money is a necessity. What's more, a strong case can be made that, at least up to a point, the more money, the better. While this isn't politically correct, it doesn't change the truth of the world.

Here are two equations that we all need to understand as far as money is concerned:

1. Resources = choices

2. Choices = safety + health + pleasant surroundings and experiences

Money represents *resources*, and the more resources we have, the more *choices* we have, and the more choices we have, the greater the likelihood we can structure the world around us in *safe, healthy*, and *pleasant ways*.

Of course, you can only buy so much safety, health, and pleasantness. That's why there isn't a simple linear relationship between money and happiness. The person who has ten million dollars isn't ten times happier than the person who has a million dollars, and neither is the person who has a thousand dollars a thousand times sadder than the person with a million. But it is true that the countries that have more money have happier and healthier people, and people who don't have to worry about money are happier than people who do. Contrary to the popular myth, millionaires don't tend to be miserable, and there is no doubt that those who are crippled by poverty are not euphoric.

Now, everyone has heard stories about someone who won the lottery but still ended up miserable. Every so often, we hear from one of these unfortunate people in the media, saying they were happier before they won the money, and their newfound wealth brought them nothing but misery and heartache. While these oft-cited stories are true, they don't come close to representing the reality of what can be done with more resources. As a quick FYI, it turns out that the vast majority of lottery winners end up having terrific lives. They pay off their bills, buy nicer places to live, give money to the people they love, leave dead-end jobs, can afford excellent educations for their kids, get to travel the world, and have happy and secure retirements. The stories of miserable lottery winners simply play to our insecurities about not having money, and thus make good press. Hearing about how wonderful someone's life became after a lottery win just makes us feel bad from a social-comparison point of view, and thus gets reported less often. (Despite my dwelling on this, please don't get the impression I think you ought to buy lottery tickets. The chances of winning a big lottery are lower than the chances of losing your life to killer bees.)

MORE OF THE SAME WON'T CUT IT

The politically incorrect reality is that money *can* buy you happiness, or at least quite a few flavours of it, but you have to spend money the right way and on the right things to achieve this end. Essentially, when money is used to remove or alter negative aspects of your life, you are buying happiness. When people use money simply to *buy more of what they have*, like a *bigger* house or a *more expensive* entertainment centre, they don't really change their lives. After the initial excitement and showing off, a more expensive car is still just a car, and for most intents and purposes it won't get you to work any happier than one that's more modestly priced.

But let's be clear: buying a safe, reliable car to replace an unsafe rattletrap will in all likelihood make you less anxious and worried, and is more likely to offer you protection if you're in an accident. If your car was so unreliable that you were worried about being able to get your kid to the hospital in an emergency, being able to buy something more dependable will in fact make you happier. Similarly, buying a bigger house in the same bad neighbourhood or a nicer house that is just as far away from work so you still have to sit in traffic for hours every day probably won't bring you much more happiness, but it will take more money. When people use greater wealth to change unpleasant aspects of their lives, they do in fact use money to buy happiness.

It would be naïve in today's world to ignore the consequences of what having and not having money will bring. So everyone needs money, and money is important. But how *much* money is needed in a relationship is a different issue, and one that is more complex than the simplistic "more money, good" way of thinking. As a fundamental part of the Money and Financial Styles conversation, both of you will have to be careful to identify for yourself and reveal to your partner the assumptions you might have about how important you think money is and how much money you think you need to create the life you want.

Why might this be important? Imagine, for example, someone putting in copious overtime, pulling extra shifts, or staying late at the office so more money can be brought into the home, working from the assumption that this extra time and work is going to be recognized, appreciated, and valued by the other partner. Then imagine that the other partner has little or no interest in the extra money, as they don't value it the same way. Rather than appreciate the extra resource that is being brought into the home, they feel the time apart simply represents being left alone and brings on a sense of abandonment and rejection. Here we have an insult added to injury situation *on both sides*: the person at home doesn't value the extra money and thus feels only antipathy toward their partner, while the one at work has the expectation that they will be valued for their extra efforts, and finds instead that they're blamed and attacked!

I've said it before and I'll say it again: the hidden or unrecognized assumptions that the two of you hold are at best dangerous and at worse fatal to a relationship, so think long and hard about what you really value and feel, and *express those needs and feelings to your partner!* The fact that you feel or believe something is a good thing, but you're playing long odds if you believe that because *you* think or feel something, your partner thinks or feels *the same way*. There is a particularly insidious quality to the hidden-assumption danger here at this point in the Money and Financial Styles conversation, because the "more money, good" concept is so omnipresent.

Try following some of these suggestions to identify whether— and how much—the two of you differ on how you value money and how much of it you think you need to feel satisfied.

The Matter in Question: Money

MONEY Q1. Pick a couple of friends and a couple of relatives. Without consulting each other further, write down what you think each of these people makes in an average year. Now compare notes. How close were your estimates? What do you think about the lifestyle these people have, and how close or how far is it from what you hope to achieve?

MONEY Q2.   What is your fantasy income? That is, short of unlimited wealth, what might your absolute pie-in-the-sky income look like? When each of you has figured this out, are there substantial discrepancies between what the two of you wished for?

MONEY Q3.   What do you *realistically* believe your annual income might be? Make estimates not just for yourself but also for your partner, and then compare figures. (The important measure is less about how accurate you are in a real-world sense than how close your estimates are *to each other*.)

MONEY Q4.   Pick a consumer product that's important to you: a house, a car, a piece of furniture, some kind of electronic or computer equipment, a type of vacation, or anything that you both value. Independently write down your predictions of whether and when you might be able to afford what you chose and compare. As a variation, set up a list based on one year, five years, and ten years from now. What type of living arrangements do you realistically hope to have at these times, what type of transportation do you hope to be using, what type of vacations might you be able to afford at these different points in time, and how do they compare to your partner's hopes?

MONEY Q5.   As a different version of the above suggestion, play a game of "nice to have versus need to have." Make a list of things, events, and/or experiences, and discuss how each of you would sort them into either the "nice to have" or "need to have" column. For example, is driving an SUV— or just owning a car—a nice to have or a need to have?

MONEY Q6. Watch the movie *Trading Places* (1983, Dan Aykroyd, Eddie Murphy) together. What are your thoughts and feelings about this particular depiction of money buying happiness?

FINANCIAL STYLES

If you're proceeding through this conversation from beginning to end, you've started talking about what money means to you and how you might use money to structure the world around you in satisfying and rewarding ways. This is a good thing. However, and as the title of this conversation implies, there are two key components to the Money and Financial Styles conversation. So let's look at what a *financial style* is and why the two of you need to know about your differences and similarities in terms of this very important personal dimension. But don't let the concept of financial styles scare you. There won't be anything in the following paragraphs to trigger any arithmetic-phobia you might have, and we're not going to get technical or jargony—there won't be any math!

Let's begin by articulating a general context: life is about managing risk. From getting out of bed in the morning (a situation where you could stub your toe on your way to the bathroom), to going to work (and you could be hit in the head by a meteorite), to eating dinner (where you could want to rip your own head off because the person you're with is so boring), you are engaging in behaviours that all have a degree of risk. As we move through our lives, our experiences, our successes, and our failures allow us to draw conclusions as to how risky certain behaviours are and how much risk we are willing to tolerate. After a time, we instinctively come to learn what behaviours worry us and what behaviours we can engage in with confidence. These experiences—good, bad, and indifferent—get summed up and evaluated by the computer that is our brain, and it produces for us feelings, thoughts, and beliefs about what is and isn't risky.

Depending upon how we have evaluated and interpreted our experiences, we will each have a sense of risk management. Seldom will two people feel exactly the same about risk and risk management, because seldom will two people have had exactly the same set of experiences and outcomes. But we don't need identical experiences to make progress here.

We do, however, have to have a somewhat sophisticated understanding of why some people are more willing to take risks than others. Depending upon any individual's experiences and outcomes, they will have come to an understanding of what makes them feel safe and what makes them feel unsafe.

The critical point of this is to recognize that no one's approach to risk is going to be right or wrong. Rather, each person's approach is going to be based on their own personal experience of the world. When someone has been hurt in a car accident, they have learned through hard-won experience how horrible it is to get injured. To the extent that they have greater fear getting into a car than does someone who has never been injured in an accident, their feelings aren't wrong, nor is any fear they experience inappropriate, despite the fact that most car trips result in no injury worse than a spilled cup of coffee. We might conclude that someone's increased sense of fear of getting into a car after having an accident might be disproportionate to the risk, but their feelings of fear *are not wrong or inappropriate!* We're all allowed to have our feelings and to do what does or doesn't feel safe.

If we turn our attention to fear and comfort in terms of how money is managed, it's pretty easy to conclude that someone's success or failure in dealing with money will inform them as to how much risk they may or may not be willing to take. For example, if you have risked money (or any other resource, for that matter) in the past and succeeded, you will be more likely to pursue other opportunities that involve risk. If you have not been so successful, you likely will feel a little gun-shy when it comes to risking money (or other kinds of resources) and take a more conservative approach. Neither position is right or wrong; it is just consistent with past experience. And, to be clear, I'm not just talking about how money might be invested in the stock market or a business venture. A decision to incur debt to buy a new couch or a preference to save until debt isn't necessary will also be informed by how one feels about risk and the use of money. And, frankly, this is where the rubber meets the road—it is often these day-to-day, mundane financial choices that have the potential to make or break a relationship.

It's also important to point out that it's not going to be just someone's success or failure with money specifically that informs their financial style. A person's general experience of the world will also influence how fiscally risky or conservative they are. Probably nobody reading this book will have lived through the Great Depression early in the twentieth century, but the conservative financial style of the grandparents and great-grandparents of many of us was profoundly influenced by living through things seeming to be safe and stable one day but lost and chaotic the next. When the stock market crashed in October 1929, the greatest period of financial instability and unemployment in modern history began, and in many places it lasted a decade. In the blink of an eye, people lost much if not all their financial security as well as their jobs, and millions of people were exposed to a new and very harsh financial reality. Eventually, the situation improved, but for many the influence of the Depression never faded. And even when things did get better, those who lived

129

through this difficult time were known to hoard money, food, and other resources to the point of obsession. The times they lived through profoundly influenced how they viewed the world and shaped how they viewed risk and money management. In more recent times, the tech crash of 2000 and the Enron scandal a few years later are modern examples of how stability and security can evaporate with little warning and affect the development of risk tolerance.

The point is that any number of factors can have an influence on how comfortable someone is with risk. The odds are not small that the two of you will have different feelings about money management and risk tolerance. But trying to resolve differences by contending that your personal comfort with risk is the "correct" position to take, that your financial style is "superior," is frankly is a waste of time.

So as part of the Money and Financial Styles conversation, spend some time thinking about where you are in terms of risk and financial management. Are you someone who is comfortable with playing the stock market, investing in higher-risk, higher-payoff startup companies, and speculating with money with the objective to increase profits quickly? Or are you someone who prefers a sure bet, looks only at blue chip stocks, and is happy to let money grow slowly and surely in the bank? Or are you somewhere in between—someone who, while happy to save money for a down payment on a house, is also likely to feel that a tax refund is "found money" and ought to be enjoyed in the here and now?

Being able to identify and describe your financial style to your partner is really the objective of this part of the Money and Financial Styles conversation. Use your answers to the questions below to help figure out your own financial style, and then both of you ought to describe your styles to each other. Words and concepts like these might be useful during this conversation: *risk tolerant, risk averse, daring, playing it safe, gambler, frugal, conservative with money, social status, materialism,* and *hedonist.*

The Matter in Question: Money

MONEY Q7.   Forced choice, fast answer—don't think about it, just choose: you're given $5,000. Do you go on vacation or put the money into the mortgage to pay it off faster? (Note: Different choices might be made given different amounts of money. See if you take the same position when you change the amount to $500 and to $25,000.)

MONEY Q8.   Your best friend tells you about an investment opportunity. He believes it will pay off big and has personally invested $10,000. He isn't trying to twist your arm, but he doesn't want you to miss the opportunity. What do you do?

MONEY Q9.   A furniture set goes on sale and it's a really good deal. You both like the set and believe it's a very good price, but you'll have to go $7,000 into debt to take advantage of the sale. What do you do? Essentially, what are your feelings about debt?

MONEY Q10.   What are you most likely to do with a $1,500 tax refund?

a.   Take it to the casino.
b.   Spend it immediately.
c.   Spend it in the next four months.
d.   Put it in the bank to save for a larger purchase (e.g., a car, a trip, etc.).
e.   Pay off debt.
f.   Put it into long-term savings or a retirement saving program.

g. Give it to charity.

h. Some other option (explain to your partner).

MONEY Q11. We have all heard the stories of a person who risked everything they owned on an investment or a business idea. Could you see yourself doing something like this?

MONEY Q12. Forced choice: Do you spend $2,000 of "found money" on a thing or on an experience? Although *materialism* is often used as though it's a four-letter word, set aside political correctness and describe for your partner the things you would like to have.

FANTASY AND REALITY: THE P-WORD

With growing passion, they both knew that the evening held promise yet to come. Others might have been more impetuous, but they've waited for this moment for a long time. And it hasn't been easy—they've wanted to for so long. But prudence had advised holding their course till they knew their relationship was ready for this next, intimate step.

Now they sit across from each other at their favourite restaurant, one sipping wine, the other a single malt. As the meal continues and the evening progresses, they come to realize yet again how deep their love is for each other. As their talk becomes more and more intimate, their sense of confidence grows. They know they were right to wait, but now tonight is the night! They are buoyed with the strength of their relationship and know that they will be able to persevere where others have faltered. They *will* make their relationship into one for the ages, one that endures, one that grows and thrives, nurtured by their mutual dedication, trust, passion, and love. And at least in part, it's the discipline they have shown that has brought them to this point.

As they gaze confidently into each other's eyes, their sense of connectedness grows and the intensity mounts. Sensing the charge in the atmosphere, she leans across the table. Her desire to take it further is unmistakable. Feeling the ever-increasing passion of the moment, he too leans in to meet her. With her lips slightly parted, she leans closer and he feels the warmth of her face and breath. The smell of the wine and her perfume fills his head and takes his mind instantly to what they both know will be the climax of the evening. He too parts his lips to meet hers. Teasingly, she drifts past his mouth and their cheeks caress. As her lips move past his, he feels the warmth of her breath on his neck. She brings her lips to his ear and at last breathes the three words he's been waiting for so long to hear:

"Let's talk prenup."

What? You thought I was going somewhere else with this? This is the Money and Financial Styles conversation, remember?

Prenuptial agreements can scare the pants off people. Just the thought of a prenup will send some screaming from the room. For many, their partner's wanting a prenup means doubts about the relationship and an attempt to hedge bets. And, no question, a prenup does represent an exit strategy for some. However, in the same way that a knife is far more often used as a tool than a weapon, so too does the prenup far more often serve less sinister purposes.

Just so we're all on the same page, a prenuptial agreement is a negotiated contract put together before you get married that describes the division of assets, including money, if your marriage doesn't work and the two of you get a divorce. These types of contracts serve a variety of purposes, but generally they allow an individual to maintain control over their assets. I believe this is a good thing and serves an extremely important purpose, but one that has less to do with assets and money and more to do with recognizing personal autonomy.

As I described at the end of the Careers conversation, it's risky to believe you can give up looking after your own personal interests because you are safely ensconced in a marriage. Building on this logic, why would anyone undermine their own independence by not looking after their own needs *before* entering a marriage? While the purpose of this book is to help the two of you develop confidence in your relationship decision-making skills, the fact remains that *all relationships remain a risk*. Good communication and informed decision making reduces but does not eliminate this risk. And, to be clear, we recognize that there's going to be risk and uncertainty in other aspects of our lives— we buy insurance to cover our car, our home, and our life.

Few like to dwell on the possibility that something catastrophic might happen, but the informed put a plan in place in case something unfortunate does. Only the superstitious would believe that buying insurance increases the chances that something horrible will happen. In the grown-up world, we do much better hoping for the best but planning for the worst. From this perspective, then, we could appropriately view a prenup as an exercise in exploring, describing, and asserting a degree of independence. When viewed from this perspective, I believe the prenup begins to lose its horns and tail.

To address the concern that the request for a prenup is an expression of doubt in the relationship, allow me to let you in on a little secret: *everyone has doubts!* A claim to the contrary is either dishonest or naïve. Simply too much about the future is unknown to claim perfect, unwavering, unquestionable certainty that a relationship will survive any and all the challenges the future may hold. Unfortunately, we have developed a culture of *relationship political correctness* where expressing doubts about a relationship is bad form. Feeling confident that your relationship is strong and healthy is a great thing, and I don't want to minimize this. However, I believe the viability of a relationship is threatened not so much by the fact that both of you will harbour doubts, but far more by a failure to have the *maturity* to acknowledge that doubts exist and the *courage* to face this reality. It seems to me that being able to admit to doubts and talk about them is a far better plan than to pretend that those doubts don't exist. Doing so actually promotes trust, intimacy, and a sense of connectedness. Romantic ideals of relationships and marriage typically don't serve us well *unless* they are balanced with a realistic appraisal of the strengths and weaknesses of that relationship. *Romance without realism is immaturity.*

If you're able to buy what I'm selling, you can see that a prenup is actually a positive marital exercise in that you are both forced to talk about one of the most ticklish subjects a marriage has to manage. Learning how to talk about money in a frank and candid way where both people are expected to be looking out for their own interests while working within a relationship is a pretty challenging skill to develop. Better you start now and learn the "how to," rather than leave it to fate and hope that your interests will somehow be looked after—better to be smart than depend on luck.

The Matter in Question: Money

MONEY Q13. **Does the thought of a prenuptial agreement create anxiety for you? What thoughts are associated with discussing a prenup with your partner?**

MONEY Q14. **I'm always telling my patients that most of psychology boils down to having the *discipline* to identify our strengths and weaknesses, and the *courage* to face both. Based on what you've learned about each other by answering the previous Money questions, what do you see as the Money and Financial Styles strengths and weaknesses of your relationship?**

MONEY Q15. When do you think it would make sense for the two of you to start putting together a prenuptial agreement?

THE THREE-BANK-ACCOUNTS RULE

Given that money is the thing that couples most commonly fight about, I'm continually surprised to learn how little effort some couples put into developing conflict-management strategies specifically to deal with this all-too-common bone of contention. In the interests of getting the two of you started on the right foot, let me clue you in to a little canon that has the potential to spare the two of you from a lot of bickering—the three-bank-accounts rule.

In the interests of conflict management, every marriage ought to have at least three bank accounts. It doesn't matter if they are at the same bank or at three different institutions; it's the number of accounts that matters. Specifically, there ought to be two separate, individual bank accounts, one in each of your names. These are personal accounts, one for each of you. The third account is a joint account that both of you can access at any time.

Here's how you make the three accounts work, and in so doing reduce a substantial proportion of fights about money. The joint account is used for all the shared expenses. These will include things like rent or mortgage payments, utilities, food, joint car or transportation costs, entertainment, household items—whatever costs the two of you decide ought to be shared. At the end of every pay period, both of you contribute to this joint account so that these shared expenses get covered. At the beginning of your relationship, both of you should be participating in this process. That is, both of you should be sitting down together with the bills and jointly figuring out how each expense will be covered. Two important things happen here: you both learn where the money goes, and you both participate in the decision-making process on how all the bills will be paid. In pretty short order, the two of you will be able to determine how much of your take-home pay will be needed on a regular basis to deal with expenses.[19] With any luck, there will be some left over, but this might not always be the case. If there is something left over, however, you now have money that gets divided up and put into the two personal accounts.

How the leftover gets divided up will likely be the subject of some lively discussion, but welcome to the world of marriage and financial management! More critical for our purposes here is the fact that the leftover does get divided and allocated into *each of the two personal accounts*. This is a critical part of the three-accounts rule. Both of you should have your own personal account and consequently your own personal money to spend however you want. I can't emphasis this enough, so let me say it again: both of you have your own personal account, so both of you have the ability to access and spend money *however you want!*

How does this reduce fights about money? Well, it turns out that one of the more contentious issues about how money is used in a relationship is when one person buys something, typically something personal, but the other doesn't agree that this was the right way to spend money. It might also be the case that one person has an interest that the other doesn't share. Let's say one person in the relationship is really into movies (but it could be anything). Spending money on DVDs or going to film festivals may be very important to this person. Let's say the other member of the couple just doesn't get that excited about the cinema but, more importantly, would be resentful if a substantial proportion of the monthly take-home went to paying for this personal

---

[19] The rule here is "at least" three accounts. Quite reasonably, a fourth, fifth, or even twentieth account could be set up to allow for things like retirement saving, saving for a trip or a down payment on a house, putting money aside for a child's education, money to invest in the stock market, or a variety of other financial products or tools. The general principle is to remember to allow for individual as well as joint spending.

137

interest of the other party. The three-accounts rule helps reduce acrimony because only money in the film fan's account can be used to explore this particular interest. If that person runs out of money, they run out of money—joint money is only for joint expenses.

The nice thing about the three-accounts rule is that it allows both members of the couple to remain connected while at the same time continuing to act with autonomy. If one person wants to buy something for him- or herself, they don't need permission from the other person to do so. You're both grown-ups. You ought to be able to act that way and exercise a degree of personal choice and discretion. You need to be able to be yourself within your relationship, and sometimes this takes money.

Of course, there will be challenges in terms of how money is allocated to these two different accounts, and the two of you will have to figure out how this is going to be done. For example, you might decide that because one of you makes more money, that person can put a greater proportion of leftover money in their account. Of course, this would have to be balanced against other things like the division of labour in the home.

Every couple will have its own idiosyncrasies, but the general concept of the three-accounts rule can apply to just about everyone. The number one mistake young couples make in this area is believing that things will simply work out because both are coming into the relationship with love and goodwill toward one another. Allow me to caution you on this type of thinking: learn from the example of all the couples that have come before you and ignore the contentious quality of the division of money at your peril! *It is so much easier* to have tools like the three-accounts rule in place from the outset. If, over time, you turn out to be the exceptional couple that agrees on all aspects of how money is managed and spent, great, you can relax as far as applying the rule goes. But if you're like most couples, you'll be able to avoid a lot of needless and potentially damaging fights over money by having these simple guiding rules in place.

The Matter in Question: Money

MONEY Q16. Have you ever set up a joint account? Do you understand how joint accounts work? Do you want a joint account where both people have to sign for every transaction (this gives equal control to the account holders, but at times will be less convenient) or where either person can sign to complete a transaction (more convenient but potentially subject to individual abuse)?

MONEY Q17. What personal, individual interests do each of you have that are not shared by the other? For example, might one of you want to spend money on seeing sporting events while the other might want to save to travel? To the extent that you can start identifying what these personal interests might be and begin discussing how the costs associated with these interests will be covered, you are well on the way to reducing fights associated with allocating money.

MONEY Q18. What do the two of you know about budgeting? Have either of you ever put a budget together? What sources of information could the two of you use to help you learn how to put a budget together? When are you going to do this?

MONEY Q19. Although it might sound strange, discuss what each of you knows about financial planning for retirement. Retirement might seem like a long way off, but as the business experts tell us, "a failure to plan is a plan to fail."

Liability, Psychologically Speaking

Increasingly, the individuals and couples I counsel are bringing up *financial debt* as a major issue that is interfering with their lives. A week no longer goes by without someone talking to me about the stress and worry that has come along as a function of maxing out credit cards, needing to defer payments for months or years, borrowing money from friends or relatives, hiding debt from a partner or family, and purchasing items with little or no plan as to how those purchases will eventually be paid for.

Somehow we have weaseled our way into becoming a culture of debt. This shouldn't really be a surprise, as on a daily basis we are bombarded with the message that if you can't pay for it today, don't worry; there's always plenty of credit. And, no question, there *is* plenty of credit. Banks and other institutions fall all over themselves trying to lend us money. Of course they do— every time they get someone to borrow money, essentially they have found a new person who is willing to go to work for them. This is what happens when you borrow money: you go to work for the lending institution. Unfortunately, because there is so much credit, it is quite common for individuals to have five or six figures of debt and for nations to have eleven, twelve, or even thirteen figures of debt. (FYI, thirteen figures translates to *trillions* of dollars of debt, and this is a number I can't even imagine.[20])

While it is completely understandable that people want to have nice things and experiences, this has to be balanced with the reality of making ends meet. Psychologically, a lot of people fail to appreciate the amount of stress that the obligation of debt

---

[20] Just to *try* to put this in context, if you live to be a hundred years old, you would have lived about three billion seconds. If you live to be a thousand years old, you would have lived thirty billion seconds. If you were to live a *trillion* seconds, that would make you about 30,000 years old, which is about three times the length of recorded human history. That's what a trillion means.

entails. And stress of this kind has a crippling quality: as debt mounts, many feel a sense of powerlessness and despondency that has them knocking on the door of depression, and this doesn't do them, or any relationship they are in, any good at all.[21]

What's more, a toxic debt situation is made even worse when there are substantial discrepancies in how much each member of a couple is doing to manage or pay down that debt. When one has been saving pennies for months to try to make a dent in the bills and the other blithely—and often without consultation— purchases a new toy or other indulgence, the fur can really fly.

Realistically Speaking: Ashley and Adrian

Poor debt management brought Ashley and Adrian to the brink. Although they both had good jobs, their debt was substantial and was creating a tremendous strain on their relationship. Or, more correctly, their different perceptions of their debt was creating tremendous strain.

Ashley had been brought up in moderate circumstances and was accustomed to delaying gratification. She was comfortable, if not happy, to save for the things that she and Adrian wanted. She would make financial plans that extended months and years into the future, and was content to acquire things and have experiences only insofar as they fell within her financial planning. To the extent that something upset her financial plan, whatever enjoyment might have come from the new acquisition or experience was lost to her anxieties.

Adrian, on the other hand, had few qualms about debt. Growing up, he'd been accustomed to a high standard of living, and he was relatively unconcerned that the couple's current combined income didn't accommodate the lifestyle that he was used to. Further, social status was very important to Adrian, and to be

---

[21] And for those of you who were left with a bad taste in your mouth when I was pontificating about how money *can* buy you happiness, go and talk to someone who was deeply in debt but then came into sufficient money to get them out of it—that's a whole new flavour of happiness!

seen within his social circle as wanting for things or experiences bordered on the intolerable. He was of the mind that things were going to continue to get better for him and Ashley, and their debt would be successfully dealt with sometime in the future. Adrian wasn't naïve or cavalier about their debt or their continued acquisition of costly things; he simply had confidence in his ability to cover their debt in the future and a history of success that was not inconsistent with this perception.

The critical problem here was not who was right or wrong, but rather that there was a failure to appreciate each other's needs as far as risk and debt tolerance were concerned. Adrian interpreted Ashley's anxieties as doubt about his plans to see their income continue to rise, and that angered him. They would fight, and occasionally he would spend. For her part, in an attempt to allay her fears, Ashley began to secretly squirrel away money that she hoped could later be applied to their debt. For a while, her secret saving seemed to work and they stopped fighting. They both knew, however, that they needed help to work through what had happened to the relationship, so they called me and began marital therapy.

Just after they started, Adrian independently made a substantial personal purchase, and this was the straw that broke Ashley's back. To see the benefit of her months of secret scrimping evaporate with one purchase felt too much like disrespect and a violation of trust, and she chose to leave Adrian. Although in subsequent sessions we tried to salvage what they had, they were both too fearful and angry that the other would not accommodate their respective financial styles and their separation became permanent.

YOU NEED TO LEARN ABOUT DEBT MANAGEMENT

Unfortunately, living within our means seems to be passé these days, and it's hard to feel good about yourself when your neighbours or friends have a nicer home or a bigger car than you do or a relative just returned from a cruise or bought a fancy new home entertainment system. Well, let me tell you a little secret: based on the current spending habits of North Americans, in at least three of those four examples those things were not actually purchased outright but were put on a credit card or a line of credit and have yet to be paid for.

This isn't a book about finance, and I don't think you want to be getting your financial advice from a psychologist (in the same way I hope you don't get your psychological advice from a financial consultant!). But, that doesn't mean there isn't a psychological cost to be paid for financial ignorance. There are tons of resources out there on how to manage personal finance and debt, and because few of us were taught much of this during our formal education, it behooves all of us to go out and learn about these things on our own. Talk to financial consultants, visit your banker, read books, and go to personal finance workshops so that you become conversant with the issue of intelligently managing debt and conducting your personal finances. Better yet, set yourselves the task of doing this together so that differences in financial style can be dealt with as you both learn and grow as a couple.

The Matter in Question: Money

MONEY Q20. How much debt are you bringing into the relationship? Have you disclosed this to your partner? Have the two of you discussed if and how that debt is to be managed and repaid? Is there any expectation that the debt either of you bring into the relationship will become a shared responsibility?

MONEY Q21. What "debt stories" have you heard from friends or family?

MONEY Q22. Do either of you know someone
you could talk to about learning how to manage
debt and start making informed financial decisions?

FINAL THOUGHTS ON THE MONEY AND FINANCIAL STYLES CONVERSATION

So couples fight more about money than anything else; we all
need money because it represents a lot of very important things;
money can't buy everything, but it can buy certain kinds of happiness (even though this isn't politically correct); different people
will have different financial styles, and these need to be acknowledged and accommodated within a relationship; talking about
prenups is great practice for a lifetime of dealing with financial
issues; the three-bank-accounts rule is a terrific money and conflict-
management tool; and debt sucks, so avoid it whenever possible.
Got all that?

As a psychologist, I can offer only so much about the specifics
of how to manage money and explore the financial style(s) that
might be right for each of you. If you're like most young people,
you have a lot to learn about how to use your hard-earned
money to your greatest advantage. Unfortunately, as a culture, we
seem to do a pretty poor job of preparing people for what they
ought to know about finance. For reasons I have never understood, our formal education seems to leave out three topics that
are of daily interest to us: sex, relationships, and finance.

Given this reality, it's important to understand that there
remains a lot to know about how to handle your money. To the
extent that you both see this as a necessary task, you are on the
right track. If only one of you (or, heaven forbid, neither of you)
decide to assume responsibility for this task, the potential for
important bonding experiences will be lost, but worse than that,

at least one of you will lack information and knowledge that is critically important to functioning in the adult world. It's downright foolish to download the responsibility of money management to your partner. We all have to develop our personal financial chops, if only to maintain our independence, and this is a dangerous thing to shirk or give up. And, of course, if each of you takes on an appropriate level of *responsibility for financial knowledge*, neither of you will ever be caught in a circumstance of not knowing "who knows *what?*"

CONVERSATION 4:
Sex

SEX IS GREAT! NO, REALLY. If no one has ever told you before, let me be the first to clue you in: *sex is fantastic!* It feels great, it's terrific exercise, it meets a tremendous biological need, it helps you sleep better, it enhances your sense of well-being, and don't even get me started on orgasms! Orgasms are killer: that sense of sexual tension building and building, your muscles tightening, the heightened sensitivity and sensual awareness that grows with the muscle tension, that growing sense that you don't think you can take any more stimulation before you explode, and then BANG! You *do* explode, and all that tension is released in a flood of relief, satisfaction, and profound well-being! It's like a sneeze, only ten or even a hundred times better!

Yep, sex is great. Sex is fantastic! Oh, and perhaps I should mention, apparently two-person sex is pretty good too!

Welcome to the wonderful and wacky world of sex, where there is so much assumption, stereotyping, and myth it's a wonder that we ever manage to disseminate any good basic information to anyone.

I have been studying, researching, teaching, and counselling about sex for the last twenty years, and, not surprisingly, I believe there are a lot of important issues to be dealt with. You may have noticed that this is one of the longer conversations in *The 10 Conversations*. For those of you who are intimidated or uncomfortable with issues sexual, try not to worry—I'll be gentle. On the other hand, as I have contended in previous conversations, if we're going to talk about getting married, we need to adopt a *grown-up*, or if you prefer, *mature* (or if even that doesn't work you, how about *courageous?*) perspective on important relationship issues, and the sexual relationship you develop with your partner will require no less candour and frankness.

SEX IS PRETTY IMPORTANT

Establishing a sexual relationship with your partner is arguably *the* defining quality of marriage. Sex in marriage is considered by many to be the most (and for some, the *only*) appropriate place for two-person sex to take place. Traditional North American wedding vows reflect this with pledges to "forsake all others, and keep yourself unto him (or her) and no other."[22] The requirement for sexual fidelity or exclusivity within marriage remains a cornerstone of what most people expect from marriage, and violations of this expectation represent for many the greatest threat a marriage can face, as well as a fundamental personal violation of trust (more on this later). And of course, without sex, we're not making any babies, which again, from a more traditional perspective, is something that goes hand in hand with marriage.

So sex and marriage have a pretty powerful association. But even without marriage, sex is pretty important all on its own.

Think about it. If it weren't for sex, you wouldn't even be reading this book—you wouldn't be here! None of us would. If our parents hadn't had sex, there wouldn't even be any "us." And, yes, that's right; your parents have had sex. They might have had

---

[22] It is interesting to me that our social discomfort with sex is evident right out of the gate, as is evident in these vows. They don't say, "And I won't have sex with anyone else." Instead, we get this "keeping" business. Imagine this as a pickup line or a sexual come-hither: "Hey, baby, wanna do some *keepin'*?" I suppose it would depend on who said it—maybe if we got Barry White it would sound better.

a lot of sex. In fact, in all likelihood, your parents are *still* having sex. Hell, they might even be having sex right now! If this observation generates a "yuck" response in you, it's time to get over that. If you're going to have healthy and productive conversations with your partner about things like sexual behaviours, sexual gratification, sexual satisfaction, and sexual needs, you're going to need to create a more mature understanding of the role sex plays for you as an individual. You were born a sexual person, you are currently a sexual person, and you will remain a sexual being no matter how old you become and for the rest of your life. Everyone else is also a sexual person, and they will all be sexual people for as long as they can draw breath. Being alive means being sexual.

This might be a good time to introduce you to an important concept that is closely related to sexuality: *erotophobia/erotophilia*.[23] We all have a personal level of comfort or discomfort with things sexual. Some will be pretty relaxed about sexual issues and could throw words like *penis* or *clitoris*[24] into a conversation without batting an eye. Others will visibly wince in just such a conversation and would rather run screaming from the room than discuss a preference for circumcised versus uncircumcised penises, changes in labial colour as a function of sexual arousal, or the volume and calorie count of the average male ejaculate.[25] To the

---

[23] Although I have tried very hard to keep jargon to a minimum, of necessity there will be times where nothing but jargon will do. While I know that a lot of professions have their own special language (I'm thinking doctors, lawyers, and engineers here), I sometimes wonder about psychology. I wonder if, because as a science we are a little late to the game (psychology as a science has really been practised for only about a hundred years), we generate these and other words and phrases—such as *transitory hyper-focus* or *scalloped reinforcement schedule* or *momentum of complacency* or *maintaining the homeostasis of the system*, and trust me, I could go on—just to make us sound legitimate.

[24] And by the way, it's pronounced *CLI*-tor-is, not cli-*TOR*-us. In its small way, *Seinfeld* has set the cause of clear and effective sexual communication back years!

[25] About a teaspoon, 3 to 5 calories max.

extent that someone is uncomfortable with sexual issues, they fall more toward the eroto*phobic* end of the erotophobia/erotophilia continuum. On the other hand, if someone is pretty comfortable with sexual issues, they could consider themselves more of an eroto*phile*.[26]

As you can imagine, someone who is more erotophobic is going to have a harder time talking about sexual issues, more difficulty taking responsibility for their sexual needs, and a really hard time considering their sexual satisfaction worthy of attention. This is a bad thing—bad, Bad, BAD! Being afraid or uncomfortable about sex *is a bad thing*. It has the potential to create substantial and even catastrophic problems with your long-term intimate relationship.

But take heart. Being erotophobic is more of a learned trait than something that is carved in stone. Every year I explain to the students taking my Human Sexuality course that one of my primary objectives is to move them along the erotophobia/erotophilia continuum, so that whatever level of comfort they had with sexuality at the beginning of the course, by the time it's over they will be more erotophilic; that is, more comfortable with things sexual. And at the end of every year, the feedback I get from hundreds of students is that in fact they *are* more comfortable with sexuality! They can now think about, ask about, and express sexual thoughts, ideas, and needs in a way they previously had never thought possible.

So it's quite possible to increase your level of comfort with sexual matters, but this doesn't happen without effort. Indeed, there are a number of social factors that have conspired to make so many people less than comfortable with sex.

---

[26] An early mentor of mine, Dr. William Fisher of the University of Western Ontario, was among those who coined the concept and phrase *erotophobia/erotophilia*, and those of us in sexology, as well as the lay public, have been made richer by this very important contribution. Thanks, Bill!

Sex Can Be Hard to Talk About

Think about how sex is portrayed in movies or on TV or in music videos. Who are the people having sex? In a nutshell, they're the beautiful people. They're young, healthy, and good looking. You don't see elderly people, overweight people, unattractive people, disabled people, ill people, or mentally challenged people regularly having sex, do you?[27] Sex, at least as it is portrayed in the media, is about health, beauty, and, for the most part, youth. The rest of us mere mortals are left only to imagine what our sexual lives might look like. With this bias, is it any wonder that many of "the rest of us" are left to wonder if we're even supposed to have sex?

For most of us, sex is poorly modelled in popular culture, if it's modelled at all. In the absence of healthy sexual models for all types of people, we could be forgiven for struggling with the creation of our own sexual image, and a sexual image that is healthy and worthy of attention and respect. So one of the reasons sex might be hard to talk about is that most of us seldom see ourselves portrayed as sexual beings. This serves to delegitimize our sexual thoughts and feelings, and creates a stumbling block to good, assertive sexual communication.

What about other models of good, representative, healthy sexuality? TV, movies, and music videos can't be the only source of our sexual information. What about what our parents taught us about our sexual desires, needs, and rights? What about all those times they brought up the topic of sex in a comfortable and casual way, and made the point that it was a really important part of our ongoing development? Remember how they encouraged

---

[27] On the very rare occasion when any of these kinds of people are portrayed as sexual beings, it is typically only within the context of a documentary or as a joke. Given the sexual exclusion or derision that members of these groups have to endure, in the language of psychology we talk about these groups being *desexualized* in our society.

us to ask questions about sex and used their own personal experiences of sexual learning to reinforce the sex-positive messages they offered us? Don't you smile when you think about how mom talked about her first menstrual experiences, and dad laughing about the thoughts that went through his head when he had his first wet dream? Remember too how they talked together about their own early sexual experiences and how awkward yet excited they felt? They'd go on and on about the mistakes they'd made, but in so doing learned more and more about each other's sexuality and how to build a healthy and satisfying sex life within their marriage. Those were good times, weren't they? That was the stuff of familial bonding and the modelling of appropriate developmental goals and maturation, wasn't it? Or were you at camp when those conversations took place?

Of course, if you did miss those terrific and frequent talks with mom and dad where the model for "frank and candid" in regard to sex was laid down, you knew you could count on getting good and complete sexual information at church. Sure, the church fathers have always been about making sure everyone hears the latest on sexual functioning. These are the institutions where sex is given centre stage, and church and religious elders make sure that all sexual questions from young adherents are encouraged, and the latest and most useful information on sex is offered to build a better, healthier, and safer religious community!

But, thankfully, for those poor underprivileged few who didn't get the good news about sex from home or church, at least there was school. Treading the halls were those specially trained and informed sex education specialists who had the answers to every conceivable question a grade schooler or, at worst, high school student could want to ask about sex. Not only could they tell you at the drop of hat about the costs, effectiveness, and availability of the latest forms of birth control, but they also schooled kids on the meaning of sex, how to make good sexual choices, favoured sexual positions, how to satisfy a sexual partner, and how, by knowing all about sex, everyone could make a clear and informed choice about when and how they were personally ready to engage in two-person sexual experiences. In doing so, they created a climate of knowledge and understanding that meant kids didn't have to satisfy their sexual curiosities by actually going out and having sex before they were ready. No, in this supportive environment, children were given clear and candid explanations of all things sexual, knowing that of course sexual knowledge doesn't cause kids to go out and have sex but does in fact mean they'll be better prepared to have sex should they choose to do so.

Now, if you're one of those rare and exceptional cases we occasionally hear about, one of those who DIDN'T get exposed to ANY of these positive sources of sexual information, I suppose it would be understandable for you not to feel immediately and totally comfortable thinking and talking about sex with your potential lifetime marital and sexual partner. This in fact might actually get in the way of your being appropriately sexually assertive. We'll need to keep these rare people in mind as we proceed through the rest of this conversation.

Setting sarcasm aside, let me just make the point that although there have been numerous opportunities and institutions that could have ushered in a more erotophilic society, for the most part those opportunities have been missed and those institutions have failed to create a healthier, more erotophilic climate in North America. This failure of modelling has left many feeling uncomfortable and sometimes overwhelmed when it comes to the necessity of talking about sex.

Just a couple of other points before we get on with the *how* and *what* of a productive sharing of sexual likes and dislikes. Even when we are relatively erotophilic—that is, comfortable with sexual issues—there are still at least two things that get in the way of this sexual comfort being turned into productive sexual communication. The first is the actual language of sex. For reasons I have never been able to figure out, we don't seem to have a nice middle-of-the-road set of words and descriptors for things sexual. Rather, we seem to have only a couple of extremes. When it comes to talking about sex, it's either all clinical and scientific like *penises* and *cli-torises* or it's street language like *dicks* and *cunts*. Given these unpalatable choices, is it any wonder we hear people say things like, "Yeah, I really like it when you do that thing to my thing," or "That stuff that you do while you're down there is nice"? Not exactly the stuff of clear and precise communication, is it?

Given the limit of these two less than desirable choices, if we want to talk about sex we either have to be wearing a lab coat or a pimp hat, and neither tends to appeal when we want to have an important sexual conversation. If we had a respectable, middle-of-the-road set of terms and descriptors, I seriously wonder if we might resolve a substantial amount of sexual misunderstanding, dis-comfort, and even sexual dysfunction. However, allow me to offer this bit of advice: when in doubt, go formal. You can always loosen up the language as you gain confidence and experience, but put-ting someone off by saying, "Let's talk about how to improve how we fuck," when they aren't comfortable with this level of vernac-ular threatens to end a conversation before it has even started. I'm not saying that using more colourful sexual language is a bad thing—far from it. For some people, it can be a huge turn-on. My point is that when you don't know the comfort level of your audi-ence (or your partner), *start* formal. As you learn more about each other, and your level of comfort and trusts develops, you'll be able to use whatever kind of language turns you on! In fact, in a per-fect example of talking about talking, one of the most useful places to get a sexual conversation started is to talk about the kind of sex-ual language you're most comfortable with.

The Matter in Question: Sex

SEX Q1. Let's get things started by establishing our terms of reference for the big three: coitus, male genitalia, and female genitalia. Tell your partner what your preferred term is for coitus: *love-making, having sex, doing it, fucking, banging, humping, making the beast with two backs, bumping uglies,* or whatever term makes you most comfortable (or least uncomfortable). Similarly, what is your preferred term for the male member: *penis, cock, dick, shlong, your (or my) thing, one-eyed trouser snake,* etc.? Finally, how would you prefer to reference female genitalia: *vulva, vagina, pussy, cunt, bird, oyster of love,* etc.? There's no rule that you have to settle on one particular term, but knowing what creates comfort and discomfort for yourself and your partner is a good place to start.

SEX Q2. For fun, but only if it's consistent with your current sexual comfort level, the two of you could get on the Internet and search for sexual slang. No area of human endeavour has ever been graced with a greater variety of descriptive terms. There are more ways to refer to sex, masturbation, and male and female genitalia than any other set of words in the English language (I suspect this is also true in other languages, but I can't make this claim with any authority). The purpose here is not to be crass but to have fun.

As though we didn't have enough to contend with as far as language issues go, there is also the whole gender problem, where men, according to our traditional set of cultural expectations, are supposed to be sexperts, while women, according to this same set of dubious rules, are supposed to be sexually naïve. There's nothing like a set of ill-informed and inaccurate set of social demands to set men and women up as adversaries. The *traditional sexual script*, as these rules have come to be called, demands that men always have to be sexually aggressive, sexually interested, and sexually proficient, while women are supposed to be sexually passive, tolerant of men's sexual interests since they as women have little sexual interest of their own, and completely unskilled in the ways of sexual satisfaction. While there is no truth to either set of these so-called rules, they are continually perpetuated, at least in Western culture (I'll have more to say about the traditional sexual script later in this conversation).

Realistically Speaking: George and Martha

This is one of my favourite clinical stories because it highlights how off base things can get as a function of our general difficulty in talking about sex.

Many years ago, a newlywed couple, George and Martha, had been referred to me for help with a sex problem. Martha was very tense when it came to sex and was seldom able to have an orgasm during lovemaking. If she did, it would only be after forty minutes or more of direct clitoral stimulation, and both parties wanted her to feel more sexually relaxed and enjoy orgasms more frequently. This is not an uncommon problem, and sex therapists are often called upon to help people become more relaxed about their bodies, more relaxed about sexual expression, and more relaxed about sexual response. I saw this as a pretty plain-vanilla case, and one that would be successfully resolved in no time.

In the sex therapy biz, we often teach clients about a series of sexual exercises called *sensate focus*. Essentially, you get both members of a couple to become more sexually expressive and responsive by first going back to basics and getting them to get in touch with the sensual potential of their bodies. They do this by exploring and touching their *own* bodies and focusing on the sensual experiences they have (hence the name sensate focus). This exercise is first done individually, where a person looks at and touches themselves all over, not to generate sexual arousal or response, but just to get comfortable with what their body can offer them. From there, clients are told to focus on their genitals and any other area that generates pleasant sexual feelings. Once someone is comfortable with this type of self-exploration, we encourage them to take it up a notch and specifically engage in sexual self-stimulation, and eventually self-stimulation to orgasm. Once they are comfortable with this, we have them show their partner what they have learned about how they like to be touched and stimulated, which eventually culminates in mutual sexual stimulation and whatever sexual behaviours the couple finds enjoyable. While a couple is going through these exercises, we put a "ban" on intercourse, explaining that only when they have learned to feel comfortable with their own personal sexual feelings will we gradually reintroduce two-person intercourse into their sexual repertoire.

I thought George and Martha were making good progress. Over seven weeks, I had explained to them the process of sensate focus and sent them home to do their sensate focus exercises and other psychological homework. In each subsequent session, they reported their feelings and experiences to me, and in no time at all they reported they were getting more comfortable with their bodies. Martha in particular felt sure that when she and George were ready to attempt two-person intercourse in the near future, she would be able to feel relaxed and enjoy her own sexual feelings.

So I was a little surprised when it was only George who showed up for the eighth session. George sat down in my office and after the standard pleasantries I asked him why Martha wasn't with us. He looked a little sheepish and, staring down at the floor, told me that she didn't feel ready to take the next step in sex therapy, that being the two of them sharing and showing each other what they had learned about their own bodies during their individual sensate focus sessions at home. I expressed surprise at this, believing that they had been making good progress. (If a camera had been in the room, I'm sure the video from this point on would have been indistinguishable from an Abbot and Costello routine.)

George looked at me in surprise and explained that what I was asking them to do next was a pretty big step. He was of the opinion that most couples I see must have a hard time with the next step and intimated that, as a psychologist and a sex therapist, I should understand how difficult this next step was—I shouldn't be surprised at Martha's trepidation! I of course was taken aback. I thought I *had* shown an appropriate level of concern and sensitivity. I thought that I had explained the rationale of what I was trying to get them to do and that we had all agreed on this course of action.

Our miscommunication went on for another couple of minutes until, in horror, a thought occurred to me. I asked George exactly what he thought the next step was. With obvious annoyance and exasperation, he explained that the next step was for him and Martha to get undressed and start showing each other what they had learned about their own bodies during their sensate focus exercises. With what I can describe only as my own clinical level of apprehension I asked him *where* he thought this next step was going to take place. "Well, where else? Right here! How else could we show you?!" he exclaimed.

I don't need a large office—there's room for three wingback chairs, a couple of bookcases, a table, and my desk. No couch, no futon, not even a recliner or a throw pillow, and certainly no bed!

In disbelief at the sound of the words I was actually required to say, I explained to George that no one, *ever, EVER* takes their clothes off or actually *has sex IN MY OFFICE!* Somewhere in the seven hours I had spent with this couple, they were both left with the mistaken impression that sex therapy involved sex in front of their therapist. In the classic words of the evil prison warden in the movie *Cool Hand Luke* (played brilliantly by Stother Martin), *"What we got he-ah . . . is failure to com-MUNicate!"*

Since that experience with George and Martha, I explain to all clients seeking sexual counselling that we only *talk* in my office. There is no sex, not even any touching (other than a handshake or a clap on the back).

Although this anecdote highlights a number of issues, for my purposes here I use it to demonstrate how difficult and prone to misunderstanding the simple expression of sexual ideas can be.

Getting a Sexual Conversation Started

Given all the impediments described above, how could a couple start to create a culture within their relationship that fosters positive sexual communication? Try starting with the suggested topics below. Even if you've covered some of this ground before with each other, it's likely that there are examples or details that remain to be described. And, to be clear, getting comfortable with talking about sex is not something you can just read about—you have to actually do it.[28]

The Matter in Question: Sex

SEX Q3.   Tell each other how you learned the "facts of life." But don't stop at the facts of what happened. What were your thoughts and, most important, your feelings when you learned for the first time where babies come from? What were the circumstances under which you learned the "facts"? Looking back, how accurate was the information you were given? Was there any opportunity

---

[28] Sadly, not everyone has benign stories about sexual experiences. The degree of trust you feel for your partner will affect whether you are ready to share painful, frightening, or traumatizing sexual events. Allow me to offer this observation: to the extent that you don't feel you can trust your partner with this type of information, we can realistically question whether the relationship in general is ready to flourish and grow. Often, the help of a skilled psychologist familiar with relationship-building issues as well as trauma (sexual or otherwise) can be tremendously useful at this juncture.

for you to ask questions and, if there was, what were they? What did you do with your new-found knowledge?

SEX Q4.   Share your memories of any formal sex education you received. Quite a few of you will have nothing to say in this regard, but for those who did receive sexual instruction at school, at camp, or in any other formal venue, tell your partner about your experience. If you had little or no formal sexual education, who did you get sexual information from? Remember, thoughts and feelings, thoughts and feelings, thoughts and feelings...

SEX Q5.   First menstruation and first wet dream are relatively commensurate coming-of-age events in women's and men's lives. Many feel squeamish just thinking about these issues, but, hey, we're here to start talking about sexuality in an open and adult manner. Share your stories about what happened to you, again concentrating on the feelings you had.

SEX Q6.   Moving on, this would be a good time to start talking about masturbation. Now, masturbation can be a huge issue for some, primarily because there continues to be the misinformed belief that there is something wrong with sexual self-pleasuring. Well, if this is the case, there is something wrong with an awful lot of us. The old saw that "ninety five percent of men masturbate and five percent of men lie" isn't far from the truth. Masturbation is simply sex with someone you love! The majority of men and women masturbate, and continue to masturbate after they're married. If you need to, limit the discussion at this point to masturbatory experiences during childhood and adolescence. As always, while the facts are interesting, it will be the thoughts and feelings that are really useful.

SEX Q7.   Finally, for now at least, do you have any funny or embarrassing stories with any type of sexual connotation that would be fun to share with your partner? Most of the guys will recall getting erections at embarrassing moments, while the girls may recall when their tops came off while swimming or some other "wardrobe malfunction." Do a little relationship building by sharing these stories with each other.

SEX Q8.   Watch *American Pie* (1999, Jason Biggs, Chris Klein) and compare and contrast how your early sexual experiences compared with the embarrassing incidents the movie depicts.

For most, the value of addressing the above questions will be less about exchanging information and more about the fact the two of you are talking about sexuality. As there are so many taboos and impediments to talking openly about sex, we often need to work just to set the stage, so to speak, if we want to make progress in increasing our comfort level in talking about sex.

"PREMARITAL SEX" OR JUST "ADULT SEXUAL BEHAVIOUR"?

Over the past couple of generations, the average age of first marriage has steadily been increasing to the point where both men and women are now waiting on average until they are *thirty* before they get married (if you want to get picky, on average women are getting married for the first time at age 31.7, while men are waiting just that much longer and not getting hitched until they are 34.3, according to Statistics Canada, *The People: Marriage*, 2004). A number of reasons have been offered for why this might be happening, including a greater focus on completing higher levels of education and the decreasing dependence of women on men to support them financially.

Another obvious contributing factor that can't be ignored is the fact that marriage is less about having sex for the first time than it used to be. Fewer and fewer people believe that sex is appropriate only between married people. As a reflection of this fact, a recent survey by the Council of Ministers of Education found that ten percent or less of adolescents intended to forgo having sex until they were married (*Canadian Youth, Sexual Health and HIV/AIDS Study: Factors Influencing Knowledge, Attitudes, and Behaviours*, 2003). Put another way, more than nine out of ten teenagers reported that being a virgin at marriage played little or no role in deciding if and when they were going to have sex. For many, the "sexual pressure" to marry has in large part been steadily eroding in contemporary society.

The most common age for teenagers to start having sex is seventeen (that applies to both girls and boys). Consequently, we have adolescents and young adults having sex for about a ten-year period on average before getting married! Now, this period of sexual activity also corresponds to a period of the life cycle when people are often at their most physically fit, their healthiest, and, applying skewed but nevertheless common standards of beauty,

161

their most physically appealing.[29] We can fairly ask if it makes any sense to expect people of this age range and with these physical attributes to forgo sexual interactions with one another.

The only reason I'm going on about this is that in my mind, talking about sex being "premarital" in this age range is judgemental. From my point of view, people are entitled to be sexual when they feel physically, intellectually, and emotionally ready to have sex, and this may or may not have anything to do with whether they're married or not. When sex was more intimately tied to reproduction, the logic was different, but that ship sailed in the 1960s with the advent of reliable birth control. What's more, not everyone wants to or even ought to get married! If someone is thirty-seven years old, and they have decided that they don't want to get married, does it make sense to label what they're doing in bed with someone else as "premarital" sex? There is so much baggage already attached to feeling comfortable about our sexuality that we don't need antiquated ideas about sex before marriage adding to the weight. Imagine if we said you don't get to vote or drive a car or play tennis until you're married. Premarital voting, premar-

---

[29] And by the way, the idea that men and woman have different "sexual peaks" or "sexual primes" is just another old wives' tale. In *Understanding Sexuality Research*, Michael Weiderman says this mistaken idea got started over fifty years ago when people misinterpreted some survey data collected by a famous sex researcher named Alfred Kinsey. Kinsey found that men reported the highest number of orgasms per year in their late teens and early twenties, while women reported the highest number of orgasms per year in their late twenties and early thirties, and this got translated into men and woman having different sexual peaks. However, men masturbate more and learn to masturbate earlier than do women, and back in Kinsey's day it often took a married couple a few years to learn how she could be orgasmic on a regular basis, delaying her experience of regular and higher-frequency orgasms. The difference between the number of orgasms between men and women was a reflection of sexual practices, not physiological sexual peaks. Contemporary sex research shows that men and women go through the same stages of sexual development at about the same time, which from a reproduction and social development point of view makes a lot of sense. Accurate data never get in the way of myth and misperception however, and you will still find references to men and women having different sexual primes in supposedly authoritative sources.

ital driving and, perish the thought, premarital tennis? What ARE we coming to?

If we drop the judgement, the presumption, and perhaps the fear of teenage sexuality, I think all we are left with is *adolescent sexual behaviour* and *adult sexual behaviour*, and these terms seem just fine to me.

WHAT EXACTLY IS SEXUAL COMPATIBILITY?

So exactly what makes a couple "sexually compatible"? I suppose the easy answer would be that they simply like having sex the same way. But what docs that mean? Are we talking about regularity or preferred positions for intercourse here? Is this about nonverbal come-hithers or desires for the often touted and seldom achieved simultaneous orgasm?

In reality, there are all kinds of dimensions that can be used to assess sexual compatibility, so let's start making a list of potential sexual dimensions for the two of you to start talking about.

The obvious place to start would be frequency of intercourse. For most, when they think sexual compatibility, they think numbers. They think how often. And no question, frequency of intercourse can be an important issue. However, assuming that sexual compatibility is just about intercourse frequency is putting the sexual cart before the intimacy horse. (In fact, it's not just in front of the horse—it's down the road and on the other side of the stream!) So why don't we break sex down a bit into some of its component parts so we can talk about all the different aspect of sexual connectedness?

SEXUAL SEMAPHORE

The first place to start assessing sexual compatibility is the way you communicate your interest and desire for sex to each other. Egalitarian protests to the contrary, sexual initiation is still primarily a man thing. In "Predicting Initiation and Refusals of Sexual

Activities in Married and Cohabiting Heterosexual Couples," E. Sandra Byers and Larry Heinlein say that men are more likely than women to offer a sexual come-hither. But here's a little secret: men often love it when their partner shares the responsibility for getting the sexual ball rolling. Think about it. Everyone, men included, wants to feel sexually desired by their partner, and one way to show this is to invite your partner to have sex! Conversely, some women are terribly frustrated that the rules that have developed in their relationship are such that only he gets to get things started. A better plan for everyone is simply to eliminate rules about who is or isn't *allowed* to express sexual interest and open up the game equally to both players.

Signals of sexual desire range from direct verbal requests to subtle verbal and behavioural cues. Direct verbal requests like, "Do you wanna fool around?" can make intentions pretty clear, but so too can more subtle comments like, "We don't have to be at the restaurant for another half an hour," or "I just changed the sheets upstairs." The range of behavioural cues is similarly broad, with prolonged, deep kisses being one of the more obvious signals, but with lingering touches, playful nudges, even prolonged glances also making intentions known.

From a compatibility point of view, the critical issue is less about the type of signals than signal recognition and fit. Sometimes what we think is a pretty hot come-on doesn't generate the heat we were hoping for. Worse, sometimes it can even serve to *dampen* the mood.

Negative feedback on the efficacy of a sexual signal can be threatening and risks hurting the other person's feelings. However, better some negative feedback now than a lifetime of sexual dissatisfaction. And, to be clear, feedback does not necessarily have be perceived as negative or threatening. For example, "I know that nibbling my earlobe is supposed to let me know you want to go to the bedroom, and I'm often keen to get there too. But instead of my earlobe, how about a kiss on the neck when you want to let me know you're in the mood?"

Poor signal reception also comes from assuming that what *we* would like to hear or see is what our partner wants to see or hear. For example, imagine a woman who loves to have her hair touched as a prelude to lovemaking. In an attempt to get her partner to do this, she frequently runs her fingers through his hair, hoping he will get the hint. But while she is doing this, all he is thinking about is how much he likes the head rub. And adding insult to injury, he is completely bewildered when she walks away in a huff after playing with his hair for twenty minutes!

So there can be all kinds of sexual-interest signals from subtle to obvious, and they can be sent in a variety of verbal and nonverbal ways, but of critical importance are *signal recognition* and a *willingness to modify and adapt signals as needed*. Use the questions below to assess the efficacy and compatibility of your sexual semaphore.

The Matter in Question: Sex

SEX Q9. To ensure that you're both on the same page, describe for each other the things that you've done in the past to let each other know that you're in the mood. Let your partner know about your preferred methods to get things started, as well as the ways you like to be invited to be sexual. (If you're a presexual couple, describe what you think you might like as a sexual invitation.)

SEX Q10. Describe for your partner a time when you thought you sent a sexual signal but it seemingly went unrecognized or ignored.

SEX Q11. If you could change or add one thing to your partner's sexual signalling repertoire, what would that be?

165

SEX Q12. Imagine that you've both been struck by a severe case of laryngitis and been advised not to speak for a week or risk losing your voice forever. What happens to your sexual signals? Freakishly, just after the laryngitis clears up, photophobia sets in and you have to wear patches over your eyes for a week. Now what? (Don't worry—you get better.)

SEXUAL SYNCHRONY

"Timing is everything" is an important axiom in clinical psychology. But as apropos as it is to therapy, so too does it apply to lovemaking. If you and your partner are sexually out of sync, frustrations can mount. However, I'm still not talking about intercourse frequency. By *sexual synchrony* I mean finding the right moments and times of day that work for the two of you sexually. For example, some people prefer to make love just before they go to sleep. However, this isn't necessarily the only or best time to make love. Just as there are night owls and early birds, so too are there genital-knocking nightingales and randy roosters. For some, weeknights are a great time to have sex, as among its many benefits lovemaking helps reduce the tension of the day, while for others the demands of work, school, and potentially child care leave them exhausted, and sexually they would prefer a quiet moment on a weekend. And of course preferences like these will change with work schedules, seasons, age, health status, etc. Again, there are no rights or wrongs here other than a demand for flexibility and a desire to offer accommodations to one another to keep things interesting and satisfying.

The Matter in Question: Sex

SEX Q13. What do you know about your partner's preferences when it comes to the timing of sex? Do they have any preferences? As a general rule, are you a morning, afternoon, or evening person when it comes to sex? Does it make any difference? How have you communicated your timing preferences to your partner? (Again, if you are presexual, with the remaining questions in this section and in the rest of the conversation, speculate and use your imagination.)

SEX Q14. Pick the time of day or week that would be least enjoyable for you in terms of making love (setting aside times that would be next to impossible: e.g., teaching a class or conducting a business meeting, riding a bus, taking ski-jumping lessons, etc). What might your partner do to make this particular moment more sexually attractive to you?

SEXUAL SEGUES

The next step is transitioning from sexual signals to more direct physical sexual contact. By *sexual segues*, I am referring to what is more commonly called foreplay.

Now, everyone knows that women like a lot of foreplay and men could care less. Women are all about romance and the lingering intimacy of touching and caressing, while the guys are about the physical and just getting the job done. Women admire the garden, but men just want to cut the grass.

Stereotypes, stereotypes, stereotypes! Adhere to stereotypes like "all women want lots of foreplay and all men don't" at your peril! Sure, some women like to spend a lot of time enjoying the closeness and anticipation that can be the wonder of foreplay, but so too can guys. There are plenty of men who get into holding and caressing, allowing sexual tensions to build. And there are plenty of women who hunger for the sex act and want to get right to it rather than slowing things down with foreplay. There is nothing wrong with either of these approaches. Sex is about having physical fun, being close, and sharing something intimate with each other. To the extent that *these* issues are being addressed, that's all that really matters. Giving ourselves and our partners the opportunity to simply express sexual appetites is a much higher-probability route to sexual happiness than trying to round-peg, square-hole each other with gender-based sexual stereotypes.

And of course there's no rule that says the same amount of foreplay has to be part of every lovemaking opportunity. Mixing things up and experimenting with types and amounts of foreplay is a great way to get to know about each other's sexual interests and turn-ons.

Foreplay compatibility will primarily be about if and how much, along with technique, so having a discussion about each of these aspects of segueing into sex will be very important.

The Matter in Question: Sex

SEX Q15. How and when have the two of you talked about what you like and dislike about foreplay?

SEX Q16. Personal opinion: Is oral sex foreplay, or do you view it as a sexual main event?

SEX Q17. What is your favourite foreplay activity? What is your least favourite? What foreplay activity might you like to engage in but been uncomfortable requesting or suggesting?

SEXUAL SUBSTANCE

While for some, sex can have a world of meaning, for others sex is better conceptualized as pleasant recreation. Both positions have merit and neither constitutes a superior truth. Sexual compatibility is about exploring the meaning and desire for a wide variety of sexual behaviours including kissing, touching, intercourse, oral sex, and other sexual behaviours. It involves evaluating needs for playfulness, tenderness, physical gratification, intimacy, trust, and sharing.

Exactly what is it you like to do from a sexual perspective? For example, some feel that oral sex is as good as it gets, while others are all about intercourse. Some couldn't imagine lovemaking without sex toys, while others get a real turn-on slipping an erotic tape or DVD into the home entertainment system to add to their pleasure.

Describing every possible variation in sexual interest would be challenging, but listed below are a range of common and not so common sexual interests. Sexual compatibility doesn't mean you have to like exactly everything your partner likes. However, it does mean that you have similar, overlapping interests. You may have done many, few, or none of the things listed below. It isn't intended as a checklist of required sexual behaviours. It is, however, representative of a wide range of sexual interests, and as such the two of you can use it to further explore sexual compatibility.

The Matter in Question: Sex

SEX Q18. Use this list to continue your discussions about sexual interests. Describe for your partner your thoughts and feelings about engaging in each of the following activities:

a. Manually stimulating a partner's genitals
b. Sexual intercourse
c. Giving oral sex
d. Receiving oral sex
e. Anal sex (again, talk about giving *and* receiving)
f. Mutual masturbation
g. Intercourse during menstruation
h. Using enticing clothing (or costumes) to enhance arousal
i. Using sexually explicit material to enhance arousal
j. Recording your own sexual behaviour (i.e., using still or video cameras) to enhance arousal
k. Having three-person (or more) sex
l. Having sex in public or risky places (i.e., where you might be discovered by others)
m. Using food for sex play
n. Using sex toys
o. Wearing each other's clothing or clothing of the other gender (i.e., cross-dressing)
p. Having phone sex
q. Sharing personal sexual fantasies
r. Being tied up or restrained during sex
s. Using various types of pain to enhance sensual and sexual feelings

t. Viewing sexual performances (e.g., strip or sex shows)

u. Attending sex shows or clubs

SEX Q19. Intercourse positions: tell your partner about your favourite, least favourite, and the one you would like to try but have been afraid to bring up.

SEX Q20. Go to the bookstore or public library with your partner and take a look at the various versions of the Kama Sutra (or any other sex manual describing intercourse positions and sexual activities). In leafing through the pages, do you see an intercourse position or activity that you might like to try? Feel free to get a copy for yourself, not so much as a sexual requirement but as a reference for a variety of positions and activities to talk about and explore.

Assessing sexual compatibility means *knowing* what the range of sexual behaviours and options actually are. But just so we're clear, the above is not supposed to be a checklist of *everything* that *everyone* is supposed to do sexually. It is, however, supposed to represent a range of sexual behaviours that different adults enjoy. Learning in a frank and candid manner what you and your partner like is the best way to evaluate the sexual compatibility that exists between the two of you.

Ignoring substantial differences in sexual preference is a risky business. When it comes to sex, people often like what they like, and if they don't get a chance to express their sexual interests in their marriage, they will be tempted to find fulfillment elsewhere.

Nothing can guarantee fidelity, however, so the fantasy that good sex at home *ensures* faithfulness is another unfounded preconceived notion.

The Matter in Question: Sex

SEX Q21. Discuss with your partner the role of each of the following in lovemaking. Do all of these things need to be present in a sexual encounter? How would you and your partner rank these qualities in terms of their importance to lovemaking? Are there other important qualities you think belong on the list, or should the list be shortened?

1. **Playfulness**
2. **Physical gratification**
3. **Trust**
4. **Intimacy**

Sexual Symmetry

With all of these other issues now covered, I suppose we can start talking about frequency of sex. But make no mistake: if the above issues have not been discussed, and sexual interests, likes, and dislikes haven't been clearly identified and understood, trying to figure out issues of frequency will be a waste of time. Preferred frequency of sex is as much about *how* and *what* sexual things are done as it is about absolute level of sexual desire. Think of it this way: how often would you want to show up at practice if your bandmates were constantly out of tune?

When they're in their twenties, couples typically have sex two or three times a week. As they age, this rate decreases somewhat. By the time a couple is in their fifties and sixties, the rate of intercourse is typically once every week or two. But don't be too impressed with statistics when it comes to sex. No statistic in the world is a substitute for what you or your partner wants. Neither does a statistic make someone correct or incorrect when it comes to sexual desire. As far as sex goes, we're all entitled to like what we like and to want what we want, and it doesn't really matter where we fall in some statistical distribution.[30] To look at it another way, even if nine out of ten people think *Casablanca* is the greatest movie ever made, this still doesn't make it the "right" movie for any particular individual.

Discrepancies in desire are among the most common sexual problems I see as a psychologist who deals with sexual issues. Most often, however, sexual desire discrepancies have a lot to do with the topics we have already touched on in this conversation and result from poor timing, bad signals, or lousy technique. But there are other reasons a couple may have very different levels of sexual desire.

Absolute libido differences—that is, when there is a difference within a couple on how often they want to have sex—can exist even in the absence of other sexual incompatibilities. That is, a couple can be in sync as far as everything else about having sex goes, but they just don't want the same amount. In these circumstances, it is often very difficult to find a middle ground that will work for both of them. For example, imagine a couple where she wants to have sex every day, but he'd prefer sex only once a month or less. Any middle ground is unlikely to be satisfying to either of them: for example, agreeing to have sex ten times a month is going to be at least nine times more often than he wants

---

[30] Although this is probably unnecessary, let me be clear: we are all entitled to have our sexual desires and our sexual likes and dislikes, and to assertively express them. However, this never gives us licence to impose our sexual desires on anyone else. Mature, responsible sex is *always* mutual sex where all participating parties are in a position to offer informed consent and have a desire to engage in sexual behaviour. Anything less than this, in any context, married or otherwise, is assault.

and less than half as often as she wants. In these circumstances, the couple needs to see the situation for what it is—they are two people who are fundamentally sexually incompatible. Neither is right or wrong, and the discrepancy is nobody's fault—they are both allowed to want what they want, and, as I've said, there is no correct amount of sexual desire to have.

Unfortunately, I have seen a number of couples who have been in this situation. Typically, one or the other knew they didn't have the level of desire the other person wanted and tried to hide this fact. In every case, however, the hiding could last for only so long before resentments started to show inside and outside the bedroom. When they finally got to therapy and we eventually discovered what the root of the marital problem was—that is, a substantial difference in sexual desire—the marriage typically ended. This falls in the sad-but-true category, and I will contend that the saddest part was that the pain suffered by both members of the couple could have been eliminated if we as a society, and they as a couple, had established a healthier culture of sexual communication to begin with. No one should be afraid or embarrassed to talk about what they want sex in their marriage to look like. We all need to take responsibility for what we want and to share those hopes and expectations with our partners. If these hopes and expectations (sexual and otherwise) match up, then we have a higher probability of having a solid union. But if they don't match up, facing this as a sad truth early in a relationship just means that people have that much more opportunity to either see if changes can realistically be made or to keep looking for someone who does have overlapping expectations and wants.

The Matter in Question: Sex

SEX Q22. How important is sex to you? What role do you see sex playing in your marriage?

SEX Q23. What do you think your preferred sexual frequency might be, and what do you think your partner wants?

SEXUAL SAFETY

It'd be nice if we could skip over this issue, but we can't. Among all the other interesting and fun things we get to deal with while we're talking about sex, we still have to talk about sexual safety. Sexually transmitted infections (STIS) aren't just painful, an inconvenience, or embarrassing; in some cases they're fatal, so ignoring them is a profoundly poor plan.

If you don't know much about STIS, you should educate yourself. Welcome to the grown-up world, where the risks are real and no one has any plan to look after you. Looking after yourself is the order of the day, and in our current context this means learning about the risks of STIS and coming up with ways to keep yourself safe. Learning about STIS is not that hard (although it can take up a lot of space and is beyond the scope of this book), and there are tons of resources out there for you to use (i.e., books, the Internet, health centres, your physician, etc). For some, the issue might be less about getting good information and more about getting past any "ick" factor they might feel about STIS, finding the time to sit down and do the required reading, and generally learning about something that is not exactly the most thrilling topic in the world.

Because many STIS have few or no symptoms, you can't reliably depend on the way a partner looks to tell you if they have an STI or not. For the same reason, someone telling you they don't have an STI is a useful but not necessarily accurate piece of information, primarily because they can't always know if they actually have an STI or not. For example, bacterial chlamydia (which, among other things, can damage reproductive organs

175

and thus prevent babymaking) produces no symptoms in a substantial proportion of infected men and women. A person can carry the AIDS virus and remain asymptomatic for years. Unless a genital wart is actually present and visible—neither of which will necessarily be the case for someone who has been infected with HPV, human papillomavirus, the virus that causes genital warts and most cases of cervical cancer—there will be no signs that they have an STI.

I could go on, but you probably get the picture. There are a lot of details about STIs that you need to know, but as a general rule know this: as soon as you touch another person in any way, sexual or otherwise, you put yourself at risk for catching something that infects humans, again sexual or otherwise. From this perspective, STIs are no different than any other type of communicable disease. One organism can infect another, and that's just the nature of being alive and choosing to be in the company of other humans.

Because we have all these hang-ups about sex, we also have hang-ups about STIs and believe them to be worse or more embarrassing than other types of infections. Don't believe me? Ask yourself if you think people would respond differently to someone who got hepatitis from a tainted blood transfusion compared to someone who got it from sexual contact?

Getting tested for STIs is a necessary step in creating a long-term relationship that includes physical contact and sex. Talking about your sexual histories isn't a bad place to start, but it's only a beginning.

The Matter in Question: Sex

SEX Q24. What do you want to know about your partner's sexual past? What do you think they need to know about yours? What might get in the way

of the two of you talking about your sexual histories?

SEX Q25. What formal education do you have on the risks associated with STIs? Did you learn about them at school, from a friend, from the popular media, from a medical professional, or from some other source? What gaps are there between what you know and what your partner knows?

As you can see, it turns out that there are a lot of important dimensions to know about in terms of assessing sexual compatibility. As I've already said a number of times, you don't necessarily have to have all these things figured out perfectly just yet (although knowing about the risks associated with STIs should not be delayed). Developing a sexual compatibility with someone takes time, learning, trial and error, a sense of humour, a degree of experimentation, and a sense of fun. But the most useful ingredient may arguably be the ability to talk about and assertively express what you want and like as far as sex goes.

COPULATORY CROP CIRCLES, SEXUAL SASQUATCHES, AND LOVEMAKING LUNACY: MYTHS AND MISINFORMATION OF THE SEXUAL KIND

There's a lot of bad sexual information out there. If I were to try to outline for you all the misinformation and downright nutty ideas about sex, I'd have to start another book (note to self: start another book). However, I *have* selected the five most common misconceptions about sex that I think everyone ought to know about, primarily because they are ones that have the potential to really mess people up by creating unrealistic sexual expectations about either themselves or their partners.

G-SPOTS AND FEMALE EJACULATION

Let's do a little Human Sexuality 101. The G-spot, or Grafenberg spot, is supposedly a small area of tissue located on the upper wall of the vagina, about a third of the way in from the vaginal opening. Some women report that stimulation of this area of heightened sensitivity, while initially uncomfortable, can quickly become pleasurable and lead to powerful orgasms, sometimes accompanied by the expulsion of fluid, referred to as female ejaculation. I say supposedly not because I don't believe that some women have a G-spot or because there's some doubt about the possibility of women ejaculating fluid when they orgasm, but because there are a lot of conflicting data on exactly what, where, and how common the G-spot and female ejaculation actually are.

A full explanation of the controversy surrounding exactly what the G-spot is or isn't gets a little bit technical and involves prenatal development, the structure of both male and female genitalia, how those genitalia are supplied with nerves, and the biochemistry of various body fluids. You're probably not reading this particular book to get into that level of detail, so let me give you the *Reader's Digest* version of the data, or at least the data I am familiar with.

Not everyone agrees that there actually is a G-spot, or at least that there is *special tissue* in the vaginal wall that could be called a G-spot. Few of the knowledgeable people in this field are in doubt, though, that a substantial proportion of women—but exactly what proportion is also the subject of debate—report that when the upper wall of their vagina is stimulated by fingers, a penis, or sex toys, they can experience a very power type of orgasm that feels different from orgasms that arise from clitoral or other genital stimulation. As far as I can tell, no one has yet identified any type of vaginal tissue in this area (or any other areas, for that matter) that is actually different from all the rest of the vaginal tissue, nor has anyone found that any area of the upper wall of the vagina itself is differently innervated—that is, supplied with a greater or lesser number of sensory nerves—compared to the rest of the vagina.

If this is true, and I think it is, how do we explain the group of women who have what are called G-spot orgasms? Are they making it up? Are they imagining what is happening when they engage in sexual stimulation? I don't think so.

It has been speculated that, while there seems to be no unique area on the upper wall of the vagina from a tissue differential or an innervation point of view, *outside and just above the upper wall of the vagina* runs the ureter, the tube that carries urine from the bladder to the urinary opening below the clitoris and above the vaginal introitus (fancy word for opening). Along with the ureter, some scientists speculate there might also be structures that are the remains of tubing that would have turned into male reproductive structures such as the prostate had the genetics and prenatal environment been set up to produce a male rather than female person.[31]

G-spot orgasms are thought to occur from pressure on the upper vaginal wall that stimulates the ureter and perhaps these vestigial structures. (This *doesn't* mean, however, that women who experience G-spot-type orgasm have male plumbing or are in any way less of a woman. *All* women have these developmental leftovers, in the same way guys have vestigial structures like nipples. For reasons not yet understood, these natural vestigial structures are just more responsive in some women than others.) For some women, G-spot orgasms are accompanied by the

---

[31] Without getting too technical, before eight weeks of gestation, we all had *two* sets of internal tubing that were designed to turn into either male reproductive organs or female reproductive organs. However, male genetics kicks in at about eight weeks and causes one set of tubes to develop into male organs and the other set to degenerate, as they won't be needed. If genetically there is no male factor, we get a girl baby and the other set of tubes that would have been male organs degenerates.

expulsion of fluid, probably from the bladder, though the fluid has a number of characteristics that make it quite dissimilar from urine (and these different characteristics might come from those vestigial structures, but again we don't know for sure yet). It seems clear that the majority of women don't experience any degree of hypersensitivity as a function of stimulation on the upper wall of the vagina or experience this particular type of orgasm. And complicating things just a little bit more, for some of the women who do have G-spot orgasms, they describe having not so much a G "spot" as a G "ridge," an extended area along the top of their vagina that seems to correspond with the path of the ureter above the upper vaginal wall. Unfortunately, this natural variation among women has led some to call the G-spot a "gynecologic UFO." Others, myself included, say that denying the existence of the G-spot in some women is just another example of erotophobia and an attempt to take sexual power away from women.

It is astonishing to me that we still don't have clear answers to basic questions of sexual anatomy, functioning, and response. On the other hand, we have never been great at encouraging sex research. (Trust me on this one, I know!) For reasons that have always escaped me, learning about sex has almost never been a priority in our society. Yet there are few subjects we are more curious about.

Here's what I think you ought to know G-spot-wise. In the same way that some women are tall and some are short, some women will have more of what we can call a G-spot or ridge and some will have less. This isn't good or bad, right or wrong; it just is. A problem arises only if you or your partner have bad information and believe that if you don't have a G-spot or ridge or G-spot-like orgasms, there is something wrong. There isn't! All of human sexuality falls on a continuum in the same way intelligence or shoe size does. There is a ton of normal variation, and getting upset about where you fall on a sexual continuum is like being upset about your natural hair colour. Be upset if you want to, but the better plan will be to love what you have and make the most of it. Think of G-spots or ridges the same way you might think about music and having perfect pitch: some people have it, and it's probably a great thing to have. For the rest of us, not having perfect pitch doesn't mean for a second that we can't make beautiful music!

The Matter in Question: Sex

SEX Q26. What thoughts and feelings have the two of you shared concerning G-spot stimulation? Is this something that you have explored or talked about? Have either of you ever felt pressured to find or stimulate a G-spot? Have either of you felt any pressure to produce a G-spot-induced orgasm?

SEX Q27. Can either of you identify any other type of sexual expectation or pressure to sexually perform or respond? For example, do you, as the guy, feel pressure to last longer before you ejaculate? Do you, as the gal, feel pressure to have multiple orgasms rather than just one?

THE "VENUS BUTTERFLY," THE "COUNTER-CLOCKWISE SWIRL," AND "... SEVEN, SEVEN, SEVEN ... SEVEN!"

About twenty years ago, there was a nighttime TV drama called *L.A. Law*. In one episode, a lawyer was told by his bigamist[32] client that a sexual technique called the Venus butterfly drove

[32] Someone who is married to more than one person at the same time.

women crazy with pleasure and, if the lawyer did a good job, the bigamist would teach it to him. At the end of the episode, we see the lawyer in bed with his wife, post-coital, and she has a look of puzzled astonishment on her face. As the camera moves in, she asserts that she just "came closer to experiencing total sexual ecstasy" than she ever had and asks what it was he just did to her. He says it was the Venus butterfly. Apparently, after this particular episode aired, the switchboards of the broadcasting network lit up with desperate inquiries as to exactly what the Venus butterfly was, and a sexual legend was born.[33]

The idea that there is some mystical and magical sexual technique that has the potential to drive a partner wild remains both a secret hope and a secret fear for many. We hope that such a technique actually exists, but also fear that others will know about it while we don't. These secret sexual techniques are often alluded to on magazine covers trumpeting "How to drive him wild with desire" or "Be a master in the bedroom" or other such promises. Other genres of popular media, such as sitcoms, also pander to this hope and fear. Remember "The Move" from *Seinfeld*? Jerry apparently had a great sexual technique that he shared with George, who found it so complicated that he had to write crib notes on his arm. The most potent part of the "the move" was "a counter-clockwise swirl," but neither the "swirl" nor any other aspect of the technique is ever explained. In a *Friends* episode entitled "The One with Phoebe's Uterus," Monica explains to Chandler how to sexually satisfy a woman. She draws a picture of woman (which we, as viewers, don't get to see) and labels seven female erogenous zones (which we also don't get to see). Monica then

---

[33] As I understand it, following this episode, a variety of entrepreneurs took advantage of the name and published books and videos supposedly explaining the mysterious and forgotten "Venus butterfly."

explains the order by which each numbered erogenous zone should be attended to, ending her description with emphatic shouts of "seven, Seven, SEVEN..." and then a silently mouthed "seven" as she herself has an orgasm just from providing the description![34]

Of course, the one thing the Venus butterfly, "the move," and "seven, Seven, SEVEN..." have in common is that none are ever explained or described. And of course the reason they are never explained is that *there is no magic technique*. By way of analogy, think of it this way: can you imagine the "perfect" make-out song, or food, or perfume, that would create sexual arousal and desire in *everyone*? Of course you can't, because intuitively we all know that everyone is different.

Why, then, is the concept of the perfect or a magic sexual technique so ubiquitous? Probably because in our culture we have done such a poor job of teaching people what they need to know about sex. By promoting sexual ignorance, can we expect anything more than fears based on lack of knowledge?

So if there are no magic or perfect sexual techniques—and there aren't—how does anyone get to be a good lover? Essentially, by listening and attending to what your partner likes and doesn't like; by being a little experimental, adventurous, and willing to try new sexual things; and by looking for good, informed sexual information to increase your sexual literacy and skill. Later in this conversation, I'll give you more specifics about good sex and how to keep having it.

---

[34] After this description, Monica, Chandler, and Rachel (who was listening to Monica's description with Chandler) all immediately and individually leave the room, slamming doors behind them, ostensibly so they can masturbate. But apparently this very funny finale to the scene is often edited out when the episode is aired in syndication. I suppose for some TV stations, talking about how to have two-person sex is okay, but even alluding to one-person sex crosses some line. This part of the scene *was* left in on the DVD version of the episode, at least in Canada, so you can still see it if you find one of these copies. It's hilarious!

The Matter in Question: Sex

SEX Q28. Have either of you heard of anything else that was supposed to be a magic technique or something that has supposed aphrodisiac powers?

SEX Q29. Can you describe for your partner any fears or worries you might have had or continue to have about being unable to provide what you think they might want from a sexual perspective?

"If I Have to Ask for it, It Doesn't Count!"

Myth number three is that sex is always supposed to be spontaneous and impetuous, that good lovers "just know" what the other person wants, and that if you have to specifically ask your partner to have sex or to do some particular sexual thing, it doesn't count.

Because there are lots of reasons we, as a culture, end up being uncomfortable with sex, I think there are lots of reasons this myth continues to thrive and grow. As I've mentioned before, we live in a generally erotophobic culture in North America, so being comfortable with talking about sex has seldom been taught or encouraged. This erotophobia reinforces the "If I have to ask, it doesn't count" idea. We also have the mistaken idea about good lovers *just knowing* what someone else wants, and the resultant fear of not wanting to appear as a bad lover or make our lovers feel inadequate by talking about the specifics of sex or making sexual requests.

And we aren't done yet! For some, asking for something sexual feels risky because they fear being seen as a pervert or sexual deviant. Also, no one wants to be rejected, sexually or otherwise, and if you don't make requests, you don't have to risk rejection, right? Finally, there is the idea that asking for something sexual could turn a pleasant sexual situation into a potential conflict, and who wants to replace a perfectly good opportunity to have an orgasm with a fight? Frankly, I think this last explanation is the only one that provides anything like a legitimate basis for not asking for something sexual, but of course there are better workarounds for this too.

It is my contention that not only should we be okay talking about sex, we should be *really good* at talking about sex and, specifically, *really good* at talking about the sex *we want!* Ideally, telling your partner about what you want and like sexually ought to be able to happen through as many channels as we can imagine, including direct verbal communication.

Subtle verbal cues are great! Using body language to get want you want sexually is fantastic! If you can find a way to tell your partner what you want from sex through smell, go for it! All of this is wonderful, but don't make the mistake that direct verbal communication is somehow less valid. Why shouldn't we be able to get all that we want from sex? Why shouldn't we feel that our sexual needs are legitimate and deserve attention? Why shouldn't we simply be able to ask in a direct and frank way for what we want? If we were playing tennis, there wouldn't be any taboos against making requests of your tennis partner or offering direction or instruction.

Good lovers are made, not born. You learn to be a good lover by looking for and accepting feedback on what a partner wants and enjoys. The more efficiently you do this, the sooner you and your lover become simpatico. Asking for something sexual just makes good sense.[35]

[35] "Too much of a good thing can be wonderful!"—Mae West

The Matter in Question: Sex

SEX Q30. Can you think of a time when you missed having a sexual encounter because you felt it wasn't going to be spontaneous enough? Describe that opportunity to your partner to see if they felt the same way.

SEX Q31. If there was one thing, from a sexual perspective, you wish your partner would do *more* of, what would that be? If there's something that you wish they would do less of, what would that be?

MASTURBATION IN MARRIAGE

As I said before, masturbation is just sex with someone you love. (I also like "Pornography is literature you read with one hand," but let's try to say on track).

Sexual sanction number four is that once you have a full-time, live-in, lifelong sexual partner, getting yourself off sexually is immature, self-indulgent, insulting, pathetic, or deviant.

If we go back to Human Sexuality 101, genital self-stimulation—and, later, masturbation to orgasm—is among our first sexual behaviours and plays a tremendously important role in learning about our bodies, our sensuality, our sexuality, and what our bodies can do for us. It is important in developing self-confidence, sexual and otherwise, and getting comfortable with our abilities to respond comfortably to sexual stimulation. Masturbation helps us learn about our body parts: what they look and feel like; how they respond to stimulation; how they can change shape, size, colour, and smell; and how this can change as we grow, age, and mature. Masturbation brings on feelings of satisfaction, release of tension, and euphoria, and is a terrific way to help fall asleep. Masturbation allows a person to engage in sexual fantasy and can be a great way to even out differences in sexual desire between two people. You don't risk catching an STI when you masturbate, and masturbating for a partner can be a huge sexual turn-on. Masturbation can be the gateway to exploring new and different stimulation techniques and sexual toys. And if all this wasn't enough, masturbation feels fantastic!

I'm going to contend that the above list of positive attributes of masturbation constitutes a group of pretty compelling reasons masturbation should be your friend and something you practise for the rest of your life. The idea that two-person sex is the only correct, appropriate, or mature way to have sex is just wrong. Anyone espousing this position doesn't know much about sex. Think of it this way: if you really love playing baseball, why wouldn't you spend some time in a batting cage? And to extend the analogy a little further, if your teammate spent some time in a batting cage, why would you feel threatened or rejected?

The Matter in Question: Sex

SEX Q32. What early messages did you receive about masturbation? Were you told it was dirty and shameful, natural and normal, or something in between?

SEX Q33. Did you skip Sex Q6 earlier in the conversation? If you did, go back and see if you can give it another shot.

SEX Q34. What thoughts do the two of you have about masturbation in marriage? Does it seem out of place? Threatening? Inappropriate? Would it be something you would want to hide from your partner?

SEX Q35. Can the two of you have a discussion about how masturbation could be incorporated into your sex play with each other?

Gender-Specific Sexual Assumptions and the Rule of "P"

The fifth and final bedroom blunder I want to talk about grows from the mistaken idea that men and women are from two completely different planets, and as such have completely different sexual needs and desires. As I have been fond of saying for years, if you believe that men are from Mars and women are from Venus, you will alienate your partner!

Gender assumptions are perhaps the most common kind of stereotype we have in our society. From the moment a child is born, the first thing we want to know is their gender, probably because we believe it tells us something particularly important about them. And as a general rule, it does tell us *something* important. However, it doesn't tell us *everything* that is important about that person and at times leads us to incorrect assumptions about who they are. Knowing someone's gender is like knowing a person speaks English. It tells you something about them, but there is still a ton to learn, and it would be ridiculous to assume that because they speak English, they're an American baseball fan.

Returning more specifically to sex, earlier in this conversation I mentioned the *traditional sexual script*, or what we will now abbreviate to the TSS. Recall that the TSS is a longstanding set of rules and expectations growing out of general gender stereotypes that apparently tell us what men and women are supposed to do when it comes to sex. Let me illustrate what I'm talking about by asking you some simple questions.

Traditionally, who is supposed to initiate sex, the guy or the girl? Traditionally, who is supposed to always be ready and willing to have sex? Who is supposed to be hesitant to have sex? Who is supposed to resist sexual advances and seldom if ever make sexual advances of their own?

If you recognized the answers as man, man, woman, woman, you're in touch with the TSS. Essentially the TSS tells us that men are supposed to always be interested in sex, always want sex, know all there is to know about sex, always be sexually aggressive, always seek out sexual novelty, and have little or no emotional connection to sexual behaviour. Women, on the other hand, are supposed to be sexually naïve, fearful, hesitant, and generally not that interested in sex. However, women are also supposed to feel there is a huge connection between sex and emotion. As a general rule, the TSS leads us to "the rule of 'P'"—as far as sex goes, men are Pigs and women are Prudes.

So what's wrong with this model of gender and sex? Well, just about everything. While it's true that *some* men are often interested in sex, few if any men are *always* interested in sex. What's more, plenty of women are interested in sex, although again few if any are *always* interested. Some men know a lot about sex, but the vast majority don't, and there are plenty of women who know lots about sex. Sure, there are women who are hesitant about having sex, but so are there men who feel the same way. And I could go on and on.

Let's look at one of the more common gender sexual stereotypes: the supposed difference between men and women as far as a desire for foreplay is concerned. Having read a ton of sexual research and having dealt with sexual problems in my office for many years, I can say with great conviction that there are in fact lots of men who love to linger, tease, and be teased before any sexual "main event" takes place, and so are there plenty of women who want to get physical and get physical fast, limiting or

189

completely eliminating foreplay. Once again, there is no right or wrong, just personal preference, and we do ourselves, our partner, and our relationship a disservice when we use gender stereotypes as the foundation for our sexual behaviour.

Gender assumptions and stereotypes are the siblings of prejudice. And prejudice in the bedroom will lead to what prejudice anywhere else leads to: misunderstanding, resentment, and even hatred. So let's be clear: it is not the man's *job* to initiate sex, and it is not the woman's *job* to be sexually resistant. Women have just as much right to make sexual suggestions and orchestrate a sexual encounter as men do, and men are allowed to say they are not in the mood, while women are allowed to say they are, and so on and so on.

The Matter in Question: Sex

SEX Q36.   The next time you watch a movie together, particularly if one of the themes in the movie is relationships, play a game of "spot the gender-based sexual stereotype" with each other. See how quickly and how many stereotypes each of you can identify. In identifying these, did you see similarities to or differences from what happens between the two of you sexually?

SEX Q37.   From your personal perspective, what do you feel is the most toxic male sexual stereotype? What is the most toxic female sexual stereotype?

There is much more that is wild and wacky when it comes to sexual behaviour, but we have other issues to cover. Just be aware that, more than any other topic, human sexuality is plagued with

myth and misrepresentation. When you want sexual information, seek out good, legitimate, informed sources, and even then
don't completely give up your skepticism. Don't let the taboo
nature of sex stop you from getting the good information you
need and deserve.

From the weird and wacky, unfortunately, we now have to
turn our attention to one of the most damaging and frightening
threats to marriage, sexual infidelity.

INFIDELITY

For most, marriage is equated with sexual fidelity. Few things feel
more threatening or turn out to be more toxic to a marriage than
infidelity. When asked, the majority of both men and women
report that their partner's having an affair would mean the end of
the relationship. However, men seem to find their female partner's
affairs more threatening than do women their male partner's—
perhaps as a reflection of the whole ownership thing some men
still have about their female partners.

I don't have stats on exactly how often infidelity ends a marriage, but based on what I have seen in my office over the years,
kids seem to be the determining factor. Marriages with kids usually survive (but not as happily), while marriages without kids
tend not to survive an affair. Even when "staying together for the
kids" becomes the implicit or explicit choice, the offended partner often never really gets past the hurt and ends the relationship
as soon as it seems viable to do so. However you cut it, if you're
thinking of having an affair, plan on it forever changing and in
most cases ending your relationship, even if the ending doesn't
come for five, ten, or fifteen years.

Infidelity is not as common as most people think, although
rates tend to be higher in the United States than in Canada. In
the United States, one out of four men and one out of seven
women have an affair while married. In Canada, the rates are
about half this. Regardless of how common or uncommon

infidelity is, the effects are often devastating for both men and women on both sides of the border.

I am often asked by couples, young and old, what they can do to prevent infidelity from ever darkening their door. While I obviously have quite a bit to say about how to improve a marriage and how to increase the chances that you get what you want from your relationship, unfortunately I don't have a slam dunk for anyone to ensure that their partner will remain sexually faithful. This is due, at least in part, to the fact that affairs come about for a wide variety of reasons. Anger, disrespect, resentment, sexual attraction to another, lack of attraction to a current partner, weakness, opportunity, sexual frustration, inebriation, a sense of entitlement, stupidity, selfishness, arrogance, a lack of self-esteem, a sense of invulnerability, a desire for excitement, an attraction to the clandestine, pressure from another, and the list goes on, can all be part of the "why" of an affair. But, perhaps at the most basic level, infidelity is about feeling that losing one's long-term partner is worth the risk.

Believing you can make yourself immune to infidelity is like believing you can become immune to sickness. While there are a lot of excellent things you can do to decrease risks, there is nothing that can guarantee absolute safety. Extending the metaphor, it would also be silly to say that because you can't be assured of absolute safety, you should throw up your hands and do nothing. For many, infidelity is such a scary issue they never want to even talk about it. Big mistake. We don't like to think about death or disability, but the informed do, and they take out insurance to try to mitigate these frightening possibilities.

Disabuse yourself right now of any *relationship immunity syndrome* you think you have. Immunity syndrome, you ask? Relationship immunity syndrome is the common, natural, but totally naïve belief that while "bad couple things" happen to other people, they could never happen to you or your relationship. With very few exceptions, when I see someone professionally and the issue is an affair, I hear, "And I NEVER thought something like this could happen to me!" Affairs happen, and no one is immune. However, telling your partner your thoughts and feelings about what infidelity would mean to you is an informed place to start in shaping a healthy relationship.

The Matter in Question: Sex

SEX Q38. What do you imagine would be most disturbing to you about infidelity? Would it be the violation of trust, the thought of your partner having sex with someone else, the loss of privacy, the sense of rejection, the threat of STIs? Would it be all of these, or is there something else?

SEX Q39. What might constitute Internet or technological infidelity as far as each of you is concerned? Does looking at sexually explicit pictures on the computer or cellphone cross a line? What about engaging in sexually explicit chat with someone else? Be very clear with your partner about what your thoughts and feelings might be in terms of how technology is offering a wider forum for sexual expression, and what your hope and expectations might be for sexual expression within your marriage.

Before we get too far down this road, another point needs to be made. Sexual monogamy needs to be understood as a choice, not a requirement or a demand. The fact is, not everyone is well suited for monogamy. In fact, a case could be made that sexual monogamy forces us into a model of behaviour that is both inconsistent with human needs and infrequent in the rest of the natural world. Genetic studies have proven repeatedly that many animal species that we thought "mated for life" and remained monogamous actually get action on the side all the time. Genetic analysis of the eggs in their nests have demonstrated that swans, for example, which have come to symbolize lifelong commitment and sexual fidelity, have mated with a variety of partners in the same mating season. Neither male nor female swans operate under the monogamous rules we presumed. My point, then, is that sexual exclusivity is neither a good nor a bad idea. The more critical issue here is choice and commitment.

So let's be crystal clear about what we are talking about: you get to *choose* if you want a sexually monogamous relationship; no one forces it on you. As a grown-up, you get to make choices for yourself, now, in the future, and for the rest of your life. If you want to be in a sexually monogamous relationship—and it turns out that this is what most people want—fine. But that doesn't make it "right" or the only way to be. If you don't want sexually exclusivity, or if you feel you can't, in good conscience, offer sexual exclusivity to a partner, *don't make the offer that you can!* This doesn't have to mean no marriage, but it likely will mean that the two of you will need to talk about what you feel is important about marriage (and hence the entire purpose of this book).

There is a variety of models of happy non-monogamous relationships. They are not for everyone, and they can fail for many of the same reasons monogamous relationships do, but they exist and they bear examination and consideration. Sexually open relationships typically allow for sexual interactions with other partners, primarily with the understanding that limiting sexual expression to only one person for a lifetime feels wrong. Sexually open couples will often establish rules about who, how often, and how much commitment is acceptable with additional sexual partners. Sometimes one-night stands are allowed, but only when out of town. For other couples, ongoing relationships might be allowed, but only with same-sex partners. For other couples still, extramarital sex is allowed, but only with other sanctioned couples, and extramarital sex happens at fixed times and locations.

Not infrequently, couples start off having a monogamous marriage, then experiment with open marriage, and later still return to monogamy. A complete discussion of all the polyamorous options is again beyond the scope of this book, but the general point needs to be made loud and clear: you get to choose what kind of sexual life you want without guilt, demands, expectation, or social obligation. The critical issue is not monogamy but, more important, the open and honest commitment you offer another person. Sticking to what you offer and what has been offered to you will be the cornerstone of long-term trust. While for most this involves sexual exclusivity, taking monogamy as a given without frank and candid discussion is a poor plan. Knowing what your personal preferences and desires are is a critical part of this portion of the Sex conversation.

The Matter in Question: Sex

SEX Q40. Perhaps you don't feel threatened by infidelity at all. Perhaps sexual monogamy feels like an outdated concept to you. Have you shared these thoughts with your partner? Do they feel the same way? Have the two of you negotiated what would and wouldn't be "allowed" as far as extramarital sex is concerned?

Keeping sex interesting seems like an obvious way to prevent infidelity, but this is based on the profoundly flawed presumption that affairs are only about sex. As described above, affairs come about for a wide variety of reasons, and there is no way these reasons can all be taken into consideration and counteracted. What's more, even if this were possible, preventing affairs would still be outside the range of the possible because there is no way any of us can have complete and total control over another person's behaviour. If someone is going to have an affair, they are going to have an affair. Odds are you won't even be in the room when they decide to cheat, so how were you supposed to control or prevent what was happening? When it comes down to it, relationships are a risk. We can evaluate and attempt to minimize risk, but it would be intellectually dishonest to believe that all risk of infidelity can be eliminated or that you have the ability and power to control what another grown-up does.

In a nutshell, infidelity sucks and it can be fatal to a relationship. It is not as common as most people think. Sharing with your partner what you think about infidelity is a really good idea. But not everyone is well suited for monogamy. This doesn't make them good or bad. We all want to believe that those we love will stick to their commitments, so if monogamy is your commitment, sticking to it is a better plan than not. If monogamy isn't your thing, or you feel you can't make this commitment, don't, and be honest about it. For the open-minded, there are a variety of ways of being with someone that don't have to be intertwined with monogamy.

How to Keep Sex Interesting

Keeping sex interesting is a great plan, not because great sex will make you immune to infidelity—it won't—but because great sex is, in a word, GREAT.

The following are the four most important things you can do to keep sex vital in your relationship. And just to remind you, there is no single secret technique or piece of sexual information out there that is guaranteed to keep your sex life fulfilling for the rest of your life. Keeping your sexual relationship with your partner interesting and rewarding is no greater or less of a challenge than maintaining and growing any other aspect of your lives together. Common sense and effort work just as successfully when it comes to sex as they do for everything else in life.

MAKE GOOD SEX A RELATIONSHIP PROJECT

Perhaps the most important step in keeping sex interesting is remembering to never take it for granted. Both because sex is thought of as something "natural" but also because it can be difficult to talk about, the idea of making sex a project seems kind of strange and perhaps even inappropriate. For many, the idea that they might need to have ongoing discussions about what is and isn't working for them sexually seems a bit like overkill. If you fall into this camp, think of it this way: does it make sense to see a doctor only once in your life, or take your car in for maintenance once during its lifetime, or think about and plan for your financial security once? Of course not. Important aspects of your life require ongoing attention, and such is the case with your sex life.

To keep sex interesting, then, essentially you need to get really good at and really comfortable with talking about sex. If you want to increase the chances that your sex life will stay interesting, you can't skip this step. If you were really interested in sports, politics, or single-malt scotch, it's unlikely that you'd feel *uncomfortable* talking about it or *learning new things* about your special interest. If you feel uncomfortable talking about sex, start taking steps to increase your comfort. Read about sex, talk about sex with your friends, watch sex documentaries on the Learning Channel, take a human sexuality course on campus, whatever. A good sex life is something that is created, not something that just happens.

REMEMBER, SEX IS FUN!

Step two in keeping sex interesting is to not take it too seriously. Sex is supposed to be fun. As a model, think about other ways you have fun. You have fun by laughing; by making jokes; by exploring new ways of doing the same thing; by looking for, creating, and taking advantage of circumstances that will increase the chances of having a good time; and by not getting hung up on mistakes. There are lots of ways to have sex, and you get to explore all the ones you want. Making sex about closeness and intimacy, about a profound sense of connection and oneness with each other, is great, but this is only one approach to sex. In the sex biz, we often suggest thinking about sex the same way we think about hunger: sometimes when you're hungry you want a five-course meal, but other times you'd be just as happy to scarf down a burger. Neither meal is right or wrong; they simply are what they are—different means to a similar end. From a sexual perspective, sometimes you might want a sexual interaction that involves lingering romance, leisurely foreplay, lasting intercourse, and lighthearted afterglow, while at other times you simply want a quick and intense sexual session. Feeling okay with both ends of this sexual spectrum and all that falls in the middle means that sex can serve a variety of purposes, and can be pursued at a variety of times and in a variety of circumstances. Sex gets to be fun, and you get to think about and explore all the ways you can make it and keep it fun without feeling shameful, dirty, guilty, or any of the other baggage that often gets dumped on sex.

Keep Having Sex

Step three in keeping sex interesting is to keep having sex. If you want to be good at tennis, just watching it on TV is unlikely to smooth out your serve or sharpen your net game. Sex, like any other physical activity, tends to improve with practice. The more you do it, the more you learn about your own and your partner's likes and dislikes. The more you develop a sense of sexual comfort and ease, the more you will attend to and respond to changes in sexual preferences and appetites that naturally occur over time. Further, the amount of intimate time you spend with your partner will increase. While the equation is not as simple as "more sex equals good sex," for most there is substantial truth to the equation "little sex equals bad sex."

LOOK AFTER YOUR PHYSICAL HEALTH

Step four is to look after your health. Again, sex is a physical activity and, like all physical activities, it is more fun when your body responds the way you want it to, is working well, and is pain free. This is not to say that you can't have sex when you're in pain or not feeling well, but the reality is, better health means better sex.

Looking after your physical appearance is also an important part of your physical health. Sex is intimately related to physical attraction, and continuing to look attractive to your partner is not something that can be taken for granted. However, trying to look like you're forever twenty-one isn't going to work either. Ideally, we love who we are and focus on doing the best with what we've got. Believing that your partner will love you "no matter what" is a needless risk from a physical health perspective. You look after your health because you want to live a long and healthy life, but a really nice bonus to this is that you increase the chances that your physical attractiveness stays at higher levels. Physical appearance definitely becomes less of a factor from a commitment point of view over the lifespan of a marriage, but it never completely disappears. Looking your best is just an added perk of physically feeling good.

FINAL THOUGHTS ON THE SEX CONVERSATION

Sex is a fundamental part of who we are, and learning to be comfortable with sexual thoughts and feelings is a critically important part of our development. Thus, the Sex conversation serves a lot of important purposes. It gets you in touch with your own ideas and beliefs about sex, it helps you learn about what your partner believes and wants from sex, and it forces you to think about sexual issues you might have avoided in the past. But something my students have taught me is that it is also liberating to learn to talk about sex. Time and again, they have told me that after taking the Human Sexuality course and learning to think about and express ideas related to sex, they were able to apply this skill and confidence to other areas of their lives. They tell me that after having met the challenge of talking about sex in a frank and candid manner, they could now talk about anything! From money to politics, from religion to family dynamics, learning to talk about the taboo of sex has allowed them to re-examine many issues they struggled expressing their feelings about. Nothing but good comes from this type of confidence and candour. When you and your partner can include sex among the things you are open and honest about, you are well on your way to building a mature and healthy relationship.

Although our society still has a long way to go, a case could be made that our language might be evolving in small ways to make sex (or at the very least gender) a more comfortable issue to talk about. Only twenty years ago, it was still common to find the pronoun *he* used to refer to any unspecified person, male *or* female. Although it might seem inconsequential to some, very seldom do we now come across a contemporary volume that uses this genderist literary device. Even though the pedants might complain, we can celebrate the fact that our language is evolving and that "women are people too" is implicitly demonstrated by the shift from *he* to the more inclusive *they*.

CONVERSATION 5:
Family

LOVE, COMPATIBILITY, UNDERSTANDING, and mutual accommodation have traditionally had little to do with marriage. Through much of history, marriage was (and in places continues to be) about connecting two families to their mutual advantage, that advantage taking the shape of political, military, or financial gain. Any consideration of the two people forming the couple actually getting along or feeling something positive about each other was at best incidental to the grander goals of melding power and resources. Fortunately, those reading this book are unlikely to be mere pawns in some Machiavellian power play, so addressing such issues as political alliance or strategic advantage as component parts of a union of powers masquerading as marriage is unlikely to be helpful to most contemporary couples.

That being said—and that was a lot to say—when the two of you tie the knot, you become members of each other's families. And like any group of people, families have rules, expectations, and standard ways of interacting with each other. Learning about your potential new family's rules and expectations is smart practice. More important than this, and more critical as far as the Family conversation goes, will be thinking about which traditions, rules, and expectations you want to reproduce in your own newly minted, nascent family.

One of the really great things about getting married is that you get to choose the customs and traditions that have value *to you*, and you can promote and nurture them as such. The Family conversation, then, is in large part about helping the two of you identify what might and might not work for you in defining and developing your OWN family culture.

Family Culture

Culture is the beliefs, customs, and traditions that exist within a group of people. Typically, people think about culture in broad terms: we are all familiar with concepts like Italian culture, North American culture, First Nations culture, or Christian culture. However, sets of beliefs, customs, and traditions will also exist on smaller scales, or, more correctly, within smaller groups, so concepts like the culture of the South, urban or rural culture, or even military or academic culture also exist. The fact is, *any* group is capable of culture, whether that group comprises millions or a cadre of only two.

It follows that a *family*, as a group of people, will also have a *culture*. That is, families will have a set of beliefs, customs, and traditions that are important to them, not necessarily because of membership to some larger cultural group, but simply as a function of being a cohesive group of people in and of themselves. Often family culture will be informed by ethnicity, religion, or other broad factors, but even then there will be idiosyncrasies across families, and thus we find that no two Christian families, Greek families, middle-class families, or artistic families have identical family cultures.

From the Family conversation perspective, thinking about and cataloguing the culture of your *family of origin* is a good place to get started ("family of origin" is the family you were born into or grew up in). With a bit of thought, each of you will be able to identify the beliefs, customs, and traditions that over time have become important within your family of origin. The factors and influences that shape family culture are many and varied. For example, religious practices will strongly influence some families, and therefore we might see family culture involving which and how religious holidays are observed or when and how a family participates in spiritual activities. For others, family culture may be focused on how leisure time is used, and thus activities like spending summers at a family cottage or attending a particular winter event will have substantial cultural resonance. For yet others, much of the family culture might be determined by vocation. From this perspective, farming families, political families, or academic families will all have their own unique sets of values, expectations, and traditions.

The list of potential issues that might inform or influence any particular family culture is ponderously long, but for our purposes it's not necessary to identify all the possible influences for all families. What is important here is thinking about what has become important for each of you in terms of the culture of your family of origin.

The Matter in Question: Family

FAMILY Q1.   Let's start exploring similarities and differences between the cultures of your two families with a simple example: birthdays. How are birthdays celebrated in each of your families? Who is expected to attend the celebration (assuming there is one)? Are birthday cards important, or are they just an afterthought? Are there presents, and if so, how much money is typically spent on them? Are there birthday traditions that are unique to specific birthdays (i.e., sixteenth, thirtieth, sixtieth, etc.)?

FAMILY Q2. List ten of the most important practices or traditions that exist within your family of origin. (You don't have to have ten or limit yourself to ten; it's just a good number to start with). These might include holiday traditions, religious practices, or customs or expectations related to eating, music, sports, politics, education, recreation, vocation, or any other area of interest.

FAMILY Q3. What are your feelings about these family culture expectations or traditions? How important are these practices or traditions to you personally? Do they serve an important purpose or have particular personal meaning to you, or might they more correctly be labelled something like, "And this is the way we (that is, our family) have always done it"? Allow yourself to be frank and candid here.

FAMILY Q4. Share your lists with each other to identify similarities and differences in these beliefs and traditions. Be careful not to let assumptions slip into this process!

FAMILY Q5. Even if these things were not on your lists, compare and contrast how each of the following issues were discussed and handled in your family while you were growing up:

a. Alcohol use
b. Learning about sex (if the Sex conversation was too difficult to handle, here's your chance to go back and start to tackle this very important issue)

c. Learning to drive
d. Cooking
e. Developing a work ethic
f. Gender differences

FAMILY Q6. Most families have occasions when gifts are given or exchanged (e.g., birthdays, graduations, Christmas, Hanukkah, etc.). However, there can be substantial variation regarding what is considered an appropriate gift. In each of your families, who gives gifts to whom on these occasions? How much money is typically spent on these gifts, and does this vary based on the occasion?

FAMILY Q7. Watch the movie *Fiddler on the Roof* (1971, Topol, Norma Crane) together. This film is filled with issues related to the various conversations espoused in this book, but perhaps more than any other it addresses the concept of family and family traditions. What parallels, if any, do you see in how the familial and cultural traditions are portrayed in the film compared with the familial and cultural traditions that exist in either of your families?

The task before you will be to shape a new family culture that uniquely works for the two of you. This means picking and choosing the aspects of your family-of-origin culture that you want to reproduce, as well as rejecting family cultural qualities that haven't worked for you. Yes, that's right, not only do you get to keep doing the things that have meaning to you, but you get to reject the things that don't! This is one of those very cool qualities of being an adult that we sometimes forget about. Simply because "it has always been done that way in my family" doesn't mean you have to keep doing it that way. I stress this point because, over the years, I have worked with a number of young couples who have failed to realize this particular opportunity associated with growing up. I call it the *failure to launch syndrome*, and it is epitomized by young people getting themselves tied up in knots due to feelings of family obligation to do something they'd rather not do.

Realistically Speaking: Pam and Dominic

One young couple I worked with hated having to attend Sunday dinner with her parents. They didn't have a particularly good time on Sundays, and this was often because during dinner the two of them would be scolded by her father about what he perceived as their shortcomings. When I suggested they express their unhappiness about how Sunday dinners had been going of late and rethink attending, they were both taken aback. The idea of doing anything other than toeing the family line had simply not occurred to them! Through the process of talking about their circumstances, they were able to give themselves permission to be adults. They quickly resolved that, as they were no longer enjoying the Sunday night tradition, they were going to make other plans. As silly as it might sound, although this couple was well beyond the age of majority, this was the first time in their lives they recognized what might result from assuming adult rights and privileges.

Grown-ups get to pick and choose who and what they want to be, with whom they want to spend their time, and how they want to spend their lives, unapologetically and with no need for obfuscation or excuses. They get to choose what is important to them, and they get to act the way they want to act. No matter what culture someone comes from, no matter what religion, no matter what gender, NO MATTER NOTHIN', anyone who is a grown-up gets to choose what they want to do and what to believe. Grown-ups get to take credit for their success and assume responsibility for their failures. And of course it is this final point that is both the great and the scary thing about being a grown-up: while you have to accept responsibility for what you do, you get to choose what is important to include in your life.

COMMINGLING FAMILY CULTURES

From a conflict-management point of view, an important point should be made: even when it comes to family cultures, there are very few things that could be considered as absolute, undeniable, carved in stone "truths." That is, simply because someone believes something or does something a certain way doesn't necessarily mean that what they believe is actually *true* or that the way they do something is the *right* or the *only* way to do it.

The point here is not to belittle or minimize beliefs or traditions, but rather to reveal them for what they are. Family culture can be a wonderful thing—it can provide a sense of purpose, belonging, stability, and predictability. All this is good, but it is also important to understand family culture from a *choice* perspective, rather than one that's perceived to be *fact* based. Our beliefs, and the family culture that grows from these beliefs, are just that—beliefs. Unless we are talking about basic, fundamental human rights, like all people are inherently equal or everyone is deserving of respect, most of culture, family or otherwise, is about things people have *chosen* to believe and practise. But all the history and tradition in the world doesn't make something *true*.[36]

Let me get back to the nuts and bolts of the Family conversation. When it comes to comparing and contrasting family cultures, a lot of intense feelings can be generated. For some, it's easy to get defensive or feel insulted when talking about what they and/or their family feel is important. Feeling strongly about what you

---

[36] And just to hammer the point home, *a lot of people believing something* also fails as a basis to presume something is a *truth*. For example, recall that a few hundred years ago, almost every living person believed the world was flat and that sailing too far in any particular direction meant falling off the edge of the world. The almost universal acceptance of this belief had absolutely no bearing on the supposed *truth* of a flat Earth!

want or believe is perfectly acceptable, and in fact, identifying exactly what you feel and believe is an important element of the Family conversation. However, defensiveness or hurt feelings that are born of a belief that what has been accepted in your family *should work for everyone* or *should be self-evident* or *should never be questioned* is a thinking style that is born of immaturity. Believe and practise whatever you want, but don't make the mistake of thinking that because you or your family of origin believes something, it must be a *truth*. This kind of thinking quickly results in intransigence, which seldom serves a useful purpose in relationship building. In fact, getting obstinate and narrow minded represents one of the greatest stumbling blocks in this part of the Family conversation. Don't do it! Understanding that much of family tradition and culture has to do with *choice* rather than *truth* frees you to explore and think independently about what you want in your own long-term relationship.

The Matter in Question: Family

FAMILY Q8.   In examining the lists from Family Q2, what family tradition would you be most uncomfortable or even frightened about eliminating or substantially modifying?

Realistically Speaking: Jessica and Tom

During a therapy session, Jessica complained that Tom wasn't talking to his brother enough. I asked for more details, and Jessica explained that she had a great relationship with her siblings primarily because they talked to each other on a regular basis. As Jessica and her fiancé were soon to be married, she wanted to have a similar relationship with her new brother-in-law but felt that this couldn't happen until things improved between her fiancé and his brother. Jessica was certain that if her husband-to-be would simply shape the relationship with his sibling the way she had with hers, things would be immeasurably improved not only in his family, but also in their marriage.

I asked for his thoughts, and while hesitant to "open a can of worms," Tom offered the observation that whenever Jessica saw differences between their two families, he felt pressure from her to conform to her way of doing things—this was the way they did things in her family, so this should be the way they start doing things in his family. While no particular issue had yet become really contentious, Tom was increasingly feeling judged and manipulated by Jessica. In his mind, one of the main reasons they had come for premarital therapy was for him to find a way to tell her just how much he resented what he saw as her meddling. Apparently, he had been feeling like this for years, and his lingering resentments were building to a point where he was beginning to question the viability of a stable long-term relationship with her.

We've got lots of fancy words in psychology, and the fancy word that applies here is *projection*. Projection can take a number of forms, but for the purposes of the Family conversation, the kind of projection I'm talking about is the kind described in the case above, where Jessica was firmly of the belief that if Tom's (and their) life was going to work out, he needed to do things the way she did. Because Jessica felt a need to have this type of relationship with her siblings, she just assumed *and projected* this need onto her husband-soon-to-be. Finding the balance between *offering an opinion* and *rendering judgement* is tricky, and the preceding is an example of how things can go awry.

Of course, the ironies in this particular case were thick and deep: Jessica really only wanted to help, not control Tom; the steps she had taken to improve her relationship with her siblings were legitimate and useful; and in her attempt to prove what a terrific long-term companion she was going to be to her fiancé, she was actually driving Tom away! Although they had their work cut out for them, over the next few sessions we talked about projection (as well as his need to speak up and express thoughts and needs in a more timely fashion) and Jessica was able to come to see that her needs were not necessarily his needs, nor was her way of going about improving or changing family dynamics the best or the only way. And this of course is my point. A lot of unnecessary relationship conflict is generated by projecting our own personal needs (or insecurities or fears or ambitions or whatevers) onto our partner. This particular bugaboo seems to show up most often when we compare and contrast our families of origin, but that isn't the only time or place that it happens.

The additional point, however, is that families and family dynamics are complicated things, and what works in one situation may not work (or even apply) in another. The danger here is not just projecting our personal needs onto our partner, but assuming that because we have a certain type of relationship with a family member, our partner should have the same type of relationship with their family. Let's be clear: some families get along, some families are close, some families are supportive, but some families are none of these and never will be.

The Purse Strings That Bind

Recall Family Q6, when I was asking you about money spent on gifts for special occasions? Let's briefly return to that territory.

One of the nice things about family is that you have people who love and support you. This support can take a variety of forms, but at this point in the Family conversation I want the two of you to be thinking about support that comes in the form of dollars and cents.

Financial support and obligation within a family can be just as complicated as any emotional dynamic. Family businesses, joint investments, family assets that entail ongoing financial obligations (such as property taxes on a piece of family land or a home), and support for family members who may be elderly, incapacitated, pursuing expensive educational avenues, intellectually challenged, or mentally ill are just a few examples of circumstances that might generate familial financial obligations. As such, the two of you need to be clear with each other about any financial obligations you might be bringing with you.

The Matter in Question: Family

FAMILY Q9. Have you disclosed to your partner any familial financial obligations you might be bringing into the marriage? Do you have any thoughts about whether or how these obligations may or may not be shared with your partner?

FAMILY Q10. Projecting into the future, can you imagine any future financial obligations that might occur as a member of your family of origin? Share any of these thoughts with your partner as well.

FIRST NAMES, TITLES, AND OTHER WAYS TO INSULT YOUR IN-LAWS

As I said earlier, describing every issue that might pose a potential problem in melding family cultures would be ponderous. However, let me draw your attention to a common and potentially divisive issue, but one that, with communication and discussion, can be easily defused.

Every family has its own expectations about how the "new" parents are to be referred to. Perhaps most commonly the expectation is that the new son- or daughter-in-law will refer to the in-laws as Mom and Dad. In other families, the in-laws' first names are the expected moniker, and the in-laws become Val and Bill or Art and Shirley. Less commonly, formal titles are expected, like Mr. and Mrs., or even less commonly, titles such as Doctor, Judge, or even some military or police rank. Again, there is no right or wrong, just differences in what different families prefer or traditionally use.

Difficulties arise, however, when there is a clash of cultures. Perhaps most common is the expectation that the new spouse will refer to the new in-laws as Mom and Dad, but this is outside the comfort zone for the new spouse. For not a few people, *Mom* and *Dad* are reserved for the biological parent or for the person or people who played that role during childhood. For these people, calling someone else Mom or Dad feels at best uncomfortable and at worst a betrayal. This is not what family melding and relationship building ought to be about. The problem is most pronounced when no one speaks up about their feelings and discomfort, and a sense of rejection and even insult are the result.

Realistically Speaking: Cora

A client of mine complained bitterly about having to refer to her new mother-in-law not only as Mother, but also by the family pet name for the mother-in-law, Nonnie. Cora felt disloyal to her own family by having to share the title of Mother with someone she didn't feel was her mother, and even worse, in using the pet name, having to engage in a degree of familiarity that she just didn't feel. The situation had become so strained that she began making excuses for not visiting her new husband's family or even talking to his relatives on the telephone. She had mentioned to her husband that she was uncomfortable with the current arrangement, but he lacked the communication skill to broach the subject with his family and was worried that a rejection of the title would interfere with his new wife's being accepted into his family.

Again, what was useful for this young couple was drawing their attention to the fact that they were grown-ups, and as such were allowed to make choices for themselves. I suggested to Cora that, while it would be nice to have her new husband's support, the issue was really her own and well within her ability to successfully resolve. With some coaching and preparation, she prepared herself to have a conversation with her new mother-in-law and explain her feelings and sense of conflict. Cora later reported that her mother-in-law was, at least initially, deeply hurt by what she saw as her daughter-in-law's rejection of not only her but her family values. Upon further discussion, however, the mother-in-law came to at least appreciate the conflict her new daughter-in-law felt, and it turned out she had already sensed the beginning of a pulling away from the family. When she recognized this as an inevitable result of someone feeling forced into a role that could not be accepted, she began to reluctantly consider alternative arrangements. Over the course of a few months, the two women finally agreed that if, over time, Cora came to feel more comfortable with her mother-in-law, she would attempt to use the title. However, and regardless of the final result, they would continue to have regular discussions about family dynamics so that future issues could be dealt with more efficiently.

The Matter in Question: Family

FAMILY Q11. What have in-laws traditionally been called in your family? (If there is no *tradition*, are there *expectations* that you are aware of?) That is, do they become Mom and Dad to the new partner, are their first names used, or is there some other tradition? How do each of you feel about the traditions in your partner's family? What are each of you willing to do to support the other in negotiating and managing this issue?

Furry, Scaly, and Feathered Family Members

So the two of you are now deeply involved in the task of learning about your own and each other's family culture, comparing and contrasting important beliefs and traditions, and determining between the two of you what you want your new family culture to look like. Great! But at this point in the Family conversation, allow me to focus on a specific quality of family culture, or at least a quality that exists for some people. I say for some people because not everyone feels the same way about this issue, and I've seen a number of couples over the years for whom this was a tremendously contentious point. The topic of this part of the Family conversation is *pets*.

For some, pets are as much a part of the family and of having a family as any other aspect of family tradition or culture. But before we go too deeply into this topic, and despite reports to the contrary, I need it on record that in fact *I don't hate pets*. I don't personally want pets, I personally experience pets as little more than an inconvenience, and I have no personal love for the mess and damage pets cause, but I don't *hate* them. On occasion I even scratch my wife's cat or put food in his bowl! Someone who *hated* pets would not do this. Also let me state for the record, however, that I don't have a pet of my own and, for the most part, I just find pets inconvenient. (I am, however, an ichthyophile and I maintain an aquarium, but I think of keeping fish more as a hobby than as having a pet.)

Obviously, my ambivalence toward pets isn't universal. The growth of the big-box, pet-superstore phenomenon speaks to a deep love and dedication to pets and their welfare. Lots of people really love their animals, are willing to spend gobs of money on them, and can't imagine their lives without them.

And this brings us back to this part of the Family conversation. As strange as it may seem to those who haven't felt an emotional bond to an animal, many think of pets as family members and wouldn't want to be without them. Consequently, part of the Family conversation needs to address the meaning and needs of pet ownership for each of you.

The Matter in Question: Family

FAMILY Q12. Share with each other the experiences of pets you may have had *growing up*. Were those experiences important, inconsequential, or somewhere in between? What were your reactions when the pet died? How important was pet ownership (or a specific pet) to your other family members while you were growing up?

FAMILY Q13. If you have been living on your own, what have been your own independent experiences of pets?

FAMILY Q14. On a scale of zero to 10—zero being not at all important, 10 being an absolute, non-negotiable necessity—how important is having a pet to you? If having pets is important, what type of pet? What number of pets? What variety of pets?

FAMILY Q15. If you have been a pet owner, take a moment and figure out the cost in dollars and cents of your pet ownership and share your findings with your partner.

FAMILY Q16. If you're not a pet person, why not? Can you identify and share with your partner the thoughts and feelings that make pet ownership uncomfortable, unpalatable, or, at the very least, unexplored for you?

FAMILY Q17.   Do you know how long any particular type of pet lives? Do you know how long-lived the type of pet(s) your partner is interested in tends to be?[37]

Special Note for Those Who LOVE Pets

As strange as it might sound, not everyone feels the same way about animals as you do. This doesn't make them right or wrong; it just makes them different. If you're one of the people who really love pets, finding someone to marry who also really loves pets is a much better idea than marrying someone who doesn't like pets. People who don't love animals are not likely to see the "error of their ways" and come to develop the same love, need, and respect for animals that you have. Those who don't really love pets as a general rule don't get the emotional attachment you feel and likely never will. Believing that a partner will come to love Foo Foo or Bunnykins or Mr. Jeepers the way you do is a bad plan. This is like believing that someone who really doesn't like opera will come to adore it. It might happen, but it probably won't.

---

[37] If I watch TV, I almost exclusively watch documentaries. As a consequence, I have come to know a lot about wildlife and nature, since there are lots of documentaries on these topics. However, these documentaries are almost always about lions or alligators, or the wildlife of Madagascar, and seldom about domestic animals like horses, cows, cats, or dogs. When my wife-to-be wanted a cat, I had no real problem with this because, extrapolating from what I knew from my documentaries, wild animals didn't live that long, given all the predation, dangers, and pitfalls of living in the wild. As it turns out, domestic cats can live twelve, fifteen, even twenty years! Who knew?! As an FYI, make sure you have a clear understanding of the longevity of the animal you plan to acquire. Some pet birds, for example, can live eighty years or more!

If that ship has sailed, however, and you, as a dog, cat, or iguana person, have fallen head over heels for a non-dog, cat, or iguana person, allow me to offer this piece of advice. For your long-term happiness and the stability of your relationship, try to make pet ownership as painless for your partner as possible. For example, non–pet people often greatly resent the mess and cleanup that pets can require. Believing that this responsibility ought to be shared equally will not be understood or well received. Holding on to the hope that some day your partner will see what they've been missing and fall in love with your pet is an equally low-probability expectation. Understanding that you need to spend money on food, accoutrements, health care, transportation, etc., for your pet can also be a source of resentment and frustration, and it is probably best for you to operate under the assumption that you will take care of these issues pretty much on your own. Trying to make a pet lover out of a non–pet lover is long-shot gambling. For the sake of peace in your home, making the issue of your pet ownership as transparent as possible is good relationship management.

SPECIAL NOTE FOR THOSE WHO DO NOT LOVE PETS

As strange as it might sound, not everyone feels the same way about animals as you do. This doesn't make them right or wrong; it just makes them different. If you're one of the people who really don't like pets, finding someone to marry who also really doesn't like pets is a much better idea than marrying someone who loves pets. People who really love animals are likely to believe that you will see the "error of your ways" and come to develop the same love, need, and respect for animals that they have. Those who really love pets as a general rule don't get that you have no emotional attachment to animals and likely never will. They often believe that you will come to love Foo Foo or Bunnykins or Mr. Jeepers the way they do. Of course, this is like believing that someone who really doesn't like opera will come to adore it. It might happen, but it probably won't.

If that ship has sailed, however, and you, as a non-dog, cat, or iguana person have fallen head over heels for a dog, cat, or iguana person, allow me to offer this piece of advice. For your long-term happiness and the stability of your relationship, try to make pet ownership as painless for your partner as possible. For example, try to temper the frustration you feel about the mess and cleanup that pets can require. Believing that you have absolutely no responsibility to help maintain the home as far as the pet is concerned will not be understood or well received. Holding on to the hope that some day your partner will understand the discomfort you feel and offer their pet for adoption is an equally low-probability expectation. Understanding that they need pets, and thus also need to spend money on food, accoutrements, health care, transportation, etc., for their pet, will also be a source of resentment and frustration for you, but it's probably best for you to operate under the assumption that your helping out will be greatly appreciated. Trying to make a non-pet lover out of a pet lover is long-shot gambling. For the sake of peace in your home, making the issue of their pet ownership as transparent as possible is good relationship management.

A POSTSCRIPT TO PET POLITICS

To conclude, let me be clear: the person who wants the pet(s) ought to be doing the lion's share of looking after it, primarily because it's an elephant of an imposition on the person who's not crazy about animals. But for those of you who don't want the pet(s), recognize that you're marrying someone who really loves and maybe even needs to have animals around and that maybe you could get down from your high horse and lend a hand.

FINAL THOUGHTS ON THE FAMILY CONVERSATION

At this point, we're about halfway through *The 10 Conversations*. If you've been doing them in order, you have talked about five issues that are critically important to building a long-term relationship:

whether having kids is a good choice for the two of you, if each of you is looking for a job or a career, how the two of you will bring together your individual financial styles, the importance of learning about and expressing your sexual needs and desires, and the challenges of developing your own family culture.

Even though every one of these topics is extremely important, aspects of each conversation often get missed by young couples preparing to marry. By using this book, the two of you are approaching these important topics more systematically, and thus ensuring that the critical points of each conversation are not missed, avoided, or glossed over.

Just as important as the topics we have covered are the experiences of communication the two of you will be having. By formally setting out to discuss important issues in an efficient, frank, and candid manner, the two of you are setting a precedent for how you will tackle the myriad issues that will present themselves over the years of your lives together. There are few steps you could take that are more beneficial than learning how to "get into each other's heads" and learning what is important to each of you. What's more, from a Family conversation perspective, taking the time to develop the skills to understand each other provides a solid foundation for creating a strong and healthy family, whether you choose to expand your own or improve the ways an existing family interacts. From my perspective, this is one of those "no lose" situations.

To those of you who have been having difficulty or are finding that substantial conflict is being generated when you tackle any of the conversations, I might suggest that you reread the fifteen rules of good communication for clues about how the two of you might be getting off track. Learning to communicate well is a substantial challenge and is seldom accomplished simply by knowing the rules. Like many things, knowledge is good, but practice is better! All the reading in the world isn't going to make someone a good hockey player. At some point, they have to strap on their skates and get out on the ice. And of course, while a few falls are expected, no one should use these falls as a justification to give up and just take a seat on the bench. Learning to talk about sensitive, important, or delicate topics is a skill set that everyone needs and, as has already been said, is absolutely necessary if you're going to make your partner aware of what you need, want, and *desire*.

CONVERSATION 6:
Location, Location, Location

WHERE WE WANT TO LIVE IS related to a number of factors, and what makes a "home a home" for one person may represent frustration and obligation to another. Proximity to family, the availability of work, the cost of transportation, safety issues, a sense of personal and familial security, and a variety of other issues will all play a role in what "home" means to anyone. Figuring out what each of you needs and wants in this regard, and where and how the two of you will be setting up housekeeping, becomes the objective of this, the sixth of the ten conversations.

Everyone has heard the old saw about how to buy property. When asked how to choose the perfect piece of property, the real estate expert sagely explains there are only *three* things that have to be considered: location, location, and location. And while the truth of this remains, my intention is to use this old chestnut to highlight other dimensions intimately related to the process of setting up house together. Allow me, therefore, to draw your attention to these other qualities of location:

1. Where your heart (or instinct) tells you to be
2. Where your mind (or logic) tells you to be
3. Where negotiation and compromise lead the two of you to settle

The Meaning of Home: Carports or Passports

You need to start the Location conversation by returning to first principles and determining what might work best for you as far as living arrangements are concerned. Essentially, you tap into your heart of hearts and decide on the kind of circumstances you want. And of course there's a range of feelings people have about home and community. For some, home is about stability and a sense of family, history, and belonging. The idea of moving to another town, city, province or state, or even country is unthinkable for these people, primarily because so much of their identity is inextricably linked with where they are in the world, who they know, what they have experienced there, and how comfortable they are with their surroundings.

For others, however, it would be a curse to remain in one place for an extended period. "Home is where you lay your hat" is their motto; wanderlust their creed; airports, seaports, and train stations their temples. Experiencing all the world has to offer brings meaning to these people's lives, while "putting down roots" has a stifling quality and risks missing opportunities for growth.

Prodomesticism

In previous conversations, we have tackled *pronatalism* and *genderism*. Here in the Location conversation, the ism we need to talk about is *prodomesticism*. By *prodomesticism* (*pro* meaning *positive*, *domestic* meaning *home*), I am referring to a set of expectations and attitudes that suggest that acquiring a relatively permanent address and spending years, if not much of your life, in the same place is the correct course of action for pretty much everyone. From the prodomestic perspective, settling down, buying a house, and establishing yourself in a community is really the expected, the best, and the correct thing that anyone could choose to do.

And for the prodomestic, denying this course of action or a failure to follow this plan will potentially result in recrimination, regret, and a loss of some of life's most meaningful experiences.

As with the other isms we have talked about, the two real problems with prodomesticism are the social momentum that sweeps so many along with it and an inappropriate "one size fits all" set of assumptions.

There is nothing sinister about a couple wanting to set themselves up in a home and establish roots in a community. Finding a place to live where you feel comfortable, safe, and wanted are eminently reasonable goals, and I don't think it's necessary to describe all the positives of feeling safe and secure, knowing you are part of a community, or having a place in the world you can call your own. No, the danger of prodomestic attitudes arises only when there's an assumption that *of course* everyone wants to do this, *of course* this is the correct thing to do, and *of course* anyone would have to be crazy to want anything else.[38] The *of courses* are the things that get in the way of building healthy and sustaining relationships or exploring your own personal needs. If we just add the proviso *for some* to each of the above prodomestic statements, we will arrive at a position that better reflects the diversity of human nature and provides a more realistic foundation for a discussion of what the two of you want from your relationship.

In the same way that some become parents not out of choice and enthusiasm but from the social momentum of pronatalism, many find themselves adhering to the tenets of prodomesticism, taking steps toward "settling down" like buying a house and making commitments to community involvement before really considering the personal "fit" of such choices.

As with many of the topics in *The 10 Conversations*, there is no demand or need to have all the answers to all these substantial life

---

[38] This is another example of those faulty *assumptions* that were described in Rule 11.

questions right this moment. There are many issues in life we can't be certain about until we have built up some experience, often on different sides of the same issue. So determining both the "if" and the "when" of settling down may take some practice and experience. One of the points, then, of the Location conversation is more to ensure that all options are being considered and respected, rather than simply following common models of decision making or social trends.

Realistically Speaking: Gary and Joanne

One couple I worked with felt particularly handcuffed by the expectations of prodomesticism. For different reasons, both had been bitten by the travel bug since their adolescence and they were never as happy as when they were wandering around some part of the world that few Westerners had visited. Because of this love of travel, both chose to pursue jobs and make domestic choices that involved little or no long-term commitment, save to each other. Putting money aside for "the house" was out of the question for this couple, as it remained unclear to them *what continent, if any*, they might eventually settle on. Instead, money was earned almost exclusively to fund the next six- or eight-month trip abroad. While other couples in their late thirties were concerned about mortgages, career development, and summer camp for the kids, this couple paid attention to the political climate in a number of African nations, hoping to choose a moment of reduced hostilities to further explore a natural environment they felt inextricably drawn to, or to take advantage of the different seasons Down Under and explore the central deserts of the Australian outback.

Unfortunately, neither of their families appreciated what was important to this couple and continually applied pressure to both of them to "settle down and get real jobs." They were accused of wasting their educations and intellect (both had post-graduate degrees) and of turning up their noses at the career opportunities their families went to great pains to create for them. Most hurtful

of all, however, was the accusation that they were purposely trying to hurt their families by staying away for such long periods
and by frequently placing themselves in harm's way in the destinations they chose to explore. So great was the pressure from
their families that this couple came to see me to try to resolve
their mixed feelings of obligation.

By taking the time in my office to fully explore their desires
and options, this couple discovered how much they resented the
deeply ingrained expectations of prodomesticism and how inappropriate that way of thinking was to their personal hopes and
desires for the future. By considering the issues from a
prodomestic point of view, this couple then gave themselves permission to explicitly reject this way of thinking and come to
accept that the way they were living their lives together was completely legitimate and in no need of defence. Together, we
generated a horticultural metaphor that succinctly described what
their lives were about: they would rather be exploring savannas
than cutting grass.

Once this attitude was more firmly established in their own
minds, they had little difficulty confronting their families with how
they were hurt by the judgement and pressure that they felt sub-
jected to. Although their families continued to eschew the
nomadic lifestyle the couple had chosen, there was no longer the
hostility toward or rejection of the couple, and their choices were
seen for what they were: a legitimate lifestyle option. For the
entire family, *recognizing and then rejecting the demands of
prodomesticism* was the liberation that everyone needed.

Forgoing home or community of origin to travel the less-well-
known pathways of the world is obviously not the only alternative
to acquiring a permanent address, but it does represent one end of
a continuum of choices as far as where and how the two of you
might want to locate yourselves and your life together.

Of course, the more common model is to acquire a more
permanent address and settle down. Rather than trips to faraway

lands, this model is about trips to the home improvement store. For many, the idea of setting up house together is one of the most appealing qualities of getting married. Finding a space that is just for the two of you, choosing how you want to decorate and arrange your things, and getting to allocate space the way you want represents for many a substantial step toward fully visible adulthood. An address, a phone number, and a place to call your own epitomizes "making it," turning a page, and starting a new phase of life. Becoming linked to a community, establishing your identity as an adult, perhaps even joining a service club, school board, or town council might be really important for you.

But let's not forget what we just talked about: while these feelings are common, they are not universal. They don't represent needs or desires that are correct, mature, or obvious; they're just common. This brings us back to the entire point of *The 10 Conversations*: finding out what each of you want and need.

The Matter in Question: Location

LOCATION Q1. What thoughts do you have about setting up (if not now, some time in the future) a permanent home or address? Is this a comforting thought, or does it leave you feeling trapped and limited? Does your partner know how you feel about this—one way or the other?

LOCATION Q2. If prodomesticism feels like a good fit for you or your partner, what are the most appealing qualities or aspects of setting up a home? Is it about setting out on you own? Is it about having control over your own space? Is it about becoming an independent part of a community?

Is it all these things, or is it something else?
Essentially, what is the meaning of home for each
of you?

LOCATION Q3. Do either of you have strong
feelings about renting versus owning where you
live? What do either of you know about the costs
associated with each option?

So the purpose of this part of the Location conversation is to establish the "what" part of location for the two of you. What does having a home mean to the two of you, and what needs or desires associated with this might you have? If seeing the world is what you and your partner are into, and the idea of settling down is not what you want to be thinking about at this time, you can go ahead and skip the rest of this conversation and move on to Division of Labour. But if home and hearth are what you're about, read on. We still have some things to discuss.

CONNECTING CONVERSATIONS

Assuming that the two of you won't be wandering around the world for most of your lives, we come to a pretty important point in the ten-conversations process. The two of you will now need to sit down, think about, and discuss the actual "where" of where this is going to happen. This book has been designed to facilitate this particular part of the Location conversation in that, if you've been doing each of the conversations in order, you already know a lot about issues that will be of critical import to this discussion. Much of what the two of you have been talking about and learning about each other in the Having Kids, Careers, Money and Financial Styles, and Family conversations will be profoundly relevant to how the two of you go about deciding where you want to live.[39] Earlier, I said this part of the conversation was about logic and practicality, and it is. But don't make the mistake of dismissing your own or your partner's emotional needs as you progress through the next series of questions—as I've said before, ignore emotional needs at your peril!

Although not universal, it is often the case that family and career issues have the biggest influence on the Location conversation. That is, with some effort, we can set up a home and bring up kids happily and safely in a number of different circumstances. The same is true for how much we earn: there are plenty of opportunities to "make do" in lots of different locales. However, it becomes obvious pretty quickly that we can live only where we can make a living. Deciding to become an actor but living where there is no theatre or opportunities to do commercials, television, radio, or movie work simply fails to pass the reality test. Similarly, and as we discussed in the Family conversation, if being close to extended family is critically important to you, exploring potential living arrangements that will situate you on the other side of the world (or at least have limited access to the family that means so much to you) is clearly a failure to prioritize what gives meaning to your life, and this is a terribly dangerous precedent to set and will substantially strain your relationship.

The work issue is a particularly salient one given the increasing reality of two-career relationships. The ideal location to further *one* person's career aspirations may be less than ideal for the other. Careful consideration and negotiation need to take place in these circumstances, and a reiteration of the point that no one's career is more important than the other's is useful at this juncture.

One helpful tool in managing conflicting needs and desires about where to live is the recognition that many currencies of exchange can be used to balance out perceived inequities.

---

[39] If what you learned about each other in the Sex chapter also plays an important role, bring that into the Location conversation as well!

What do I mean by this? Let me provide an example from my practice.

Realistically Speaking: Samantha and Shane

For one couple I saw, she was in a career that demanded domestic stability and security. If Samantha was going to do what she wanted to do, she was going to have to establish herself in a particular community and stay there for the duration of her working life. Shane, however, had designs on applying his technical training to a military career but had come to learn that he would have to be flexible in where he would be posted, particularly in the early years of his career and quite possibility for most of his working life. There would be none of the stability she needed if he were to pursue what he wanted to do. In short, what the two of them wanted from their careers was incompatible as far as location was concerned. However, their desire to be a couple outweighed the career demands of either. After much negotiation and discussion, they settled on a compromise achieved only by expanding what could be traded and exchanged in this Location conversation. Rather than thinking only about fixed careers or locations, we looked for other ways he could find what he wanted from life.

The solution for this couple came when they recognized that time and money could be exchanged for career opportunity. They decided that they would choose a community and settle down, allowing her to establish herself as a professional and build her career. However—and this was a big however—Shane still wanted to serve, but they came to believe that this could take the form of service to his community instead of his nation. The new currency of negotiation then became time and money for him to train and engage in community policing, not as a police officer, but as a community police volunteer. Shane applied his technical training to a field that had little to do with the military but allowed him to make a reasonable financial contribution and establish a career for himself. The point here is that a location issue was resolved by recognizing all the different things that can be exchanged and traded when trying to resolve a problem.

Another couple I know faced the problem that he needed to locate in another country, but she was very attached to her family. The resolution for them was that, in addition to travelling to be with her family for most of the major holidays, they would set aside enough money so that at least once a year, and for no specific reason, she could buy a ticket to come home for a visit and he would accommodate her absence by stepping up and assuming all the responsibilities of looking after the house and children for the time she was away.

Solutions are often there to be found, even when issues seem intractable.

CURRENCIES OF EXCHANGE

The different "currencies of exchange" that can be used to help ensure both of you are feeling equally benefited in your relationship are limited only by your imagination. Anything that's considered a resource can become a currency of exchange to help maintain balance in the relationship: time, money, authority, first choice, etc. For one couple, looking after the pets, which required time, effort, and considerable inconvenience in the winter months, was a currency of exchange; for another, the biyearly ritual of rotating warm- and cold-weather clothes out of storage was considered an onerous task and became a currency of exchange. In the category of every rule having an exception, however, I would caution against using sex as a currency of exchange. Sex can be a complicated issue all on its own, and specifically making it a commodity where one person can demand sex in exchange for some other favour or to balance out an inequity sets a dangerous relationship precedent.

In the self-disclosure department, to become the clinical psychologist I wanted to be, my graduate training required that I move 1,400 kilometres away from where I'd been living. This was not what my girlfriend and soon-to-be-fiancée wanted, nor was it consistent with her career aspirations. There were a lot of tears and hand wringing as we discussed alternatives, but eventually it was decided that I would move away and sometime in the near future she'd follow. As part of the deal, we agreed that the next time we relocated, which was going to happen upon the completion of my graduate training, she would get to choose the location that was best suited to meet *her* career needs. Essentially, we adopted a "taking turns" approach to the location question: I got the first turn and she got the second one. (I suppose if we were to pursue a third relocation, it would be my turn again. Note to self: fantasize about a third relocation.) Taking turns as a potential path to finding agreement is explained in more detail in "Troubleshooting."

The Matter in Question: Location

LOCATION Q4. How, if at all, does what you learned about each other in the Having Kids conversation influence where you want (or will be able) to live? From a location perspective, talking about the following issues will be useful: the time it takes to get to and from work; daycare quality and availability; location, cost, and proximity to schools; the safety of the neighbourhood; traffic flow around your home; and the presence of public facilities like parks, rinks, and pools.

LOCATION Q5. How, if at all, does what you learned about each other in the Careers conversation influence where you want (or will be able) to live? From a location perspective, talking about the following issues will be useful: the stability of the job market and future opportunities in the area; any potential need for further career development

or education that might require relocation; the likelihood of a job transfer and subsequent need to liquidate real estate holdings; and the advisability of renting versus owning, given the likelihood of career changes.

LOCATION Q6.   How, if at all, does what you learned about each other in the Money and Financial Styles conversation influence where you want (or will be able) to live? From a location perspective, talking about the following issues will be useful: are differences in financial styles likely to lead to different opinions concerning the kind of home you can afford? Do either of you already own property? If so, how will that asset be respected and brought into the relationship?

LOCATION Q7.   How, if at all, does what you learned about each other in the Family conversation influence where you want (or will be able) to live? From a location perspective, talking about the following issues will be useful: how comfortable are you being close to or far away from your family of origin? Do either of you have plans to have a family member come and live with you, now or in the future? Does pet ownership need to be taken into consideration when thinking about a home's location? Does the location of a family business play any role in where the two of you might want to live?

LOCATION Q8.   Finally, and even though we are getting ahead of ourselves here, do either of you have any special leisure needs, requirements, wants, or desires that ought to be taken into consideration when you're having the Location conversation? For example, if one of you is passionate about rowing, deep-sea scuba diving, rock climbing, or downhill skiing, the geographical features of where you live could have a substantial influence on the quality of your life.

LOCATION Q9. Location issues can be contentious, and as is always the case with potentially intense issues, starting the conversation with statements of feelings is far more useful than making statements of fact or taking a position. Starting with comments like, "Well, I have to live here and that's all there is to it," will not be helpful in moving the conversation forward. Can the two of you start this part of the conversation by making a statement about feelings, attitudes, or needs rather than drawing a line in the sand? Try opening lines like, "My preference would be to live..." or "I would really like being close to..." or even "I love the mountains. How do you feel about them?"

LOCATION Q10. If the two of you have identified incompatibilities in your needs and desires on a location, what have you done to identify the various currencies that could be exchanged to balance the needs that each of you might have? (Keeping a list of these currencies in mind is a very useful marital tool, as they can be applied in a variety of circumstances, not just in disputes about location. For example, we will return to this issue in the next conversation, Division of Labour.)

Painting, Maintaining, and Repairing the White Picket Fence

Forgive me for this next short diatribe, but I wouldn't be doing my job if I skipped over this next issue.

Don't ignore the practicalities of setting up a home together. What do I mean by *practicalities?* Setting up a home can take a lot of time and effort. Now, I don't know anyone who actually wants a home with a white picket fence, but the picket fence has come to be the symbol of idealizing what living together might mean. This is my caution against too much idealizing. The reality of setting up a home is that, while it can be a tremendous amount of fun and a wonderful growing experience, it's also filled with the mundane practicalities of everyday life. Having to buy waste paper baskets, curtain rods, picture hooks, bath mats, floor cleaner, and those little things you have to put on the bottom of chair legs so they don't wreck the hardwood floor all cost money (and time to get), and are thankless and unappreciated tasks that still need to be done. Cleaning and painting and repairing and replacing and maintaining are dull and boring chores but still ones that need be accomplished, and again there is the time, effort, and money involved.

As a parallel, studies have shown that new mothers who have *only idealized* the concepts of baby and parenthood make poor mothers and are more prone to postpartum depression because they didn't have *realistic expectations* about the reality and hardships of parenting and baby care. I'm not aware of any studies that specifically support this effect with new couples and living together, but I will strongly suggest that the same thing happens if the reality of the work, time, and effort of setting up house together are not taken into serious consideration.

> ## The Matter in Question: Location
>
> **LOCATION Q11. How many times have you moved before? What did you find to be the most onerous part(s) of the process? What surprises and unexpected expenses did you incur?**

HOUSE RICH, CASH POOR

There are many other practical aspects of setting up a home together that need to be considered. For example, the idea of being *house rich and cash poor* has to be seriously considered. Financial institutions will happily lend us far more money than we should practically accept, but some people make the mistake of believing that if a bank will lend them X amount of money, that's how much they can spend on a house, a condo, or something else they can live in. Perhaps you know people who have fallen into this trap and have a lovely home, but it echoes for lack of fixtures and furniture. This might be the same couple who can never take a vacation with you or go out to the movies because they're forced to watch their pennies—house rich, cash poor. Every couple has to find a practical and realistic balance between what they can afford versus what banks and credit card companies are willing to lend them.

A DOMESTIC THOUGHT EXPERIMENT

Here's a little exercise I recommend you try when the two of you are considering any particular change in living circumstance: as you go through your current daily routine, imagine what that routine would be like *living in the new situation*. As an experiment, compare and contrast what might be the same and what might be different about the new digs compared to where you are currently situated. Think about this all day, starting from the moment you get up and have your first cup of coffee, using the question, "What might this be like in the new place?" Think about it when you're travelling to work and when you're coming home. Think about it when you're shopping, picking up the dry cleaning, dropping a vehicle at a garage for a tune-up, getting home, making dinner, watching TV, talking to a friend on the phone, paying the bills, using the bathroom, doing the laundry, and eventually going to bed. In every one of these situations, give yourself a moment to consider what these tasks and routines might be like, living at the new location.

Once you've done this, do it again, except now imagine it during *each of the four seasons*. For example, that beautiful, winding driveway at the new place might look spectacular in the summer, but who's going to find the time to shovel it in the winter? Gardens look wonderful when they're maintained, and the new place has a terrific one. Do either of you have an interest in maintaining a garden, and the time to keep doing it? That potential new condo or apartment next to the school looks terrific and will be tremendously convenient if you end up having children of your own, but have you thought about what living next to a playground full of kids in September (and October and April) might be like? What seems like a great view in January from the new townhouse might be completely lost when the trees are in leaf.

Exploring thoughts and asking questions like these increase the chances that the two of you will have realistic expectations about where you might be living together.

The Matter in Question: Location

LOCATION Q12. Prepare a list of "nice to have" and "need to have" features you would like in a home and share it with your partner.

LOCATION Q13. Do either of you have any immediate or long-term plans to work out of your home? If so, have you told your partner about it?

LOCATION Q14. Do either of you have health or medical needs, or any other kind of special requirement, that ought to be discussed and considered from a location perspective?

SETTLING (IN ITS MANY FORMS)

I apologize for beginning this section with platitudes and clichés, but I've really got no other place to go. If the two of you are going to make a life together that works, you're both going to have to recognize that marriage is about *negotiating and compromise*. While this will be true in many marital circumstances, when it comes to figuring out questions of location, sometimes Gandhiesque conciliation is needed to keep things moving forward. Finding a place where the two of you can both be happy is no small chore but will be made easier if you cut each other some slack and listen intently to what the other wants and needs. Here are some pointers on how to talk about and resolve location issues.

TO APPEASE OR NOT TO APPEASE

First, don't strong-arm your partner into a choice about which they are expressing doubts or that they really don't want. You have to think about picking a place to live the same way you'd think about naming a baby—ideally, you both really have to love it if it's going to be something you'll be happy with for years to come.

Now, when I say "ideally," I mean this: few couples get everything they want when they're looking for a home. But don't mistake a need to settle for the best you can get as a way to legit-imize forcing your partner to live someplace that will make them unhappy. Even if you don't understand why something is impor-tant to your partner, you do them and your relationship a disservice by ignoring their wants and needs. There are good compromises and bad ones, so don't force your partner to become Neville Chamberlain![40]

MIND READING CONTINUES TO BE A BAD IDEA

The Location conversation provides a great opportunity to review the communication rules, but in particular Rule 11, no mind reading. What you think might be important or obvious when it comes to deciding where to live may not have even occurred to your partner, and that's exactly the kind of thing that leads to unnecessary acrimony and distress. If something is important to you, you need to speak up about it, regardless of whether or not you believe your partner will find it impor-tant. A failure to do this increases the chances of minimizing the compromises you might make, and this in turn leads to the particularly insidious and toxic *lingering resentment*, where you're walking around with unspoken anger and frustration with your partner.

TAKE THE TIME IT TAKES!

If at all possible, *take your time* when deciding about a place to live. It's easy to get swept up in the excitement and anticipation of finding a place the two of you can call your own, but some-times this excitement and anticipation leads to impetuous and poorly thought out choices. Good options are almost always out there, and deciding (or compromising) too soon has the poten-

---

[40] Neville Chamberlain was Prime Minister of Britain between 1937 and 1940 and is famous for his policy of appeasement to Hitler. Chamberlain thought that by giv-ing a bully what he wanted, the bully would go away and everyone would be happy. Of course, we all know things didn't work out that way.

tial to take us back to lingering resentment. Don't be pressured by others to make a choice the two of you haven't had enough time to think about, and completely dismiss the idea that you're under some obligation to make a purchase or choice to do someone else a favour (some salespeople love to play up this angle). The two of you are full-fledged members of the grown-up world, so you get to make grown-up choices with grown-up consequences—be a grown-up and take all the time you need to decide!

THINK OUTSIDE THE BOX STORE

Feel free to think outside the box, particularly at the beginning of the Location conversation. For example, maybe living in the city isn't the only option the two of you could consider. Perhaps the responsibility of a mortgage is not something the two of you are ready for or ever want to have. It might even be possible that the world won't come to an end if the two of you break the family tradition of living in the same neighbourhood and decide to live somewhere else. Let me reiterate the part about being grown-ups and all the rights, responsibilities, and range of choices you're allowed to explore.

Building a life together is a marathon, not a sprint. Similarly, establishing the ideal home together is something that seldom happens all at once. Usually it is done in stages, including the occasional misstep. Just as a sense of humour is important in learning how to be good sexual partners, so too does that same sense of humour come into play in negotiating and choosing where the two of you will live.

Finally, consider talking to others you know about their experiences with making challenging location choices. One of the greatest strengths of the human species is our ability to pass on knowledge from one person, as well as one generation, to the next. Take advantage of this quality and ask around.

The Matter in Question: Location

LOCATION Q15. Watch the movie *House of Sand and Fog* (2003, Jennifer Connelly, Ben Kingsley) together. While not specifically related to premarital issues, the two main characters' struggle over the home has the potential to generate important discussions between the two of you. For example, which side did you sympathize with? What do you think would have made a better compromise and ultimate solution?

FINAL THOUGHTS ON THE LOCATION, LOCATION, LOCATION CONVERSATION

When it comes to location choices, few if any decisions ought to be made independently. The two of you are in the "find a great place to live the three-legged race" of your lives and, just like at the family picnic, neither of you are going to make any meaningful progress without working and coordinating with the other. The two of you need to establish a partnership where important decisions like where to live are made together so you both feel committed and responsible for a positive outcome for what the two of you have decided to do. A sense of shared responsibility not only fosters a greater sense of connection, but also helps avoid the two of you descending into the "blame game" when things don't go perfectly or as expected. By setting up things correctly from the beginning (i.e., both participating, negotiating, and compromising), both of you will take a role in fixing whatever might need fixing and equally taking credit for the successes and victories.

Here's one final thought on location that I want to leave with you. Symbolically, as well as practically, setting up a home together is a statement to the world that the two of you are now an independent unit, a couple, and the beginnings of a new family and potentially new traditions. Figuring out what you, as a couple, want to do and how you are going to solve the many problems that come along with setting up house together is accomplished far better when the two of you accept responsibility for working out your own problems. When problems arise—and they will—the simple act of committing yourselves to working them out *between the two of you* is an important, even vital component of healthy relationship building.

Some are accustomed to having parents, other relatives, or friends work out their problems for them, and there is no question, having family and friends in your back pocket is a great comfort. But if you're going to go down the road of marriage and home, *learning to solve your couple problems as an independent couple* goes hand in hand with the symbolic and practical statement you are making by setting up a home together. Millions of couples before you have learned how to handle their own problems, and so can the two of you. Having the courage and discipline to work the problems out as two members of a couple, rather than bolting or immediately calling for reinforcements, is another skill set common to successful couples, no if, but, or *and*!

CONVERSATION 7:
Division of Labour

THE SEVENTH CONVERSATION IS about the division of labour and household chores. In the grand scheme of things, I wouldn't blame you if you found this topic as boring as unbuttered toast. Sorry, there's not much I can do about that—dishes have to be washed, bills have to be paid, and tires have to be rotated. If there's any solace I can offer as we plow through this issue, it would be that because most people are already familiar with doing chores and at least some forms of housework, we're not going to have to spend a lot of time justifying or describing the tasks that need to be done. On the other hand, the Division of Labour conversation tends to be closely tied to gender expectations, and when things come down to gender, some people foolishly become intractable. So let me encourage you to open your minds, press on, and let's get the Division of Labour conversation started and finished as quickly as possible.

GENDERISM REARS ITS UGLY HEAD AGAIN

As we discussed in the Careers conversation, while we have made progress toward a more egalitarian society, we still have a long way to go. Although there have been definite improvements in some areas, women are still not privileged with the same range of opportunities and advantages as men (conversely, and in the double-edged sword department, men still don't enjoy the same degree of freedom in expressing emotions and continue to die younger than women do). And as far as the Division of Labour conversation is concerned, while in recent years things have come close to parity between men and women, the fact remains that women still do more hours of housework a week than do men.

As a starting point for the Division of Labour conversation, the two of you need to explore what your expectations might be as to who is "supposed" to do housework, or perhaps more to the point, *certain kinds* of housework.

The Matter in Question: Division of Labour

DIV. OF LAB. Q1.   The grass needs to be cut. Who's going to do it, but more important, why that particular person?

DIV. OF LAB. Q2.   A pair of pants needs a hem. Again, who's going to do it, and why that particular person?

DIV. OF LAB. Q3.   When you travel by car, who does the driving? When you're watching TV or a DVD, same question? Why?

DIV. OF LAB. Q4.   When new bedding or curtains need to be chosen, who makes the choice, and why?

I am unaware of any research that shows that women are better cooks, menders, or cleaners than men. Similarly, I'm unfamiliar with the data that support the contention that men consistently do a better job of rotating tires, cutting grass, or searing animal flesh on a barbeque.[41] Why a penis would mean that you have mechanical skills and a clitoris would mean that you have cooking talent has never been made entirely clear to me. And, yes, men can have a sense of style and opinions about curtains, flatware, or art. And, no, just because someone has a vagina doesn't mean they know which wallpaper goes with which fabric, how to arrange furniture to achieve the greatest functionality, or the colour a room needs to be to set off a new bedspread. Applying gender expectations to interests and talent are, as always, a dangerous place to start.

The Matter in Question: Division of Labour

DIV. OF LAB. Q5. Double standards[42] in gender expectations are pretty common, but this doesn't mean we all agree on what they are. What is your definition of a double standard? What is your partner's? What double standards do the two of you see in the world around you? What double standards did you see in your families as you were growing up?

From a household-maintenance perspective, the division of labour still often falls along gender lines, with certain jobs being done or assumed by one gender or the other. While the clarity of this echo from our more genderist past decreases with each generation, we have yet to experience the days of its dying decibels.

---

[41] In fact, even the oft-touted but dubious data that suggest women are better at language-based tasks and men are better at spatial and math-based tasks are increasingly (and vigorously) coming into question.

[42] Defined as having rules, opportunities, or principles applied differently and often unfairly, based on being part of a group.

The point I want to make is not that there's something wrong with women mending or men cutting grass. Rather, there is nothing innate about women doing some tasks and men doing others. The reality ought to be that *we get to choose* what we want to do, and if this still means some of the division of labour falls along stereotyped gender lines, fine. The problem is less about doing gender-specific duties than it is feeling pigeonholed into taking on those tasks. If you're a woman and you like sewing, great. If you're a guy and you like raking leaves, more power to you. But the idea that sewing is supposed to be done by a woman, and thus the "she" in the two of you will be *assumed to take on this responsibility*, or that yard work will be completed by the "he" in your couple and *of course he will look after this*, becomes problematic, even dangerous, and potentially constitutes the beginning of lingering resentments.

As I have frequently espoused, ideally the two of you will check any of your gender assumptions about the division of labour at the door as you begin to build a life together. Playing to strengths and preferences rather than gender dramatically improves the chances of finding an appropriate balance in this conversation. Operating from an assumption of reciprocity and equality will beat gender assumptions hands down.

Answer the following questions honestly and share your thoughts with each other to try to identify how gender-based thinking might inform how you feel about the division of household labour.

The Matter in Question: Division of Labour

DIV. OF LAB. Q6.   Although it might not be politically correct, when it comes to household chores what, if anything, do you think of as "women's work?" How about "men's work?" Conversely, are there any household chores you feel a woman (or a man) should *not* have to do? If possible, spend some time trying to figure out how you arrived at these thoughts and feelings.

DIV. OF LAB. Q7.   Watch the movie *A League of Their Own* (1992, Tom Hanks, Geena Davis). Note the reversal of some of the traditional gender roles and the juxtaposition of various household and professional tasks.

FAIR AS OPPOSED TO THE SAME

Some make the mistake of believing that a *fair division of labour* is accomplished by having the *same division of labour*. This means that both partners wash the dishes exactly half the time, do the laundry exactly half the time, cut the grass exactly half the time—you get the picture.

To my mind, the two of you don't have to be doing exactly half of everything to ensure that neither is being disadvantaged. It seems to me that if he cooks the meal, she can do the dishes. Tit-for-tat. If she does the laundry, he could do the vacuuming. If he consistently does the bills, maybe she could consistently do the shopping. In finding a balance, you're both allowed to play to strength and preference. If he really hates dusting, maybe he's willing to trade this off for cleaning up the backyard after the dog has been let out. *Fair* doesn't necessarily have to mean *the same.*

While the above point is a bit of a no-brainer, we still have to be careful about recognizing and ferreting out any assumptions that might interfere with getting all the various jobs done. However, the more critical issue, and one that often gets left out of this particular part of the Division of Labour discussion is, *when will the equity of the negotiated division be revisited?* Whenever the two of you reach an agreement on who is going to do what, you need to explicitly add a proviso that will help determine at some point in the future (say after a month or two) that whatever was agreed upon will be revisited *to see if it is continuing to work.* This little bit of extra negotiating is absolutely critical for the long-term viability of the division-of-labour agreement between the two of you, and I can't stress its importance enough. Complacency is one of the biggest threats to a healthy relationship, and putting mechanisms in place to avoid it is one of the best things you can do to keep a relationship vital.[43]

DOMESTIC DEXTERITY AND DIVERSITY

Another point that fits under the "fair as opposed to the same" heading is the ability to do at least a bit of everything. A dangerous precedent is set when one member of a couple assumes *all* the responsibility for any particular task *all the time.* For example, when only one person does the bills and the other never participates, all kinds of problems can arise. Imagine that the bill payer suffered a prolonged illness or became incapacitated. Or imagine that she does all the car maintenance, but while he is out driving, he gets a flat and doesn't know how to fix it. He always does the laundry, but while he's away on a business trip, she needs something specific washed for an important meeting and doesn't have a clue about how this can happen.

The point is that everyone should know at least a little bit about everything that needs to be done around the house. Both

---

[43] Three or four years after we were married, I was on a ladder in front of the house, installing some window shutters I had built, when Jennie came home with our eight-month-old bundled in his car seat after having done the grocery shopping for the week. Seeing me up the ladder in all my masculine glory with tool belt and power tools while she schlepped baby, infant accoutrements, and grocery bags from car to kitchen caused her to exclaim, in frustration and anger, "Whatever HAPPENED to us?!" (She might even have kicked the ladder as she went by, but that has never been proven definitively.) It was at this moment that I first realized *I* needed to revisit the Division of Labour conversation.

of you ought to know how to do the laundry, pay the bills, do the shopping, cut the grass, change a tire, sew on a button, etc. Not only does this fall under the category of fair as opposed to equal, but also is simply part of being a participant in the adult world.

Everyone Ought to Get Cookin'

Developing household skills in areas that are unfamiliar doesn't have to be onerous. Believe it or not, learning to do something with a degree of competence and skill can not only be fun but also foster feelings of self-reliance, independence, and self-worth.

Learning some basic cooking skills is a good example. When assisting couples with the Division of Labour conversation, I often make the suggestion that both of them, no matter how low or even non-existent their level of cooking ability, learn and practise enough culinary arts to have at least ten different meals that they can prepare *by themselves*. Learning to cook is a basic skill, and one that everyone should have, and with a little practice can actually be something that is a source of pride. With a little effort, many even develop a "signature dish" that they enjoy preparing and feel competent to make. Break down the ten meals any way you want, but I often suggest being able to prepare a couple of decent breakfasts, two or three good lunches, and at least five quality dinners. And remember, these are meals that each person ought to be able to prepare *independently*.

For the naysayers, let me assure you that learning how to prepare an omelette, a club sandwich, and a decent pot roast won't consume your life, nor is anyone suggesting you have to become a *saucier* or a cordon bleu chef. However, knowing how to do something well improves one's sense of self-worth and confidence. And, as I've said, everyone should be able to do at least some of everything that needs to be done around the home.

More than that, being able to prepare a few decent meals means that, even if you don't end up being the one who does the lion's share of the cooking, there will be times you can spell off your partner from cooking duties. Can you imagine, for example, your partner having a longtime friend visit unannounced and your being able to offer to do the cooking so they can have more time to visit? A broad set of skills in all the categories of household maintenance means greater opportunities to do favours or, in the language of marital therapy, offer positive exchanges to a partner, which in turn builds goodwill and goes a long way to developing a sense of couplehood.

Incidentally, this type of skill development happens only if and when you have a *plan* put in place to make it happen. Waiting for happenstance to put all the pieces in place is just poor planning. The point also needs to be made that doing some task or household chore badly so you won't have to keep doing it isn't clever or cute. It's just another form of lying. And this type of subterfuge is not only dishonest, but sets a dangerous precedent for a relationship you probably wanted to be based on trust.

So everyone should be able to change a tire, cook a decent meal, and do a load of laundry and ironing without destroying everything they touch in the process. Take a look at the list of basic household chores below[44] and start thinking about what you know or perhaps don't know about each, and what you might need to do to develop at least some competence in each area. No one expects you to be happy or enthusiastic about each and every area of household duty (I have yet to meet someone who has turned dusting into an art form). These are all things that will need to be done on a regular basis, however, and being able to do them competently is just smart time management—better to know how to do an unpleasant task quickly and efficiently than have it drag out or, worse, have to do it over! Sorry to resort to a cliché again, but if it's worth doing, it's worth doing well.

---

[44] If I have missed a particular chore or task, particularly one that is important to you or your partner, make sure you add it to the list.

The Matter in Question: Division of Labour

DIV. OF LAB. Q8.   As thrilling as this is going to
be, discuss what each of you know about completing each of the following household chores:

1. Cleaning bathrooms[45,46]
2. Picking up and tidying
3. Making beds
4. Dusting
5. Cooking
6. Washing dishes
7. Shopping
8. Laundry
9. Ironing
10. Folding and putting clothes away
11. Vacuuming and cleaning floors
12. Cleaning windows
13. Plant maintenance
14. Garage maintenance and cleanup
15. Storage maintenance and cleanup
16. Yard maintenance and cleanup

---

[45] Frankly, I have never understood the "up or down toilet seat" debate: if men can lift it up, why can't women put it down? Why are there such heated debates about this simple and minor issue?

[46] Let me say UNEQUIVOCALLY and CATEGORICALLY that there is *ONE AND ONLY ONE* way toilet *paper* should come off the roll: any right-thinking person knows the paper should come over the top of the roll, presenting its flap to the front rather than dangling behind. To those who think differently—probably the same people who drink blended Scotch—my only hope for you is that you learn the error of your ways and join the chorus of the enlightened, the pure, and the educated. Don't make me tell you again!

17. Appliance maintenance

18. Car maintenance

19. Pet care[47,48]

20. (Add your own tasks, chores, or duties)

21.

22.

23.

24.

25.

MINIMUMS, STANDARDS, AND THE DIFFERENCES BETWEEN "DIRTY" AND "CLUTTERED"

Life would be wonderful if dealing with division-of-labour issues were as simple as, "You do this and I'll do that." I love the world where this happens. Unfortunately, that world also has elves, unicorns, and people who remember to turn off their cellphones in restaurants and movie theatres. We have to deal with the world we have, and it's a more likely reality that deciding "who does what" is *a beginning rather than an end* of the Division of Labour conversation.

---

[47] Recall the discussion of pets from the Family conversation if and when this issue comes up.

[48] Obviously, if kids are already a part of your relationship, child care will be a HUGE part of the Division of Labour conversation, and in fact deserves attention as a conversation topic all on it own. However, for the purposes of *this* book, I am operating on the assumption that kids haven't shown up yet. Don't worry, though—I'll be giving this issue much more attention in a future *10 Conversations* book.

FOAB: Fingernails on a Blackboard, or Chores That We Hate

It's pretty obvious that all chores and home-maintenance requirements are not the same in terms of effort and time. Doing the
dishes one particular evening doesn't equate to the hours of
preparation and thought required to do the taxes. Stripping and
waxing the kitchen floor isn't the same as wiping down the
kitchen counter. Replacing the toilet paper[49] is hardly the equiv-
alent of weeding the garden.

Pretty obvious stuff, but just to make sure that we're all on
the same page, the point is that a simple chore count is unlikely
to result in an equitable division of labour. The two of you must
include some discussion of how much difficulty, time, effort, discomfort, preparation, inconvenience, sacrifice, or whatever you
feel goes along with any and all household chores and maintenance tasks. What might be a walk in the park for one could be
"fingernails on a blackboard" (FOAB) for another, and consequently the "meaning" of doing a particular chore could be
completely different for the two of you.

Not a startling or particularly insightful point, I know (but to
be fair, can there *ever* be a startling or particularly insightful point
when it comes to cleaning and household chores?). However, I
also know of case after case of couples who ended up in vitriolic
fights about household chores that could have been more easily
negotiated had they taken a little bit of time to talk to each other,
not only about what needed to be done around the house, but
also about which household tasks bother them more than others.
And just to drive the point home, it might be useful to remind
you once again of the mind-reading and assumption rule and
encourage you to avoid division-of-labour problems by making
sure the two of you have a clear idea of what the "FOAB factor"
of any particular task might be.

[49] Don't make me tell you again.

The Matter in Question: Division of Labour

DIV. OF LAB. Q9.   Of the household tasks listed in Div. of Lab. Q8 (including any the two of you added), which would each of you rank as an 8 or higher on the 10-point FOAB scale,

* 0 (zero) being "least onerous, don't really mind,"
* 5 being "not a fave, but it has to be done," and
* 10 being "completely FOAB—I would rather rip my own head off than do this chore."

Similarly, which tasks score only a 2 or lower? To the extent that an 8 or higher on one person's list shows up as a 2 or lower on the other person's list, some of the work of figuring out who's doing what has just been done for you. Unfortunately, all the rest still needs to be negotiated.

DIV. OF LAB. Q10.   When you look at other couples you know, what do the two of you think about *their* solutions to division-of-labour issues? Have these other couples developed division-of-labour patterns you might want to emulate or avoid?

In addition to talking about the FOAB factor of each chore, the two of you might also benefit from talking about any pet peeves you might have as far as chores or household maintenance is concerned. For example, my own personal household bugaboo is clutter. I hate clutter; it drives me nuts. Clutter bugs me to the point that if I want to relax and the room I want to relax in feels the least bit cluttered, I feel I have no other choice but to straighten things out and put things away before I can put my feet up, no matter how tired I might be. Like I said, clutter bugs me.

That being said, even I would have to acknowledge that clutter isn't exactly the greatest evil in the world, and what *I* might see as clutter, someone else may *barely notice*. If an empty juice box one of the boys left on an end table feels like clutter to me, I'm allowed to feel that way. What's more, I'm allowed to do something about it. I get to have my own standards, I get to have my own feelings about clutter and how it bugs *me*, and I get to take steps to fix the things that I don't like. However, and as annoying as I might find it, it would be a mistake to conclude that because I feel really uncomfortable about the juice box, *so should everyone else*. It would be a further mistake to assume that everyone else has to feel the same sense of urgency about fixing the problem, and to fix it in the way I believe it should be fixed. And this is where so many couples start sailing into stormy seas in terms of division of labour.

What annoys one person may not even register with someone else, but of course the mistake is to waste time arguing about how much something *should* annoy someone. Again, we're all allowed to have our own thoughts and feelings, but it's simply an error of logic to believe that because we think or feel something, that makes our thought or feeling good, true, and obvious for the world to see. I pontificate on this point—and, yes, I know I've made it before—because I spend so much time trying to get this point across to so many couples. You don't have to think and feel the same way about everything to get along, particularly when you understand that at least one very important part of the "meaning of life" is to *respect* that others might think or feel differently than you and that this is okay! Further, couples wasting time and emotion and risking needless acrimony in convincing one another that their household pet peeve or particular standard of cleanliness is the "correct" way things "should" be has people sleeping on the couch far more often than necessary.

This becomes a particular sticking point in the Division of Labour conversation because some people get all high and mighty about "standards of cleanliness," or "living like a civilized person," or "it's obvious that this is the way things should be done!" In these circumstances, we have what amounts to a relationship "perfect storm" brewing. Some of the most toxic ingredients get thrown into the communication mix in these division-of-labour circumstances. First, we have one person judging the other, or at the very least what is felt to be judgement, and this is never a good thing. Second, we have frustration about basic living conditions, which can feel akin to a human-rights issue, which then fans the flames of righteous indignation. And last but not least, we not infrequently have the use of inflammatory language like "This place is a garbage dump," or "Who could live in this pigsty?" or "I won't be forced to live in a sewer!" With these three rancid elements thrown into the pot, we pretty much have all that's needed to eliminate any chance for a useful discussion of what each of you want the home to look and feel like.

The Matter in Question: Division of Labour

DIV. OF LAB. Q11   Can either of you identify any pet peeves you might have in terms of chores, household maintenance, or how things are "supposed" to be done?

If and when pet peeves get identified, we have another assist in how chores get divvied up during the Division of Labour conversation. When "how something looks" or "the way something ought to be done" is a real issue for one of you, that task or standard or particular piece of maintenance will likely be best placed on that person's particular list of things to do, right from the very start. The logic of this is pretty clear: if you really care about how something looks or the way something is done, rather than trying to impose how you think it ought be done on your partner, do it yourself!

In rare circumstances, a couple might find substantial discrepancies between what each puts on their list, with one person having a great long list of needs or demands compared to the other. I can't say I've actually seen this happen, but I imagine it could, and I suppose that a couple's viability could reasonably be questioned if this were to occur. However, I would also find it hard to believe that a couple who had many of the other fundamentals going for them couldn't work out some sort of reasonable compromise as far as chores go. As with so many things in marriage, a can-do attitude, informed by what works in a couple rather than what doesn't, goes a long way toward finding solutions to problems like these. And as I've said before about other conversations, you don't have to have every detail worked out this minute. And here in the Division of Labour conversation, nothing could be more appropriate than a frequent revisiting of what needs to be done, who's doing what, how well tasks are being done, and how fair each of you feel the division of labour continues to be.

MISERY LOVES COMPANY

Although I've spent a lot of time talking about the "division" of labour, ideally, and from a healthy-couple perspective, doing chores together is an entirely workable option! At the very least, you've got someone to talk to while you're cleaning the toilet or scraping the gunk off the inside of the stove. Here we are in "misery loves company" territory. However, there's another, often unrecognized benefit of working together on household chores. When you're doing the scut work together, not only do you immediately resolve issues of chore equity and balance, but you're left with the same leisure time when the chores are done!

Few things are more frustrating than knowing you have some lousy chore to do while your partner gets to kick back because their work has already been completed. But I'm not talking so much about reducing envy as I am of the benefit of maximizing quality time together. When you do the chores together, or at least different chores at the same time, you increase the chances that you're both going to be able to enjoy the same period of leisure time. It doesn't take long for life together to get complicated with work and career, family, and social obligations, and very often, shared leisure time is one of the first casualties of this Western reality. One of the simple steps the two of you can take to counteract this temporal disconnect is to get in the habit of working on chores at the same time. It's like learning to like your coffee black right from the get-go: due to informed initial planning, you save yourself a lifetime of cream and sugar calories without ever missing them.

WHY A LISTING (RELATION)SHIP IS ACTUALLY A GREAT PLACE TO START

I want to make one more point about lists of chores and why the two of you ought to spend some time talking about this. It's a general truism, from an interpersonal management perspective, that the best time in a relationship to establish boundaries, rules, or expectations is right at the very beginning. While this little bit of wisdom is typically applied to work or professional relationships, it is equally applicable to social and romantic ones. With this axiom, we're in the same territory as Robert Frost's observation that "Good fences make good neighbours."

The two of you are much more likely to do better from a division-of-labour point of view the more actively you try to manage and organize what needs to get done. However, while lists of chores and responsibilities are pretty obvious management tools, a lot of people see them as unnecessary and even threatening. The thinking goes something like this:

> We already get along really well and agree on so many things. Heck, we're planning on getting married—you can't get much more simpatico than that! So why would we need to formalize

257

something as trivial as who's going to vacuum or do the dishes? If problems like this arise, we'll work them out as they come along. We're such good friends and have such an interest in making each other happy that little issues like chores and division of labour won't bother us. In fact, just the process of coming up with chore and responsibility lists might *create* doubts that we're not as solid as we think we are, and this could lead to further disagreements and fights. Better just to let sleeping dogs lie.

Engaged couples aren't the only ones who think like this. New roommates tend to entertain a similar thought process, but to equally dysfunctional ends. Perhaps it's counterintuitive, but the more work a couple does at the beginning of a relationship to come up with problem-solving mechanisms and processes to work through disagreements, the more likely they are to have the tools they need to manage the inevitable moments of conflict. From this perspective, the absence of a list of chores and responsibilities is actually increasing, not decreasing, the chances that there will be trouble. In the same way that new roommates do better to sit down as soon as possible and divide things up, so too can the two of you benefit from such a list and process. With roommates, we often recommend that even silly things like shelves in the refrigerator and room on the towel rack get assigned early so things like this don't become sources of friction. And of course, when time goes by and the roommates learn that they *can* trust each other to respect each other's needs, space, and responsibilities, the need for and use of the chore and responsibility lists begins to dissipate. However, this dissipation and relaxing of vigilance comes about *as a function of experience and good management, rather than wishful thinking.*

Try considering chore and responsibility lists as efficiency rather than threat. When the two of you work to come to a common understanding of what needs to be done through an active rather than a passive process, you decrease the chances that you will have to endure conflict or that important issues will fall through the cracks. And getting in this habit early rather than late in your relationship is also just good practice. Next to learning how to speak respectfully and efficiently to each other when issues are heated, getting division-of-labour issues right from the beginning may be one of the most effective ways of calming rough waters. A lot is required to keep a (relation)ship running, but when the crew already know what is expected of them and what to do, smooth and efficient sailing is far more quickly accomplished.

The Matter in Question: Division of Labour

DIV. OF LAB. Q12   Are you "list people?" Have lists of tasks or chores worked for you in the past, or have either of you had a bad experience or felt overly controlled when lists were used to structure how and when tasks got done?

Realistically Speaking: Every Couple I've Ever Dealt With!

I can't recall a couple who came to see me *specifically* because a division-of-labour issue was actually threatening their relationship, but it's fair to say that every couple I have ever dealt with has brought division-of-labour problems. Disagreements about division-of-labour issues, as well as disagreements about money, are as common in marriage as wedding-day jitters. The best clinical observation I can offer you is simply to acknowledge the ubiquity of this type of problem. On the up side, if you follow much of what I have described above, the two of you will minimize if not eliminate the friction and misunderstandings that come from the inevitable differences that arise as a function of having to do household chores.

Final Thoughts on the Division of Labour Conversation

As promised, I tried to make the Division of Labour conversation one of the shortest in the book, because at the best of times, it's hard to get excited about discussions of chores and household maintenance. You're never going to find the meaning of life in a clean house, a sparkling set of dishes, or a perfectly organized closet. That is not to say you can't appreciate or enjoy them when the work has been done. There's no doubting that a pleasant place to live, however the two of you end up defining this, reduces stress and can make life easier. The mistake, I believe, is to think that a clean and organized house makes you a better person. The "tyranny of a clean house" syndrome continues to be alive and well, and while men are occasional victims, women continue to be the prime sufferers of this sad and unnecessary social malady. Putting housework in a more appropriate context is, I think, the solution to this problem.

Sometimes we need to remind ourselves that the reason we do all the chores and work that we do is so that we can enjoy the other parts of our lives. We want to do our chores well and efficiently not because that makes us a better husband, wife, or partner, but because spending time with people who love us and who we love really *is* the meaning of life. In the same way that no one pronounces on their deathbed that they should have spent more time at work, I don't think anyone claims a cleaner floor or more thorough dusting would have brought greater peace to their final moments!

It's no accident that the next conversation is about making quality leisure time for the two of you a priority. Unfortunately, and just like our grade school teachers taught us, we had to get our work done before we could play. But now that we have, let's move on to see what types of fun the two of you can *share*.

CONVERSATION 8:
Leisure

FEW OF THE PREVIOUS *10 Conversations* topics required justification; the import of each was self-evident. But the same can't be said of leisure. You could fairly ask, "Aren't there more important topics to talk about, particularly if you're contending that there are only ten important issues to discuss?! We all crave leisure, so aren't we already predisposed to take advantage of and maximize our leisure opportunities?" Perhaps, but on the other hand, the fact that we all get hungry doesn't mean we've all learned to be good cooks, does it?

In the therapy biz, we have known for a long time that happy (or, technically, non-distressed) couples spend more time being pleasant to each other than do couples who are not so happy (i.e., distressed couples). Doing or saying nice stuff to or for a partner is referred to as a *positive exchange*, again by those of us who do therapy. A "You look nice today" comment, a peck on the cheek, holding open a door, or an "I was pouring myself a cup of coffee, so I thought I'd get one for you" kindness would each be considered a positive exchange, along with a host of other helpful or supportive comments or behaviours. *Negative exchanges* are exactly the opposite and include, but are not limited to, behaviours like insults, ignoring each other, and frequently finding fault. Rather than being helpful or complimentary, negative exchanges have the effect of being hurtful and destructive.

Why the description of positive and negative exchanges here in "Leisure"? Think of it this way: when you're having a good time, when you're relaxed, when you're enjoying what you're doing, you're more likely to be feeling good. When you're feeling good, you're more likely to project those good feelings onto other people. If one of those other people is your partner, we have just increased the chances of your offering them a positive exchange, and we know that more positive exchange is associated with less couple distress. Essentially, when the two of you are having a good time together, you increase the chances that you will be making each other feel positive about the relationship you've both created.

Even with the above justification, it might seem a little self-indulgent to specifically focus on leisure as an important topic of premarital conversation. But, as the old saw goes, "The couple that plays together stays together." Too many times I've seen couples evolve in directions that increasingly had each of them "doing their own thing" at the expense of "together time." Although there is no way to know, I have often wondered: if they had made leisure time *together* more important earlier in their relationship, would I even be seeing them in my office? So strap on your rollerblades, pack up the beach towel, and tuck those theatre tickets into your pocket, and let's review why, as individuals, you need to get serious about having together fun.

Fun Is Where You Find It

According to one definition, *leisure* is a label for a kind of time; specifically, free time, or time without obligation. Other sources define leisure as an activity or amusement that generates pleasant feelings. Still others claim that leisure is about increasing one's sense of well-being. And I suppose if we kept looking, we could find more definitions, but I don't think we need them to make the point: *Leisure is what each one of us decides it is.* For some, leisure will be about kicking back and relaxing; for others, it will be about having new experiences or sensations or learning new facts and skills; and for others still, it will be about competition or pushing oneself to the limit.

As has so often been the case in *The 10 Conversations*, the place to start the Leisure conversation is an examination of any assumptions or stereotypes you might have about the subject. For example, if you believe that leisure can include only sand and sun, that's fine; just don't work from the presumption that everyone else, including your partner, feels that way. If ideal leisure for you involves quiet and a good book, get yourself curled up in that comfy couch and go to it, but don't necessarily expect that your partner wants to get ensconced on the sofa as well.

The Matter in Question: Leisure

LEISURE Q1. Describe for your partner what you would do if you unexpectedly found yourself with the following amounts of free, no-obligation time:

a. **Two hours in the middle of a workday**
b. **Two hours in the middle of the weekend**
c. **A completely free evening**
d. **Two days off**
e. **Two weeks off**
f. **Two months off**

You can stay grounded in reality if you want, or for fun you can pretend there are no limitations as far as money or practicalities are concerned, or you can do it both ways.

The Six Categories of Leisure

For some, answering the above question may be too difficult due to the huge range of options they'd like to explore. For others, a lack of experience or permission to fantasize may make it a challenge to come up with even one idea. If you found the question hard to address, allow me to offer a little bit of structure to help shape the Leisure discussion. Sometimes it's helpful to think about potential leisure activities by using the following six categories:

1. **Hobbies and pastimes:** Model building; crafts; woodworking; gardening; singing; acting; coin, stamp, or barbed wire collecting; bird or whale watching; reenacting Civil War scenes; learning to write people's names on grains of rice, etc.

2. **Sports:** Team sports (baseball, soccer, underwater hockey, etc.), individual sports (horseback riding, figure skating, river pole-vaulting, etc.), group sports (scuba diving, water skiing, spelunking, extreme fighting, etc.), and sports that aren't really sports (bowling, darts, pool and billiards, fishing, participating in reality TV shows, etc.).

3. **Projects:** Renovating, upgrading a garden, learning a new language, restoring furniture, fundraising for a favourite cause, attending community service group meetings, building a perpetual motion machine, removing your telephone number from telemarketing lists, etc.

4. **Travel:** Afternoon and day trips, local destinations, national destinations, international destinations, catching a cab when it starts to rain, shopping at one of the big-box stores, etc.

5. **Entertainment:** Television, movies, live theatre, concerts, music, video games, podcasts, police radio frequency scans, parent-teacher nights, etc.

6. **Socializing:** Dining out together, having dinner parties with others, spending weekends at the cottage with family and friends, going to drug seizure auctions, standing in line to obtain government services, etc.

As you can see, what leisure can be is limited only by your imagination. Leisure is where you find it, and the choices can be limitless. And, by the way, the categories above are not meant to be hard and fast divisions but general ideas to help the two of you think about the myriad options before you.

The Matter in Question: Leisure

LEISURE Q2. Share with your partner two activities from each of the six categories above that might be a favourite of yours. How similar or dissimilar are the favourites the two of you have chosen?

LEISURE Q3. Watch the movie *Fever Pitch* (2005, Drew Barrymore, Jimmy Fallon) together. Does the commitment to a pastime, as portrayed in the movie, reflect anything you see in each other?

Returning to basic principles of attraction and liking, we know that the more similar a couple is, the more attractive they find each other. There are multiple levels of logic here that make this so. When someone likes what you like, their liking it acts as a kind of confirmation that what you like is good and appropriate. When the two of you like the same things, it's more probable that you prioritize those things in similar ways and allocate time and resources to do those things in a similar way. You're also less likely to dispute how time and resources are allocated because you both want to do the same things (so we've got that increase in positive exchanges and decrease in negative exchange thing going on here). When you like the same things, you're more likely to spend time with each other, which increases the probability that you will learn more about each other and become more accustomed to each other's company. This feeds directly into the "familiarity breeds liking" rule of attraction. When you like the same things, you not only have the opportunity to do the thing(s) you both like together, but also generate a topic of conversation that is interesting to both of you, which then doubles up on everything I've already described.

All this talk about similarity, liking, and attraction makes the obvious point: deciding to be with someone who likes the same things as you do is a much better plan than trying to make a relationship work where there are few common interests. When you start off liking a lot of the same things, you already have a leg up as far as relationship stability is concerned.

That being said, understanding the basic principles of similarity, liking, and attraction means that you can also make a good thing better. Specifically looking for and developing new shared interests and leisure activities is a great tool for relationship growth and management.

The Matter in Question: Leisure

LEISURE Q4. Returning to the six categories, can the two of you choose or generate at least one activity from each category that neither of you have ever tried before but both might like to pursue? What would prevent the two of you from pursuing these activities? What could be done to remove any of those impediments?

From now on and for the rest of your lives together, revisit the six leisure categories periodically. Check in with each other and assess if you are consistently finding things from all six categories to do and enjoy together. You'll recall that in the communication rules, the last one, the "How We Doin'?" rule, is about having a regular discussion about the ongoing health of your relationship. Through the use of this communication technique, you dramatically increase the chances of solving or eliminating relationship problems in a timely fashion, rather than seeing those problems evolve into lingering resentments and relationship-threatening crises. With no difficulty at all, you can expand your "How We Doin'?" conversations to include a return to the six leisure categories and an opportunity to further push the boundaries of how you can enjoy the pleasure of each other's company.

To Nest or to Quest: Styles of Leisure

Just as we identified financial *styles* a few conversations back, so too are there leisure *styles*. Having different styles is not at all fatal to a relationship, but understanding the styles means you'll be better prepared to consider and make the accommodations necessary for the two of you to get along and enjoy leisure time together. From a leisure perspective, essentially there are "Seekers" and "Relaxers." Seekers quest, while Relaxers nest.

Seekers like to be doing things. They like to be learning things and going places. They're not terribly comfortable sitting around and waiting for things to happen; they would prefer to be making things happen. They tend to be curious and can really get into the details of things. Seekers often fall into the "work hard, play hard" category, and enjoy challenging themselves and others as part of their leisure. On vacation, Seekers want to go on *all* the tours to learn *all* there is to learn about wherever they are, whatever they're doing, how something works or is done, and what's going to happen next. They are likely to be the ones who research their destinations before they arrive so they'll have a clear idea of what leisure and learning activities will be open to them. Seekers ask questions and tend to be more critical than Relaxers.

At the far end of the Seeker spectrum, we approach a seeking style that borders on the neurotic. For the extreme Seeker, not only do they prefer to be doing, seeing, and learning things, but they HAVE TO be doing, seeing, and learning things. Sitting around is not an option, and what was supposed to be leisure actually becomes a frenetic search. Unfortunately, at this far end of the Seeker spectrum, there is the risk of completely missing the point of leisure. The neurotic Seeker is constantly dealing with the anxiety and fear that there may have been some little thing they didn't get to see, do, or learn during their leisure time. This completely undermines the benefits of leisure and represents a style that requires a little bit of work on a personal level to correct.

On the other hand, leisure for the Relaxer is about kicking back and taking a load off. Relaxers enjoy the ride, rather than where it's taking them or what's going to happen next. Relaxers are accommodating, less critical, and have the wonderful ability to find the positive in many situations. These are the "glass half full" people, the "when life hands you a lemon, make lemonade" people. While Relaxers don't mind getting active and involved from a leisure perspective, they are not driven to this level of activity, nor do high-intensity activities need to be part of their leisure. Relaxers are far more about the big picture rather than the details of a situation. While nobody likes standing in line, the Relaxer has the capacity to find something positive about the experience, while the Seeker will constantly be dealing with their own sense of frustration and being thwarted. On vacation, the Relaxer is happiest by the pool or in the deck chair. Relaxers are less concerned about what there is to do, as long as there are lots of opportunities to do nothing. At the farthest end of the Relaxer spectrum is the "Slug"—someone who actually resists becoming involved and has the expectation that others will focus on and accommodate their needs. A Slug travelling with a neurotic

Seeker would be about the worst combination imaginable (but would probably make a great movie!).

While these styles are best understood as generalities—and it is seldom the case that a person manifests the same style in *all* circumstances and situations—it is very important to determine for yourself and your partner how compatible your leisure styles are. Incompatible styles will lead to frustration, anxiety, and avoidance of leisure-time opportunities, which itself is problematic in terms of building a mutually rewarding relationship.

The Matter in Question: Leisure

LEISURE Q5. When it comes to leisure, are you more of a Seeker or a Relaxer? How would you categorize your partner, and how do they categorize you?

LEISURE Q6. Thinking back to the last time the two of you vacationed or travelled together, can you identify any circumstances where your leisure styles were in conflict?

LEISURE Q7. Describe for your partner your perfect vacation and have them describe theirs for you. From the descriptions, can the two of you identify similarities or conflicts of leisure style? Is someone nesting while the other is questing? How might the two of you accommodate each other?

Realistically Speaking: Nathan and Jill

Nathan and Jill illustrate how differences in leisure preferences contributed to the disintegration of a relationship.

269

Both Nathan and Jill had low-paying jobs, and as a consequence had little money to spare at the end of each month—or the year, for that matter. So it wasn't surprising that issues of travel had never really come up, primarily because there had never been any money for this kind of activity. Further, given their work schedules and tight budget, Nathan and Jill had little time or resources for most other forms of leisure. Most of their downtime was spent watching TV after they'd put the kids to bed or socializing with other couples. Even then, however, he would spend time with the guys and she would spend time with the gals. As their lives progressed, they found that they were growing further and further apart. They had never been cued to the need to develop and nurture mutual interests to keep their relationship vital. The growing distance between them eventually brought them to my office and, try as we might, it was very difficult to identify anything other than the children that they had in common.

Ironically, it was a change in fortune that ended their relationship. Jill was finally recognized for the good work she'd been doing at her job and was given a promotion. Not only that, as a perk she was also awarded a trip for her entire family. While Jill was overjoyed with this development, Nathan's reaction was markedly cool. It turned out that he had no interest in travel whatsoever. In fact, his more modest career accomplishments suited him just fine, and he had no desire or ambition to change his station in life. What's more, not only did Nathan not find the chance to travel exciting or rewarding, but he was averse to it. For weeks, he made excuses about why they couldn't take advantage of the trip Jill had been given and demanded that they cash it in and use the money to purchase a larger TV. Jill was just as adamant that they were going to take the trip, particularly in light of the fact that they had gone so long without experiencing rewards and leisure of this kind.

Jill eventually decided to take the children on the trip without Nathan. During her time away, she realized how much she enjoyed travel and resolved that in future she would find more opportunities to do so. She also recognized how unacceptable this would be to Nathan. Upon her return, she asked that they separate.

WHEN LEISURE SUCKS: THE TYRANNY OF RESPONSIBILITY

Q: When does a moment of leisure lose its considerable ability to charm?

A: When the effort that went into creating an R&R opportunity goes unrecognized, unappreciated, or, worst of all, criticized.

Making anything worthwhile happen takes work. This is true of developing a talent, learning a skill, or creating something new. We've been taught since grade school that "nothing great was ever achieved without effort" and that "something doesn't come from nothing." Few have a hard time getting their heads around this concept, particularly when we're talking about building a bridge, getting an education, or learning a complicated job skill. Less obvious is the fact that, in most circumstances, thought, effort, and organization are also necessary ingredients to having a good time. While opportunities to kick back or socialize just fall into place on occasion, with a little investigation it consistently emerges that even the apparently serendipitous had an agent. Try having a dinner party, a baseball game, or a weekend with the boys or girls without some organization.

Although it may seem a trivial point, arranging time off and maximizing pleasant outcomes usually requires someone to step up and take responsibility for getting things organized. Having friends over, taking a vacation, even just going out to a movie usually requires that someone seek out information, voice an opinion, or risk a choice. Acknowledging the effort and time that went into making a good thing happen is good manners, and once again represents an opportunity for positive exchange. But letting that effort go unnoticed and unacknowledged is bad precedent setting and puts you both on the slippery slope of apathy and taking each other for granted.

A related point concerns criticism. If it's a misdemeanour to fail to acknowledge the effort, then criticizing that effort is a felony. As a classic "adding insult to injury," nothing stings more than rebuke after some effort has failed.

When I'm doing marital therapy, its standard operating procedure to see the couple together for the first session and then each individual on their own in a private, confidential session. This allows both parties to have a turn to speak a little more freely, perhaps divulge a secret or two, and maybe describe issues they want to tackle in therapy but are having a hard time finding the courage to bring up in front of their partner. It would be a tall order to enumerate all the issues that come up in these sessions, but it may come as a surprise to readers to learn that hurt feelings associated with leisure-time disappointments are frequent complaints in these meetings.

In good, professional language, leisure-time disappointments are double whammies. With leisure opportunity comes heightened expectations of good feelings, bonding moments, unique experiences, and maybe even a chance for personal growth. When something goes awry and these expectations aren't realized, the hurt is acute. To be kicked when you're down and have to endure criticism from a partner for the steps you took to try to arrange the vacation, party, or get-together more often than not leaves a dark, indelible psychological stamp in the minds of many.

Realistically Speaking: Jack and Shannon

Shannon arranged for herself and her partner, Jack, to take a weekend ski trip. She organized the transportation, the hotel, the lift tickets, even après-ski events and fine dining. He happily attended, but when it became clear that the snow conditions were not going to be ideal, he started to complain and didn't stop until they returned home. In her private marital therapy assessment session with me, she explained that she'd been so hurt, first by his lack of acknowledgement of her efforts and then by his continued bellyaching about the poor snow conditions, she silently swore she would never go to the trouble of arranging a leisure event again. When this was eventually brought up in therapy weeks later, Jack actually acknowledged what he had done and disclosed his suspicion that the reason they hadn't taken a vacation in the past three years was because of his initial ungrateful behaviour.

This is the tyranny of stepping up and putting a leisure activity together. Organizing the camping trip, packing the sports gear for the weekend, or just choosing the movie can feel risky and unpleasant if you worry about having to accept blame if things don't go as smoothly as hoped. And here we see the seeds of another marital melanoma: once unfairly criticized, the partner who used to try to initiate leisure activities finds it's easier to either plan things for only themselves or to stop altogether making any effort to arrange leisure time.

If someone steps up and tries to put a leisure activity together, or even just makes a suggestion about something the two of you could do, show appreciation for the effort and check at the door any criticism you might have. If you're unhappy with what might have been suggested or planned or with how things turned out, grow up and recognize that perhaps next time you could take a more active role in figuring out how to ensure that leisure time together produces what both of you want. It's just as they say about democracy and participating in elections: if you don't vote, you don't have the moral authority to criticize!

The Matter in Question: Leisure

LEISURE Q8. Have you ever been hurt when your efforts to arrange a leisure activity went unacknowledged or criticized by your partner? If so, try to find the courage to tell them about it with a focus not on blame but on feelings. If you were the one to be critical, try to find the courage to listen without defensiveness.

Of course the easiest way to avoid the above problems is to operate under the assumption, right from the start, that leisure planning is best conceptualized as a joint responsibility. Getting in the habit of joint decision making is an excellent strategy, particularly at the beginning of a relationship. As time goes by and you develop a greater understanding of each other, more delegation of tasks and decision making will just naturally occur. However, this delegation and task differentiation will be based on experience and proven talent, not faith and wishful thinking.

SPECIAL NOTE ON SOCIALIZING: WHEN SHOULD WE ARRIVE AT THE PARTY?

An issue that becomes particularly contentious within some couples is when they should arrive when they've been invited to someone else's home or a party. The "fashionably late" school of thought prescribes arriving at least an hour or more after the official start time of the event and contends that to arrive any earlier would be gauche. The "scrupulously punctual" school of thought eschews this laissez-faire and takes the stance that if you were asked to arrive at 7:30 p.m., you arrive at 7:30 p.m., give or take a minute or two. When both members of a couple share the same arrival philosophy, there's no issue. However, it seems that, more often than not, one person is in one camp while their partner is firmly entrenched in the other. Perhaps surprisingly, I've seen quite a few couples where this has turned into an ongoing and contentious issue. And, unfortunately, this problem has the potential to spin out of control, perhaps because there is already tension and expectation surrounding attendance at the event and this pre-existing arousal inappropriately fuels anger and indignation. There is, however, a mechanism that helps to resolve this fundamental schism in social etiquette and threat to relationship harmony.

The solution is essentially based on who is most connected with the host of the invited event, and we apply the "my friend, my choice" rule. If the host is primarily one couple member's friend or relative, that person's preference for arrival time is the one that is used, no arguments. So if Barb's best friend is hosting the party, Barb gets to decide when she and Bob will arrive. If the host is primarily someone Bob chums around with, Bob gets to decide which arrival style will be used. In situations where the degree of connection between the host and both of you is about the same (e.g., a mutual school friend you've both known for the same length of time), you take turns, in the alphabetical order of your first names (for Barb and Bob, Barb would get to go first).

For this to reduce acrimony, the two of you have to do three things. First, you have to agree well beforehand that both of you will adhere to the "my friends, my choice" rule. Second, there has to be agreement, again well beforehand, on who has what degree of connection with the host so there's no dispute on whose preference will be respected. And, finally, when the taking-turns part of the rule is invoked, you have to agree to write down on the calendar who made what choice so there is a record of who gets to go next when the issue arises again.

As childish as all this sounds, it's amazing how often this rule settles this issue. In a related vein, some couples argue about the degree of preparation or cleanliness of their own home when *they* are to host an event. The same dispute resolution mechanism can be applied: if the guests are primarily hers, she gets to make the preparation and degree-of-tidiness or cleanliness call, while if the party is primarily about his friends, the call is his. If there's no clear distinction, people take turns.

The Prophylaxis of Leisure

For better or worse, the age of first marriage falls for many around the same time as does completion of advanced academic degrees, immersion in specialized trade training, or the early years of career development, when the desire to make a good impression and cement one's position in the company goes hand in hand with long hours and extra projects. At this stage of life, it's easy to believe the first thing that can be eliminated from the demands on your dance card is the time you spend relaxing or doing things you enjoy. And of course there is a logic to this: we can't play all the time; we have to take our professional or academic or training obligations seriously if we want to get ahead, yadda yadda yadda.

All well and good, but as your psychologist, I'm obligated to cue you in to the fact that in these situations it also doesn't do anyone any good going all Jack Nicholson from *The Shining*. Rest and fun are good for us, and actually help us to learn and to do our jobs better. I don't think anybody wants me to get into the neuro- and biopsychology of this, so just take my word for it. We need R&R: it calms us down, it helps us sort things out, it improves our memory, it recharges our batteries, it reminds us of why we work so hard, it helps us feel closer to the people we love, it allows us to develop other types of skills, it's an opportunity for us to feel good about ourselves, and the list goes on. Essentially, leisure—that is, good, restorative leisure—has the ability to protect your health and your relationship, both physically and psychologically.

But here's the problem. When we feel pulled in a bunch of different directions, it's not only hard to find kick-back time, it's also *really hard to enjoy* that kick-back time, primarily because of a sense of *guilt*. Intellectually, we know that a bit of time to relax is probably good for us, but intellectually we also know there is always another paper we could be reading, there are always more skills we could be developing, and there is always another phone call that could be made, another form that could be filled out, and another tweak that could be made to the PowerPoint presentation for the meeting next week. It's hard to enjoy doing something—or nothing—for fun when there seem to be so many *more important or necessary* things to do! To help deal with these competing demands, allow me to introduce you to the concept of *structured leisure*.

Structured leisure—which I know sounds like an oxymoron—is another of those common-sense ideas that everyone recognizes when it's described but few ever actually put into practice (kind of like flossing). Structured leisure means you start attending to time-management issues in your life and make plans to fit in all the important things, *including R&R time.* This is the opposite of working from the seat of your pants, hoping you'll find time to get everything done and leisure time will just magically materialize. But it isn't a demand to get anal about organizing your life and start accounting for every single minute of your time, though you do have to attend to some of the details.

When you put effort and consideration into structuring your time more carefully, *and you ensure that leisure activities are worked into that structure,* two really good things happen. One, you get more efficient at running your life, which is just generally a good thing. The second benefit is that *your leisure time really becomes leisure time.* You really get to enjoy it and relax because you know you've earned it. You've worked it into your schedule, and there *is* nothing else you're supposed to be doing, because you've scheduled those other things to get done at other times!

Now, it would be fair if you're wondering why I've gotten into this particular little life-management tool as part of *The 10 Conversations.* Sure, it makes sense, you say, but perhaps it would be better placed in some other popular psychology diatribe. Well, there's a method to my madness. Structured leisure is a good life-management tool; it's true. But structured leisure is a terrific relationship-management tool as well! In the very act of sitting down and thinking about how you need to budget your time so there will be moments and opportunities for quality leisure, almost by definition you're going to need to consult with the one you love. In so doing, now the two of you are talking about priorities, dealing with limited resources and competing demands for your time, and a host of other complicated issues you will be dealing with for the rest of your lives. As the saying goes, there's no time like the present, and in the case of learning to budget and negotiate with each other, the sooner the two of you get started, the sooner you'll develop the tools you need to feel confident and skilled at the process.

To formalize the idea of structured leisure as a relationship-management and -building tool, it might be helpful to set yourself goals or objectives. For example, you might decide that every week, you want to have at least one dinner out together and one evening socializing with friends (of course the actual events and amounts of time you choose can be whatever you want). You then prioritize this and ensure that it gets worked into your weekly schedule. Perhaps you pick a specific date or socializing night and stick to that every week. Perhaps you need more latitude and determine that sometime before Wednesday every week you'll get together with friends, and either Thursday or Friday night you will have dinner out. Perhaps time is too precious this month, so you decide to combine the two events and have friends over every other Saturday while the two of you have a date night on the other Saturday nights.

While the two of you are working out how to have some regular fun on a weekly basis, you also start thinking about more long-term or elaborate leisure activities. Planning for a trip, saving for equipment that will allow you to go skiing next winter, looking into a subscription for theatre tickets next fall, or drawing up plans for what you would really like the back deck to look like, with a built-in gazebo and a hot tub, are all examples of more long-term leisure planning.

In reality, the details are less important than the process: putting a system in place where you prioritize leisure and you engage in that process together is a terrific way to accomplish a lot of useful relationship stuff: you find time to relax, you start planning things together, you start talking about mutual future goals, you create opportunities for pleasant experiences to look forward to sharing in the future, etc.

Here's the final cool thing about structured leisure and why it definitely has a prophylactic quality: when the demands of life build up and we feel run off our feet, taking time to relax seems like the last thing in the world that would be possible. With everything that's going on, the additional effort that would be required to rearrange and coordinate schedules, find coverage, or dig up money to pay for a little downtime all but eliminates the possibility of that downtime ever happening. As the saying goes, when you're up to your ass in alligators, it's hard to remember you wanted to drain the swamp! But when structured leisure has been incorporated into your lives, this particular impediment evaporates. Lives that already include structured leisure and have prioritized large, medium, and small amounts of happy, fun time together negate the problem of having to figure out the "what" and "when" of relaxing—the thinking, prioritizing, and planning of leisure have already been done and regular kick-back time has been worked into the schedule.

So many times in my office have I met with distressed couples who are seeing me for help with coping and stress management, and they stare at me blankly when I ask them about how they currently or in the distant past went about formally inserting leisure into their lives together. So let me make the point again: couples who have more positive exchanges tend to be happier couples. Formally sitting down and figuring out the "how" and "when" of having fun together is very likely to increase the chances that you have a larger number of positive exchanges, and this is good for your physical and psychological health and for your relationship.

When the Party's Over

Leisure is about fun, relaxing, and a bunch of other good stuff. It's not about getting "blotto" or "shit-faced" or "polluted" or developing a drug or alcohol problem. Confusing having a good time with the slippery slope of substance abuse is a measure of immaturity and poor planning.

Just for the record, I'm in no way "anti-alcohol" or a proponent of abstinence. You may recall a mention or two of my own personal affection for single malt earlier in these pages. In fact, I'll suggest developing an interest in viniculture, usquebaugh, or some other distillate fits perfectly well under hobbies and pastimes. Further, if you're into some other chemical or substance that gives you enjoyment and serves as a potential social lubricant, more power to you—you're both grown-ups and you're allowed to make your own choices. However, and if we want to remain in grown-up territory, let's be clear that enjoying a drink or a toke is not the same as allowing a substance to adversely influence your life and, particularly for our purposes here, your life with a partner.

Sorry if I'm sounding like Dad here, but a week doesn't go by in my office that I'm not helping someone deal with the adverse effects of substance use and the devastating effects it can have on relationships. Since I'm quite sure no one has ever told you this before, let me be the first: substance abuse is not pleasant.

Leisure that is in large part about drinking or substance use, as I said above, puts you on the slippery slop of abuse and dependence. Abuse and dependence ends relationships (as well as educations, careers, and parenting opportunities). If you have a drinking or substance abuse problem, get help. If you're with someone who has a substance abuse problem, don't marry them until they've fixed the problem. And by the way, this pearl of wisdom is completely consistent with one of the most important points in the "Troubleshooting" chapter. There, you'll find the recommendation that if you or your partner believes that some critical aspect of one of you needs to change and that *getting married will cause that change to occur*, you're kidding yourself and each other. A new marriage will not end substance abuse, but substance abuse almost certainly will end a new marriage—I'm just trying to save you the heartache.

The Matter in Question: Leisure

LEISURE Q9. Do you have a substance abuse problem? Have you ever had one? Are you trying to hide a substance abuse problem from your partner? If you have a problem, have you sought professional assistance?

LEISURE Q10. Do you have worries about your partner's use of alcohol or recreational drugs? Have you expressed your concerns to them and explained that this is often a marital deal breaker?

LEISURE Q11. Have you told each other about any experiences you've had with alcohol or substance abuse growing up or with other family members?

LEISURE Q12. Do either of you spend a lot of time socializing with people who have substance abuse issues? If yes, do either of you see this as any kind of threat to your relationship?

Joined at the Hip?

Although there's a wealth of empirical investigation on what does and doesn't make a good marriage, I have taken pains in this book not to get bogged down in research or statistics. So don't accuse me of going all medieval on you if I bring in just a touch of marital theory for a moment.

People far more clever than I tell us that marriage is best understood as a dance between three important concepts: attachment, autonomy, and equality (see Susan D. Cochran and Letitia G. Peplau, "Value Orientations in Heterosexual Relationships," in *Psychology of Women Quarterly* 9, 1985). *Attachment*[50] is about feeling connected to each other, *autonomy* is about maintaining your identity while being part of a relationship, and *equality* is about making sure both people in the relationship are getting fairly treated and feel that both are benefiting from the relationship in commensurate ways. If we entertain this conceptualization of marriage for a moment, we'll see there's some good advice here, not only about marriage in general, but also about how your thinking about leisure can evolve.

In many relationships, particularly in the early months and years, there is a joined-at-the-hip quality about everything the two of you do. This is nice: it promotes bonding; you learn more and more about each other; you find shared interests; there's lots of kissing, hugging, and sex, etc. Over time, however, while you've found out what you like and love about each other, you almost certainly will have also found out that there are interests and pastimes you don't care to share. Her enthusiasm for rock concerts may not be what his is, and his passion for gardening may not be what she feels. Again, no surprises here—we all like

---

[50] This is *not* the concept of attachment psychologists are talking about when they discuss *styles of attachment* and the ways early infant–caregiver interactions potentially influence the shape of future relationships.

different things no matter how similar we might be. From a leisure perspective, then, it's important to recognize that in healthy relationships you don't have to be doing every single thing together and enjoying every single thing the same amount. Essentially, it's okay to have and pursue personal interests that are not shared by your partner.

So while I have made the point throughout this conversation that discovering the things you like to do *together* is a good thing, I now want to expand this somewhat and say that doing things *on your own* is okay too and in fact has the potential to make your relationship even healthier. If we return to the marital theory previously mentioned, we are told that balancing *couple* needs (attachment) with *personal* needs (autonomy) is the task that all couples need to successfully negotiate if they want their marriage to be one that is healthy and sustaining. This means that while you need to attend to what will make the two of you work together (i.e., pursuing attachment), doing this at the cost of losing yourself is a bad idea (i.e., losing your autonomy). Essentially, giving up on what you like, what has meaning for you, or what might make you feel special for the sake of the relationship is actually a pretty big threat to the marriage. Eventually, denying yourself what you like to do becomes a lingering resentment, which, as I've said before, is the metaphorical pebble in the marathon runner's shoe: a lot of ground can get covered, but the potential to end the race now exists.

We've all heard, "There's no 'I' in T-E-A-M." But guess what? There's a great big one in the middle of W-I-N. Much of what we've been talking about through *The 10 Conversations* is learning about each other's needs and desires, and finding ways to accommodate what both of you want. Don't let that general philosophy get put aside when it comes to having fun or expressing yourself. While it might be more obvious to assert yourself when it comes to financial or career choices, the necessity of being your own person, even within a marriage, needs to take many forms, including the choices that are made about leisure. It's not dangerous or inappropriately self-indulgent to continue to think about and pursue things that make you happy, even if your partner doesn't share that interest.

The Matter in Question: Leisure

LEISURE Q13. Have the two of you identified any significant personal interests that are not shared by both of you? If yes, how have each of you felt about how money, time, and opportunity to pursue those individual interests have been allocated thus far in your relationship?

LEISURE Q14. Have you completely set aside a personal interest "for the sake of the relationship"? Does your partner know about this? Do you know or suspect that your partner has set aside a personal interest? Knowing that this could lead to a lingering resentment, is there room to rethink the choices the two of you have made about what to pursue in your leisure time?

FINAL THOUGHTS ON THE LEISURE CONVERSATION

In the Sex conversation, I made the point that you need to make sex a project: you need to think about it, plan for it, talk about it, look after your physical health so you can continue to enjoy it, stay creative about it, and never take it for granted if you want it to remain a rewarding and healthy part of your relationship. The same thing can be said for leisure. Like sex, leisure is something we often take for granted and assume it will look after itself. It won't. You need to keep it interesting, challenging, stimulating, rewarding, and mutually beneficial. Complacency is once again a major threat to keeping the fun and reward in how the two of you play together. Talk, talk, talk; plan, plan, plan.

Even though I've touched on this issue before, it bears repeating here as well. The purpose of *The 10 Conversations* is to break down the critical task of assessing the viability of your relationship into smaller, manageable chunks and to draw your attention to issues the two of you have to be talking about. The "segregation" of the ten topics into ten separate conversations has been meant only to make this task easier, not to limit the scope of any particular conversation. The Money and Financial Styles conversation will obviously be informed by the Careers conversation, in the same way that the Location conversation will be informed by the Family conversation, and so on.

From a Leisure conversation perspective, you can easily imagine how discussing issues like finance and location could play critical roles in what leisure-time opportunities are explored. Avid downhill skiers could find themselves feeling pretty frustrated living in the Prairies, and you're not going to have a lot of beach days living north of Lake Superior. Similarly, if money isn't budgeted for travel, it's unlikely you're actually going to see the Great Barrier Reef, and if there is an assumption that every New Year's is to be spent with family and that family doesn't live in New York, you won't be seeing the ball drop, at least not in person.

So while I suspect it doesn't really need to be said, let me disabuse you of the notion that you must abide by any kind of *topic or conversation apartheid*. Breaking complicated issues down into smaller pieces is excellent stress management and often results in effective problem solving, but never at the expense of fearing or avoiding complexity. Lives lived together create complication. Don't be afraid of *it*.

CONVERSATION 9:
Spirituality and Religion

THEY SAY WE SHOULDN'T TALK POLITICS, sex, or religion in
polite company. But clashing views on the "unwarranted influence of the military-industrial complex" or the "inequitable
division of resources between private and public school boards"
have never been presented as either common or divisive premarital issues, so politics has been set aside here in *The 10
Conversations*.[51]

Turning to sex, while unquestionably there is a dearth of
authoritative sexual information and couples undeniably have
legitimate queries, issues, and problems in regard to copulatory
capering, as you know, we have already dealt with reproductive
recreation in Conversation 4.

Of the three taboo topics then that leaves us with religion,
and since it's already been demonstrated that we go boldly where
angels fear to tread, let's get the ninth conversation started and
begin talking about the role faith might play in building a life
together.

It isn't an accident that spirituality and religion is the subject
of the ninth rather than the first or second conversation. Its standing within the taboo three remains secure, given the depth of

---

[51] Please note: I'm not saying politics *can't* be a premarital issue, it's just that in my
experience it seldom, if ever, is an actual deal-breaker.

feeling that many have on their faith, religious belief, or adherence to dogma. So many atrocities have been committed in the name of some god or system of faith that they don't need to be enumerated here, but they do stand as testament to the volatility this topic can incite. Questioning or critical examination of a person's belief system is often far too threatening and seditious, and as such leaves no room for rational discourse for some. To those in this camp, let me say two things.

First, even such great spiritualists and profound thinkers as Mahatma Gandhi, the Dalai Lama, and Albert Einstein saw (and in the case of the Dalai Lama continue to see) issues of belief and faith as a journey of discovery and enlightenment rather than a "Truth" or a completely known and rigid set of precepts, so if smart guys like these saw room to manoeuvre, you might consider lightening up. However, and second, to the extent that you can't lighten up and your belief system does not allow accommodation, critical examination, or a tolerance for other belief systems, *skip this conversation*, as it will have nothing to offer you. The entire purpose of next few pages is to help couples consider and negotiate room for multiple and potentially *evolving* spiritual beliefs, and intransigence is antithetical to this objective.

For those whose certainty in a "Truth" is less than resolved, petrified, and absolute, read on, as there might be something of value for you. Hopefully, what you have learned from the experience and accomplishments of the previous conversations will allow the two of you to tackle this touchy issue with greater equanimity than if I had thrown this particular topic at you right from the start. Like they say, nothing succeeds like success, and hopefully the momentum of learning what is important to each of you and the depth of those feelings, as was demonstrated in some of the prior conversations, will make the Spirituality and Religion conversation a positive, building experience, rather than one that is divisive. And given both the intensity of how some feel about their spirituality, and the complex and esoteric nature of spiritual thought and language, I might have to ask you to work a little harder in this conversation to wrap your heads around the different options you have in talking about what spirituality means (or doesn't mean) to both of you.

Fire without a Spark: The Absence of Faith

While having a faith or experiencing some form of spirituality is common, it is neither universal nor necessary. Plenty of folks have no spiritual faith whatsoever and have never experienced what might be called the spark of the divine. There is even growing evidence that the experience of the divine is actually related to activity in a very specific part of the brain, and those whose brains don't experience activity in that small cluster of cells see and experience the world differently than do those for whom those cells are active. As with musical skill, artistic talent, or any of the multitude of other human attributes, the experience of or need for the divine simply falls on another continuum, with most falling somewhere in the middle and a few falling at either end.

Rather than a fervent belief in the "non-existence" of something—if that's even possible—many who claim to be atheists don't define themselves by what they are not but by what they are. They neither are nor feel broken or deprived as a function of their non-divine view of the world. In simple terms, they are those who, when confronted by existence and the various and complex patterns of the world, see a natural order whose beauty is most appropriately appreciated by what is actually known rather than what might be supposed. A fear of death, a need to bring order to chaos, or any supposed "self-evidence" of design all fail to demand in the faith free the imposition of a creator, a plan, or any imposed flavour of morality. Rather, existence simply is, and a need to "round hole, square peg" that existence runs the risk of denying the challenge of learning all there is to learn.

Extremism by Any Other Name...

However, as there are different degrees of spirituality or religiosity, so too are there different degrees of being spiritually unencumbered. The devotionally devoid may have nothing but casual feelings about their beliefs, or they may be strident, vocal, and challenging in their personal convictions.

Ironically, it is at this end of the spectrum where atheists and religious zealots have more in common than might initially be supposed. The smug and superior atheist can be almost as offensive as the religious fanatic (although, in complete fairness, I'm unaware of anyone killing in the name of the natural order of things). Proselytizing, *of any stripe*, whether spiritually informed or not, is one of the most offensive human behaviours that exists, and the self-righteous atheist strays into the same camp as those who knock on doors (metaphorically or otherwise) and use self-righteousness and fear in an attempt to swell the ranks of their faith. Despite claims to the contrary, demanding that others feel embarrassed, childish, or naïve *as a function of having faith* is invidious and not far removed from the divinely irrational making others fearful about choosing the "wrong" faith.

Conversely, exposure to the diversity of belief systems and unencumbered encouragement of free choice might represent the best in any spiritual philosophy. So while the atheist may feel immune to spiritual concerns, the absence of spiritual faith does not necessarily leave one immune to what amounts to intolerance. Extremism, in either the presence or absence of spirituality, is still extremism, and should be revealed as such.

Consequently, the ninth conversation has to have as its very basis a tolerance for what others think, feel, and believe, regardless of what end of the spirituality spectrum you feel most comfortable with. No one system of belief has the human condition figured out. Claims to the contrary are actually a clarion call for self-examination and a red flag to others to be wary of the potential for obstinacy. If you want to find out what's important to someone, you need to listen and listen, and then listen some more while checking your own judgement at the door.

The Matter in Question: Spirituality

SPIRITUALITY Q1. Tell your partner how and where your religious or spiritual beliefs, or lack thereof, came about. What were the familial and social influences? Were there any specific events or "epiphanies" that corresponded with the development of these belief systems?

SPIRITUALITY Q2. During adolescence and high school, it's common to have dust-ups with friends about spirituality and belief. Do you recall any of these? Did they leave any lasting impression on you? Can you share any of these experiences with your partner?

SPIRITUALITY Q3. Describe for your partner an example of when you were exposed to religious or spiritual intolerance. What were the circumstances? What were your thoughts and feelings?

SPIRITUALITY Q4. How consistent are your personal spiritual feelings with those of other family members? If there have been differences, how were they minimized, handled, honoured, or accommodated?

SPIRITUALITY Q5. If you were to name for yourself a "metaphysical mentor," someone whose guidance or wisdom on spiritual matters has been important to you, who might that be? Similarly, has there ever been an article, book, movie, etc., that strongly influenced your spiritual or philosophical beliefs? If your partner could identify this kind of material, would you be willing to read or to see it?

MARRYING OUTSIDE A FAITH

While in some quarters of Western culture, and certainly in other parts of the world, there is still tremendous pressure to marry within a faith, this type of intolerance seems to be somewhat in abeyance. I suppose time will tell whether this hopeful trend will flourish or become an historical footnote, but in any event we are currently living in a somewhat more enlightened time in human history as far as moving beyond the demand of marrying only within a faith is concerned.

At the most basic level, I'm puzzled by the idea that to make a religion stronger, you limit the opportunities for happiness among its adherents. However, I remain disheartened and at times enraged that some clients still come to me in desperation, feeling great love for each other, and yet are forced to choose between their own union or their religion, there apparently being no room within the prescribed belief system to accommodate a non-adherent. Unfathomably, these unfortunates have been told that marrying outside the faith is heretical or sinful—as though deeply loving and respecting someone represented anything other than one of the highest and most satisfying of human virtues and achievements!

For the unfortunates who find themselves trapped between a zealot-inspired Charybdis and Scylla, I wish I had some easy answer to offer you and, trust me, if I did, I'd put it down on paper.

Your pain is born of intolerance, and your strife comes of the confusion of faith and tradition with capital "T" truth. *Of course* there is nothing wrong with wanting to be with someone you love, wanting to be with someone who makes you a better you, and wanting to be with someone who feels about you what you feel about them, regardless of their faith (or race or gender or anything else, for that matter).

A Personal Act of Creation

Faith ought to enrich lives, not punish them. If you find yourself trapped in this circumstance, the good news is that you, as an adherent, can actually choose to modify your belief system to accommodate any partner you choose. Spiritual faiths, every single one of them, *were created by people*, and these faiths, every single one of them, have changed over time, and those changes were instigated and perpetuated by people. Since you're a person, you can choose to make alterations in what you want to believe. For the truly courageous, you can even consider constructing your own form of faith! Fundamentally, you ought to adopt a system of belief only when that system of belief makes sense to you, not because you have been told by others that it is the true, correct, or only form of belief to have. Within this context, who is to say that you are any less divinely inspired in constructing a method of faith, belief, or worship than any other adherent before you? The spark of the divine you personally feel may in fact be there for that very reason. Thus, on a personal level, you actually get to *choose* how trapped or conflicted you feel.

Adopting this perspective creates the potential for liberation from at least part of the morass that comes from a union that challenges spiritual or religious demands. But, if this option is beyond what you can personally accept, perhaps you can find solace and comfort in talking with others of your faith. You won't be the first person within your belief system to experience this kind of conflict, and those who have come before you may have ideas or techniques that can bring you some peace. Revisiting the

Family conversation might also be useful when struggling with these issues.

The bad news is that any spiritual or religious adaptation you entertain may mean nothing to other persons or institutions that are important to you, and consequently could amount to little more than cold comfort. The enthusiasm you might feel about finding something that is new, good, true, and right for you, spiritually or otherwise, may not be shared by important others, and few can easily dismiss the sting of familial or cultural rejection.

The burden of feeling or actually being rejected can be made somewhat lighter when the two of you have spent time identifying and expressing to each other your fears and concerns about potentially leaving the fold and finding your own personalized spiritual path. There is no easy or obvious method to accomplish this, but feeling that the two of you are figuring things out together brings with it a sense of union that helps combat fears and doubts. From a relationship-building point of view, addressing this adversity together has the potential to strengthen and mature your relationship.

Again, in the good news category, over the years I've seen more situations where, over time, the faith-inspired rejecters became more conciliatory than entrenched, settling for an uneasy truce of accepting the mixed couple while still holding on to, if not constantly displaying, their disapproval. I can't offer any guarantees, but in the majority of cases that I've seen professionally, over time—sometimes years—families or friends find ways to come back together even when fundamental religious differences initially drive them apart.

Unfortunately, the bad news here is twofold: first, this marginal solution does not emerge consistently and, second, I have been unable to identify the conditions under which one outcome is more likely than another. I can, however, offer this little bit of advice: intolerance or bigotry *on both sides* of a spiritual or religious divide seldom bodes well and dramatically extends the timeline of potential solution finding and reconciliation. Meeting intolerance with intolerance provides only resources for a completely unproductive psychological and emotional arms race.

I Shall Fear No Evil

Arguably, the faith-inspired intolerance described above represents the most incendiary of the spiritual issues a couple may need to talk about, negotiate, and potentially accommodate. However, fanning the flames of relationship discontent are other belief-related issues. Because forewarned is forearmed, let's see if we can avoid feelings of being burned by looking at how "degrees of faith" can inadvertently throw fuel on the fire of non-spiritual issues.

Faith can do strange things to people. We've all heard the news stories of how someone of faith has refused a life-saving medical intervention because it contravenes their religious beliefs. Thankfully, these sad circumstances are relatively rare. For our purposes here, we don't need to invoke such dire circumstances to reveal how a lesser and more subtle form of this kind of thinking can bring conflict to a relationship and for this reason is something that the two of you need to be talking about.

Realistically Speaking: Jodi and Brian

When treating sexual problems in a couple, it is necessary to assess how positively and negatively each person feels about the other. Positive feelings are used to enhance sexual opportunities, while hidden or unspoken hostility toward a partner can play a major role in both initiating and maintaining sexual dysfunction, and as such always need to be assessed. In exploring these types of issues, it became clear how a spiritual difference was exacerbating the sexual problem Jodi and Brian were confronted with.

While both couple members shared the same faith, worshipped together, and in general had no obvious spiritual conflicts, Brian's faith, or more correctly the *degree* of his faith, was substantially greater than Jodi's. In fact, Jodi felt Brian had developed an air of invulnerability as a function of his deep sense of personal spiritual connection, which troubled and at times angered her.

For example, because Brian felt so secure that a higher power was looking out for him, he made financial choices that, at least in her estimation, were less than prudent. When she challenged his preferred financial course of action, Brian consistently cited the strength of his faith and asserted that their higher power would ensure that their investments would always realize gains. He was also firmly of the opinion that his personal relationship with a higher power brought with it a sense of well-being and in subtle ways absolved him of more earthly concerns. A physically fit man, he would constantly push himself in sports and leisure activities, in ways Jodi thought were needlessly reckless and grew from his spiritually inspired sense of imperviousness. While she dearly loved her husband, her anger continued to grow in response to the financial and physical risks he chose to take. As she became increasingly angry and frightened, her desire to make love with him began to fall by the wayside.

For another couple, the same issue of invulnerability had less to do with money or personal adult risk and everything to do with differences in how they each assessed the degree of risk to which their children were exposed. For this second couple, he was frightened by her lack of vigilance when their children were skiing or engaging in contact sports, while she was certain that a higher power would always pay special attention to her children and keep them safe.

In both cases (and many others), the problem amounted to the same thing: differences in degrees of faith fostered different views of the world, different evaluations of risk and safety, and different feelings about vulnerability.

The Matter in Question: Spirituality

SPIRITUALITY Q6. How does your faith influence the other important aspects of your everyday life? For example, do you compartmentalize your faith, and as such see it as having a limited influence on your day-to-day decision making? Or perhaps you are defined by your faith, and it influences much of what you think and do on a daily basis. What role does faith play for your partner in this regard?

SPIRITUALITY Q7. Building on the clinical examples above, explain to your partner how your spiritual thinking has influenced any previous important financial or career choices you might have made. Similarly, are there any other important aspects of your life that have been strongly influenced by your spiritual beliefs?

THE FREE SPIRIT(UALITY) AND THE BIG QUESTIONS

For some, spirituality has little or nothing to do with formal religion or an organized faith. For these people, spirituality is about feeling connected to the world, natural or otherwise, and while believing there is more to existence than what is immediately perceptible, they feel no particular need to join a specific faith with canon and prescribed rituals and ceremonies. And once again, there is a wide range of feelings and degrees of belief among those who have this approach to spiritual practice. Some come to this form of spiritual conviction following a rejection of more dogmatic faiths, while others have found this less formal approach to spirituality has always been more consistent with their world view.

Regardless of the flavour of spirituality that someone practises, there remains a set of fundamental questions that most of us ask in regard to existence, the meaning of life, and our place in the universe. As I've already harped on the need to listen and be tolerant when wading through territory such at this, I won't bore you by climbing on that soapbox again. To get things started, use the queries below as points of departure for the two of you to explore some of the "Big Questions."

The Matter in Question: Spirituality

SPIRITUALITY Q8. If you believe in such a concept, try to explain to your partner what "god" means to you. Similarly, many spiritual beliefs espouse the idea of "fate" or a "plan." Can you offer your partner your thoughts about either of these concepts? Finally, if you engage in prayer, can you explain to your partner what role prayer plays for you? For example, is it simply a demonstration of faith? Is it an opportunity to seek higher intervention? Or is it perhaps more akin to meditation? Does it have other meaning(s) for you?

SPIRITUALITY Q9. Share with your partner your thoughts and beliefs about the moment of death and what might happen when we die. Do you believe in a soul, another plane of existence, reincarnation, nothingness, or some other consequence at death?

SPIRITUALITY Q10. Sadly, many have experienced the loss of a loved one. For some, this loss is turned into something positive through a belief in a "hereafter" and the belief that somewhere there is now a spirit predisposed to watch over them. What are your thoughts in this regard? Do you believe it is possible to talk to or be in contact with someone who has died?

SPIRITUALITY Q11. What do you want done with your remains upon your own death? How do your wishes correspond with those of your partner?

SPIRITUALITY Q12. What similarities and differences do you see between the human species and other species of living things? For example, do other animals have "a soul"? Are we, as humans, qualitatively different from other living species, or are we just an animal with a large brain?

SPIRITUALITY Q13. Do you believe that life exists on other planets? If you do, what do you think that life might be like? How, if at all, would the discovery of life on another planet influence your personal belief system and sense of spirituality?

SPIRITUALITY Q14. Should evolution and religion be given equal time in schools? Do you see them both as sciences? As philosophies? Or as unrelated concepts?

SPIRITUALITY Q15. Are you "pro-choice" or "pro-life"? What is your partner? How important is

this issue to each of you? (For the scientifically inclined, extend this discussion to include your thoughts about embryonic stem cells and their potential for use or misuse.)

"WE'RE PREGNANT"

Not infrequently, the option of one person converting to the other's religion becomes part of the Spirituality and Religion conversation. Conversion, when allowable, can solve a number of thorny issues, not the least of which might be simply making the union possible.

If you've got this far in the book, it won't come as any surprise that I will contend there's no right or wrong choice to be made in this circumstance. If converting to another faith feels like the right thing for one of you to do, as I've said, this could solve a lot of problems. However, I'd like to suggest a somewhat novel approach to thinking about the meaning and process of converting to another faith.

In the bad old days, it was the woman who went—alone—to the doctor's office to find out if she had a "bun in the oven" or was "with child." It was the woman who delivered the news, happy or otherwise, that conception had occurred. It was the woman who went into the delivery room. And it was the woman who, following birth, took on the burden of breastfeeding and bringing up baby. In the bad old days, even though it was too startling and offensive to call it this, it was the woman who "got pregnant."

Thankfully, in more recent decades we have seen a rethink and a more equitable or inclusive distribution of these parenting responsibilities. It is now commonplace for the father-to-be to be present when testing and ultrasounds are done to determine if conception has taken place. Similarly, it's commonplace for the wannabe daddy to be present in the delivery room and an active participant in the birthing process. Finally, it's commonplace for Pa to share the responsibility of feeding and bringing up the child. With this rethink has come a new conception of what "pregnant" is about. Today, it is far less often just the woman who gets pregnant. Today, the announcement is, "We're pregnant."

Borrowing a page from this more enlightened book, you might consider the necessity of a religious conversion to allow a marriage to take place in a similar, shared-experience kind of way. Certainly if someone were to convert for their own reasons, this would be a personal thing (in the same way an individual might seek to have a child on their own rather than as part of a union). However, if the primary purpose of the religious conversion is to make the union possible, both parties taking ownership of the process increases the palatability of the conversion process.

Again, using the more contemporary model of couple pregnancy, the need for both parties to be members of the same faith is a *couple requirement*, not one placed on an individual. Classes, meetings, reading material, and whatever else might be required to bring someone into a faith are attended, read, and participated in by *both parties* rather than only the initiate. If it's not a part of the standard way things have been done, ask the powers that be to accommodate this approach. Even a change in how the process is described can facilitate this more enlightened tactic, so it is *the couple who will be entering the new faith*, not a particular individual.

The method to the madness here is twofold. First, in the lingering resentment category, I have frequently heard from one member of a couple about how they were required to make a religious conversion for the marriage to take place. Their true adoption of the new faith is less the issue than is the lack of appreciation they felt from their partner. In the convert's mind, they felt they "took one for the team," yet their work, sacrifice, and commitment to the relationship feels to them minimized and unappreciated by their partner. If the "we're pregnant" approach is adopted, the other party will in fact better understand this work and effort. More than that, going through the conversion process together dramatically increases the opportunities for the couple to be discussing the feelings that arise from the process. The point of this book is to get the two of you talking about important issues, and adopting a new religion and religious conversion tends to be a pretty important issue for some.

I will also quickly remind you of a point made back in the Location conversation. For some, converting is no small task. To the extent that it feels like a major imposition or cost—which isn't uncommon—the wise couple will search out ways to compensate or balance out what might feel like disproportionate sacrifice. In "Location," we talked about exploring alternative currencies of exchange to find balance when one person has to relocate for the sake of the relationship. Here in Spirituality and Religion, we can legitimately suggest the same kind of thinking. As we explored the alternative-currencies concept sufficiently in Location, I don't think we need a substantial rehash here, beyond reminding you that finding balance is made so much easier when you open your minds to different kinds and levels of exchange.

The second advantage to this approach is that it sets the stage for the practice of faith to become a regular issue that gets talked about, not just during the conversion process but for the rest of your lives together. As we age and mature, our views about existential issues can undergo substantial modification. This is a natural part of the process of growing up and comes about as a function of a wider breadth of experience and an accumulation of successes and failures in dealing with life's myriad challenges. Issues of faith and belief ought never to be taken off the table, so to speak, and remain topics that get knocked about, challenged, modified, solidified, abandoned, readopted, etc. If we conceptualize faith and spiritual belief only as monolithic and fossilized systems of thought, we fail to demand of them all that can be offered. And while a religious conversion might be required to get married and makes sense at one stage of life, it is quite reasonable to presume that other conversions or modifications of faith and belief might be needed at other stages of life. Adopting the "we're pregnant" model for the initial conversion process fosters the idea that both of you may need to consider future opportunities to take a hit for the team. Keeping minds open is best done when nothing is taken for granted, even when it comes to something that might have the never-changing quality of a system of religious belief.

The Matter in Question: Spirituality

SPIRITUALITY Q16. Does the faith that either of you practise demand that only adherents can marry? If yes, is the idea of conversion palatable to either of you? Is it even allowed within the specific faith?

SPIRITUALITY Q17. What might be done, offered, amended, modified, etc., to balance out the requirement that one party convert to make getting married possible?

AND WHAT ABOUT THE NEXT GENERATION?

What about the kids? So far, we've talked about exploring and describing personal beliefs, along with ways that different faiths and spiritual needs might be accommodated in a marriage. The other big spiritual issue that needs to be talked about is what role, if any, faith, religion, or spirituality will have as far as potential kids are concerned.

For some, "family worship" is a critically important part of their faith, and bringing children up "within the faith" is a demand of certain religions. Accepting or rejecting such institutional demands is of course a personal choice. For our purposes here, however, expressing that choice to a potential partner is the critical piece of information we need to get on the table.

You might want to prepare yourself for surprising contradictions that could arise during this part of the Spirituality and Religion conversation. For example, there are those who have extremely strong faith and might regularly attend church and observe a plethora of religious practices, yet when it comes to their children feel no great compunction to inculcate their beliefs in their kids nor to demand, force, browbeat, or otherwise manipulate children into becoming adherents themselves. Conversely, there are those who by all appearances have no great spiritual belief, and certainly maintain few religious observances, yet when children come along insist that those children be brought into a faith, attend religious schools, etc.

To be clear, resolving contradictions like these is *secondary to the immediate purposes of this book*. Rather than challenge people with inconsistencies in their thinking, the purpose of the Spirituality and Religion conversation is simply to reveal whether such feelings or desires exist, and in so doing to get them out in the air, where they can be known and further examined within the context of a developing relationship. If things go by the numbers here, you are setting yourselves up for a lifetime of figuring out what you want to do with these issues. Right now, we just have to make sure that you both know what issues are important to each of you.

The Matter in Question: Spirituality

SPIRITUALITY Q18. Consider returning to the Having Kids conversation at this point. Does anything you have learned during the Spirituality and Religion conversation alter how you or your partner might answer any of the questions there?

SPIRITUALITY Q19.   Watch the movie *Dogma* (1999, Ben Affleck, Matt Damon) together. While potentially an acerbic tale for some, the movie challenges the idea of dogmatic religious adherence and raises some interesting questions about the differences between faith, spirituality, and religion (if you are offended by coarse language, this may not be a great pick for you). Do you think the distinction director Kevin Smith tries to make between belief and faith is a valid one?

FINAL THOUGHTS ON THE SPIRITUALITY AND RELIGION CONVERSATION

This conversation can be tough. More than any of the others, the Spirituality and Religion conversation has the potential to not only touch a nerve but also do a mosh pit on it. So it might be useful to keep a few things in mind.

First, remember that the initial purposes of this conversation are to expose what each of you believes as far as some of these more existential questions are concerned, not to judge or evaluate those beliefs. As I have said throughout this discussion, being judgemental or intolerant about someone else's beliefs does nothing to move this conversation forward and demonstrates a marked lack of maturity. You're here to learn, listen, and express, not spurn, piss on, and repress! If you're going to make this thing work together, you're going to need to have the discipline of listening and consideration.

Second, the intensity of what someone feels in regard to a spiritual or religious belief might best be understood as a "feeling of the moment" rather than an intractable position. With time, consideration, and a cooling-off period, what seemed like an incredibly important point can lose some of its significance. I'm not suggesting that a strongly held spiritual belief is really just a will-o-the wisp or a casually constructed cognition. It's more that the need for that belief to hold sway within the evolving context of a relationship can change over time. For example, most of us have had the experience of being in a huge fight, but weeks or months later we're unable to recall what that particular knock-down, drag-out was initially about. It doesn't happen all the time, but it does happen. Even in *Fiddler on the Roof*, the profoundly devoted Tevye claims he can't accept his daughter marrying outside the faith, saying, "If I try and bend that far, I'll break," but after a period of time offers her the blessing "And God be with you."

Believe it or not, when people look for commonality rather than disunity, they often find it, and this is just as true when it comes to contrasting spiritual belief systems as anything else. In fact, comparing faiths is like comparing men and women. On the surface, there seem to be some pretty big differences, and it's those that we notice and magnify. But if we look below the surface, with only a few exceptions, men and women are pretty much the same: they are made of the same stuff, have the same needs, and are organized pretty much the same way. In fact, when you factor out prejudice and assumptions, it's almost impossible not to come to the conclusion that men and women are far more similar than they are different. Sure there are differences, but those differences tend to be in the details rather than in the overall design. And doing the hard work of finding the commonality is worth the trouble, particularly if the result is you finding the person you want to spend the rest of your life *with*.

Conversation 10:
(W)rapping Things Up

Hey, we've made it! We've gotten all the way to the last of the ten conversations. That's no small accomplishment!

If you've done the previous nine conversations, the two of you have now had serious and detailed discussions about a number of really important issues. Specifically, you have talked about

1. The choice to have or not to have children

2. The process of selecting accommodating career paths

3. How differences in financial styles need to be given consideration in your relationship

4. How to discuss and explore a variety of sexual behaviours and desires

5. The need to meld and blend different family-of-origin priorities and cultures

6. The potential challenge of finding a location to set up a home together that suits the many needs you both have

7. How to ensure that the task of maintaining that home feels equitable

8. A bunch of different ways the two of you can think about having fun together and how addressing leisure needs ought to be made an evolving and ongoing project

9. The different degrees and flavours of spiritual belief both of you might bring to the relationship and how to potentially accommodate these differences

As I said, if the two of you have navigated your way through all of those issues, this is no small accomplishment! Why don't you take a moment and chat about the process so far?

The Matter in Question: (W)rap-Up

(W)RAP-UP Q1. The order of the previous nine conversations was very specific. However, you might have different thoughts about how to arrange them. Would you have arranged them differently and, if so, how and to what purpose?

If you followed my suggestion on how to use this book to best advantage, you have also made yourself familiar with the fifteen rules of good communication. Hopefully, by working through some if not all of the varied topics above, you've also begun to see how *necessary* these rules are if you want to engage in respectful and meaningful communication. With any luck, concepts like "I language," "Never using absolutes," and the "24-hour rule" have crept into your everyday vocabulary and the two of you are more skilled at recognizing how to keep a communication productive and on track.

With all that good stuff accomplished, some of you could rightfully be asking, at least from a communication perspective, what could there possibly be left to cover? We've talked about a whole bunch of important stuff, and in the process we've learned how to talk efficiently and productively with each other. Surely we can put this premarital communication thing to bed, feeling confident we've covered all the important issues, can't we?

If it feels like you really have hit the highlights and taken on the pressing premarital issues that must be dealt with, take off your shoes, kick back, and give each other a well-deserved pat on the back and peck on the cheek. The fact is, you *have* covered the most important issues, *the* issues you *must* talk about, and thus the sense of confidence you have is well deserved.

But before we go too far down this road of self-congratulations, and perhaps develop a false sense of immunity to relationship strife, there actually might be a few other important things you both will profitably benefit from talking about. These additional issues won't take that long to cover—actually, they're kind of fun—and they're really useful in the "getting to know each other better and solidifying our relationship" category.

Uniquely You

We've all got our little peculiarities. Some have to have the dinner table set just so; others will have a conniption if the bathroom towels are not folded exactly in thirds before they're put away; and still others consider the choice of either Coke or Pepsi a cause worth dying for. We all like what we like, even in the absence of an obvious or universally agreed upon rationale or logic. It is this diversity of needs and tastes that both make us so interesting to each other and work to ensure our survival as a species: because our tastes and preferences have evolved to be so varied, we have successfully populated almost the entire Earth's surface, finding ways to live in and enjoy a vast array of habitats, foods, living circumstances, social systems, forms of entertainment, etc.

As a show of respect for this diversity of human need, taste, and desire, let me invite the two of you to explore the list of "ponderables" presented below. Ponderables are those common daily choices and those personal preferences that shape our existence and in totality make each one of us unique. The set of ponderables I've provided below is wide ranging but far from comprehensive—it's unlikely that a complete list could ever be generated given the constantly changing quality of human preference and choice—so feel free to add your own as required. If you want, you can even use the lists below as a kind of game, not just to play with each other but with friends, family, and other couples. The most important point here is to have fun. There is, however, also all kinds of conversation potential in the list below, so to the extent that a ponderable leads you to discuss something important, take advantage of the opportunity, apply the fifteen rules, and get into it.

PONDERABLES

Spend some time with the list below, offering an opinion to your partner as to which choice you would make. How often are you in agreement? Are any of the listed items pet peeves or of particular importance to you? If you have strong feelings about something, make sure that this issue gets talked about. For the most part, however, this little exercise is more likely to just be a few laughs!

Technology
Computer: Mac or PC?
Portable music: iPod, MP3 player, or cellphone?
Telephone: land line or cell?
Radio: AM, FM, or satellite?
Scheduling: PDA or traditional paper and pencil datebook?
The multi-channel universe: satellite or cable?
Car: front, rear, or all-wheel drive?
Car transmission: standard or automatic?

Lawn mower: gas, electric, or push?

Barbeque: gas or charcoal?

Cooking: gas or electric?

Refrigerator: side-by-side, freezer on top, or freezer on bottom?

Bedroom: TV or not?

Big screen: LCD, DPL, or Plasma?

Camera: digital or film?

Digital photos: print them or leave them on the computer?

Snow removal (Canadian respondents only): snow blower or shovel?[52]

Add your own:

Add your own:

Add your own:

Entertainment

DVD rentals: full-screen or letterbox?

Old movies: black and white, or colourized?

Star Trek: favourite captain?

Sitcoms: favourite character from *Friends*, *Seinfeld*, and *The Simpsons?*

Puzzles: crossword or Sudoku?

Puzzle confidence level: pen or pencil?

Advertising: mute or listen to TV commercials?

Movies: *Citizen Kane*—best movie ever made?

Good movies: all-time favourite? Guilty pleasure? First movie you actually bought? First movie to make you cry as an adult (and as a child)? Best date movie?

Bad movies: first movie you walked out of? Worst movie you sat through? Worst movie ever rented? Movie that was the biggest disappointment?

At the movies: popcorn or no popcorn?

If popcorn: insist butter be spread throughout or settle for it just on top?

---

[52] Okay, border-state people in the United States can answer this one too.

At the movies: up front, in the middle, or at the back of theatre?

TV news: 6 o'clock, 11 o'clock, or not at all?

Reality shows: a legitimate form of entertainment or fluff?

Newspaper: every day, weekends only, or not at all?

Magazines: subscribe or buy single issues?

Books: buy or get from the library?

Novels: hardcover or paperback?

Radio: talk, news, or music?

Tip: ten or fifteen percent?

Add your own:

Add your own:

Add your own:

Sports

Cross-country ski, downhill, or snowboard?

Bike, rollerblade, or both?

Protection: wear a helmet or risk it?

Canadian or American football rules?

Winter or Summer Olympics?

Water ski, wakeboard, or tube?

National or American Baseball league?

Darts, bowling, and billiards: are they really sports?

At the gym: weight training, aerobics, or both?

The *one* national sport (again, Canadian respondents only): hockey or lacrosse?

Add your own:

Add your own:

Add your own:

Food

Scotch: blended or single malt? (I know, I know, there really isn't a question here. Just seeing if you've been paying attention.)

Rum: light or dark?

Mixed drinks: use a jigger or wing it?

Wine: red or white?

Beer: bottles or cans?

Beer and wine: domestic or imported?

Drinking water: bottled, filtered, or right out of the tap?

Soft drink brand: Coke or Pepsi?

Soft drink temperature: ice or no ice?

Soft drink ingredient: artificially or naturally sweetened?

Spread: butter or margarine?

Chicken: white meat or dark meat?

Milk: whole, 2%, or skim?

Bread: white or whole grain?

Cereal: sugar coated or plain?

Yogurt: fruit on the bottom or already stirred?

Coffee: black or bastardized?

Tea: same question.

At Starbucks: do you use their weird names or just ask for a small, medium, or large?

Any fast-food joint: decide while in line or figure it out at the counter?

McDonald's: Super-size?

Peanut butter: smooth or crunchy?

Ice cream parlour: cup or cone?

Red meat: rare, medium, or well done?

Chicken wings: mild, medium, hot, or suicide?

Pizza crust: thin or thick?

Pizza topping: regular or extra cheese?

Spaghetti: al dente or soft?

Orange juice: pulp or no?

Cheddar: mild, medium, or old?

Eggs: white or brown?

Yolk: hard or soft?

Scrambled eggs: add milk, add water, or leave unadulterated?

Chinese food: chopsticks or cutlery?

Hot sauce: a regular condiment or a special seasoning?

Chocolate: milk or dark?
Oatmeal cookies: with or without raisins?
Chocolate chip cookies: with or without nuts?
Brownie: same question.
Add your own:
Add your own:
Add your own;

Education

Focus: arts or sciences?
Textbooks: underline or leave unmarked for resale?
Notes: loose-leaf or notebook?
Note taking: print, script, or keyboard?
Attendance: all classes all the time or skip some?
Studying atmosphere: music, TV, or silence?
Studying style: alone or with other(s)?
Type of school: private or public?
Type of dress: regular dress or school uniform?
Lesser of evils: essay or exam?
Add your own:
Add your own:
Add your own:

Around the House

Personality: morning or evening person?
Type of bathing: bath or shower?
Time of bathing: morning or the night before?
Soap: bar or pump?
Toothbrush: standard or electric?
Floor covering: carpet or hardwood?
Furniture: cloth or leather?
Cookware: nonstick, ceramic, or metal?
Christmas tree: real or artificial?
Christmas gifts: open one Christmas Eve or all have to wait till the morning?

Clock radio: awake to music or alarm?

Snooze alarm: always, sometimes, never? If at least sometimes, how many times?

Wrist watch: set accurately or a few minutes fast?

Bed: electric or regular blanket?

Footwear: socks with sandals?

Winter: gloves or mitts? Hat or no hat?

Getting dressed: sock, sock, shoe, shoe; or sock, shoe, sock, shoe?

Add your own:

Add your own:

Add your own:

Sex

Preferred position: top or bottom?

Preferred time: morning or evening?

Pubic hair: trimmed or au natural?

Friction reduction: lube or no lube?

Add your own:

Add your own:

Add your own:

Manners

Sneezing: "Bless you," "God bless you," or nothing?

Flatulence: leave the room first, offer an "excuse me," or just let it pass?

Seasoning: pass salt and pepper together or separately?

At the table: if the phone rings, answer it or not?

Telemarketing: politely decline or just hang up?

Dining out: who gets to sit facing the restaurant and who faces the wall?

Social injustice: tell them they have butt in line or quietly seethe in anger?

In the elevator: ask riders for their floors or let them push the buttons themselves?

Toilet paper roll: replace when empty or let someone else do it?

Milk bag: same question?

Add your own:

Add your own:

Add your own:

Travel

Preferred season to travel: winter, spring, summer, fall?

Preferred destination: hot or cold?

Arrangements: travel agent or book yourself?

Itinerary: active or relaxed?

Seating: window or aisle?

Luggage: carry-on only or carousel?

Pets: boarded or come with you?

At the border: declare everything?

At the hotel: mistakenly pack a towel?

At the amusement park: front or back of the roller coaster?

Driving: get there as fast as possible or enjoy the ride?

Cellphone: talk while driving or pull over?

Lost: ask for directions or figure it out yourself?

Long-distance driving: in the fast or slow lane?

Add your own:

Add your own:

Add your own:

The Matter in Question: (W)rap-up

(W)RAP-UP Q2. In all the other conversation chapters, I have made a movie recommendation related to the topic of the conversation. This time, you guys make the selection. Can each of you identify your *favourite movie of all time*, and then make arrangements to sit down and watch both of those movies together? In making plans, make sure you leave time to talk about what makes the movie so special to you. As an added bonus, do the same with your favourite piece of music and book.

(W)RAP-UP Q3.   Describe for your partner the three most influential events of your life. These could include events that were pleasant, like a graduation or a promotion, or they might be distressing, like the death of a loved one or some sort of trauma. They could be discrete events that happened over a short period, or they could be ongoing issues.

Uniquely Together

As unique as you are as individuals, so too is your relationship. What exists between the two of you has never existed before, nor will it be reproduced anytime in the future. The two of you create something new, special, and distinct when you come together. There are some grand and philosophical realities to this small act of creation, and if you want to, the two of you can explore the deeper and more esoteric implications of this particular gestalt. On the other hand, it might just be fun to identify what each of you thinks makes you exceptional as a couple.

The Matter in Question: (W)rap-up

(W)RAP-UP Q4.   What is the "elevator pitch" for your relationship? That is, if you had to describe

the relationship the two of you have in fifteen seconds, what do you think you might say? Alternatively,
suppose another couple were to sum the two
of you up in fifteen seconds or less. What might
they say?

(W)RAP-UP Q5.   As a couple, can you identify any
"Top Threes"—foods, restaurants, bands, pieces of
music, vacation destinations, TV shows, sports figures, books, etc.—that the two of you share?

(W)RAP-UP Q6.   As a couple, consider the question "What is our greatest strength?" Are the two
of you on the same page as far as this is concerned? After this, try the more challenging, "What
is our greatest weakness?" (As scary as this might
sound, this issue still needs to be covered. Courage!)

Exploring what makes the two of you "uniquely together" is an
important relationship-building exercise. It creates a sense of
belonging and promotes the idea that you "have each other's back."
A clear concept of what makes the two of you "work" is also
extremely helpful in getting through stressful circumstances and
conflict. Having a clear sense of what it is that makes you comfortable, better, safer, stronger, happier, etc., together is like having
money in the bank during hard times: it gives you an emotional
reserve to draw on when things aren't going smoothly. Giving serious consideration to the "uniquely together" aspects of your
relationship is a necessary and ongoing task that the two of you
ought to undertake. In fact, this "ongoing quality" brings us to the
final issue and represents the last part of (W)rapping things up.

In the previous nine conversations, issues crucial to contemporary relationships have been presented. Each of the

conversations represents an important aspect of modern relationships, and though the degree of applicability to each relationship will vary, none of the conversations should have been skipped or minimized. In fact, in clinical psychology we often offer the axiom that the issue you want to talk about the least is probably the one you ought to talk about the most. Having come this far, you might ask yourselves if there was any particular topic the two of you made light of or even agreed to leave out. If only to humour me, consider going back and reviewing that particular conversation in greater detail.

In addition to exposing you to a list of the most important issues the two of you must be talking about, it's my hope that the particular problem-solving process of breaking down issues into smaller and smaller pieces, and then dealing with only a piece or two at a time, has been clearly demonstrated. As I'm sure you've noticed by now, each of the conversation chapters presented an issue, but then, rather than demanding that a position be immediately taken and defended, broke that issue down into smaller and smaller topics and questions. In so doing, feelings and implications could be considered without the burden of having to have "an answer" right from the beginning.

Realistically Speaking: Safi and José

Safi and José came to see me specifically for premarital counselling. As young bank executives, they were both accustomed to applying rationality and logic to the business problems they confronted. But when it came to emotional issues, they felt overwhelmed. Safi was terrified of commitment, as she had been profoundly hurt in a previous relationship as well as having been rejected by her father. Her willingness to risk emotional exposure to a man, let alone believe she could ever come to trust one, was practically a non-starter in her mind. José, while sensitive and caring, felt overwhelmed by Safi's sensitivities, frightened to express *his own* emotional needs for fear of overwhelming Safi, and frustrated with what he saw as the intractability of their problem: if they couldn't become more emotionally expressive and trusting, they could never marry. They loved each other deeply and shared many common interests. However, they both felt it was going to be impossible to actually express their emotional needs and have them met in a marriage.

Therapy for Safi and José was a somewhat drawn-out affair with a number of hiccups along the way, but the basic approach we took was to build up confidence in expressing emotions by taking one small emotional step after another. We started by looking for small, innocuous issues where there was just a hint of emotional content and then used these minor issues to explore whether they could generate any emotional tolerance and connection. Believe it or not, I used the necktie José was wearing as a first (and silly) example. Safi quite liked it, but José didn't and wore it only because it was a gift from Safi. I made the point that knowing about and tolerating this emotional discrepancy must have brought their relationship to the brink, given how incapable they both were in dealing with differences in feelings and needs. Of course they looked at me as though I had just stepped off a spaceship (and likely doubted that I was going to be able to help them). Having a difference of opinion about a tie was different from feeling emotionally exposed and unable to trust, they explained. Feigning ignorance, I asked them (sometimes repeatedly) to explain how one emotional situation was different from another. Eventually, we all agreed the only difference was one of degree.

With this realization in place, we were then able to reconceptualize their problem as one of emotional training and skill building, not one of absence and inadequacy. By breaking down the serious and substantial issue of lack of trust and emotional connection into smaller and smaller steps, over several months we three generated dozens of examples of thoughts and circumstances of increasing emotional import and intensity that they were able to explore and process together. Via these experiences, both their expression of emotions and their confidence increased.

319

After four months of therapy, they were engaged, and a year later they were married. Currently, they continue to come to see me once every few months to check in, and though they occasionally fail to recognize an opportunity to apply their emotional training, they are doing extremely well.

The Final Part of the (W)rapping Things Up Conversation

As I have said, the nine prior conversations contain issues that all couples need to tackle. However, as comprehensive as this list is, no list of issues is going to completely capture what *all* couples might need to talk about. I have seen a lot of couples over the years, and while it's quite common to find similarities between what one couple brings to the office compared to another, it never ceases to amaze me how often each new couple I see presents some new wrinkle, issue, or dilemma. And this brings us to the final component of the (W)rapping Things Up conversation. Building both on the "uniquely you" and the "uniquely together" theme, the final issue the two of you must talk about before you marry is simply EVERYTHING ELSE THAT'S IMPORTANT TO THE TWO OF YOU.

Now, That's a (W)rap

In its simplest form, the "everything else" portion of the (W)rapping things up conversation consists of whatever one-of-a-kind issues or challenges the two of you might have in front of you. These issues could be related to one of the previous nine conversations or could be completely unrelated. By way of illustration, let me use a couple of examples from the movies. In *Waking Ned Devine* (1998, Ian Bannen, David Kelly—and a great movie), a star-crossed couple are challenged by the fact that Finn is a pig farmer and Maggie can't stand how he smells when he comes home from work. This issue stands in the way of them getting married. In *Diner* (1982, Daniel Stern, Ellen Barkin—and another great movie) because of his passion for his favourite sport, one of the main characters insists that his female counterpart be an expert on his favourite team before he feels he can commit to marriage. In the same movie, another couple starts drifting apart as she fails to attend to his interest in music and he fails to understand how lonely she feels. For both couples in *Diner*, these differences represent "make or break" issues.

"Everything else" issues often have the quality of seeming meaningless to outsiders yet hold a world of meaning for specific individuals. The fact that the "rest of the world" might not appreciate how significant the issue is to you is a poor reason to leave the issue off the table. How someone smells when they come home from work seems like a pretty specific and potentially minor issue and would likely be out of place if I tried to put it in one of the nine conversations that everyone has to talk about, but if I were dealing with the fictitious Finn and Maggie, both would feel neglected if this issue wasn't given significant attention. If the issue has importance to either one of you, it must be given attention regardless of how the rest of world might minimize or misunderstand!

Alternatively, "everything else" issues might feel as though they are large and complicated and have seldom been settled by other couples. For example, a couple might have a fundamental philosophical or political difference. Or there could be what we call an "age and stage" difference where one person feels ready to settle down, but the other doesn't feel ready to commit. The grander nature of the problem might make a couple feel the issue has no solution and as such should just be left alone. When there are "everything else" issues of this type, hopefully the model of breaking the problem down into smaller pieces and dealing with those pieces one at a time will come to mind and potentially bring a solution closer to hand.

Essentially, big or small, there are no limits to what an "everything else" issue might be, and consequently no list of premarital issues can realistically claim to have captured all that is significant to everyone at all times. As a category, however, "everything else" is intended to cue you to the idea that *you're never done* talking about what's important.

The Matter in Question: (W)rap-up

(W)RAP-UP Q7. You've probably realized that Rule 15, "How we doin'?" is supposed to set you up for a lifetime of "everything else" type conversations. To make sure that these actually happen, think for a moment about what might get in the way of the two of you having "How we doin'?" conversations every few months. After you have identified what might prevent those conversations from happening, what can the *two of you* do to work around or at least lessen those impediments?

Lasting relationships are always works in progress. In any realistic way, there is no "finish line." Because people are dynamic entities, their relationships will always be dynamic as well. This is not to say that you can never feel safe or secure in a relationship—far from it. In large part, relationships are *about* feeling safe and secure. The challenge is to recognize that safety and security, like all other human dimensions, are on continua, rather than being black and white dichotomies, which you either have or don't have. Feeling really secure in a relationship, particularly when the two of you have made a project of keeping the relationship strong and vital, is eminently reasonable. Conversely, assuming a relationship is secure without checking in with your partner, without assessing your ongoing and changing needs, and without addressing problems as they arise is simply foolish. Even buildings made of stone and steel are regularly inspected to ensure that tragedies don't occur. And, sadly, when those regular inspections fall by the wayside, the possibility of failure and heartbreak dramatically increases.

FINAL THOUGHTS ON THE (W)RAPPING THINGS UP CONVERSATION

To conclude, this final conversation might best be thought of as a twofold challenge of responsibility. The first challenge is to accept the responsibility that your relationship is a powerful, ever-changing thing, and as such requires ongoing attention. Essentially, you're never done assessing and evaluating how the relationship is or isn't meeting the needs you both have.

The second challenge of responsibility is to doubt experts like me who tell you that if you just do what you're told, everything will be all right. It may seem like I'm shooting myself in the foot, but there is a method to my madness. Pundits can offer advice, ideas, and new ways to conceptualize old problems, but we can never know as much about what is working and not working in a relationship as do the two people who experience it every day. There is an inescapable logic here that needs to be accepted and embraced. Folks like me can help you improve your relationship, but we can never offer you a guarantee that if you do what we say, the way we say to do it, you can ignore the informed position you have within your relationship to render your own informed judgement. Finding out what works for you can be accomplished only through examination, experimentation, and work, not by absolving yourself from that responsibility and simply trusting what you're told by others. Nothing can replace your own instincts, and you're wise and informed when you listen to *them*.

TROUBLESHOOTING

As with any troubleshooting section, the purpose of this final chapter is to provide you with additional assistance should you encounter substantial difficulties making your way through *The 10 Conversations*. For example, if you seem to have hit a stumbling block on a particular issue, or if you have fears that you're not taking full advantage of the conversations, read on—it's likely that among the topics I cover here, there is something that can help. However, and just to remind you about what I said in the introduction, I don't have anything that can *make* the two of you *more compatible*. The purpose of this book is to help you determine how compatible you are, not to morph one or both of you into someone new. Also, if you feel you've successfully completed each of the conversations and managed any resulting difficulties on your own, you could actually set this chapter aside and save it for future occasions when you feel challenged by a communication or relationship problem.

PATHS TO AGREEMENT: OPTIONS FOR MANAGING CONFLICT

Sometimes the best way to resolve an important difference is to clearly understand what your options are. Essentially, in any conflict situation where one of you says black and the other says white, you have four paths to agreement.

The Four Paths to Agreement

1. One person changes their position.

2. The two of you negotiate a middle ground where it is clear that both are *giving up something* to get *some* of what they want.

3. Both agree to take turns in getting what one person wants.

4. Terminate the relationship.[53]

From a troubleshooting perspective, sometimes the simplicity of these four choices helps to bring focus to potential solutions.

To illustrate, let's say a couple disagrees about whether or not they should draw up a monthly budget. For the members of this couple, it's a black-and-white issue where he wants to and she doesn't. After much discussion, expression of needs and desires, and display of feelings, along with a sincere attempt by both parties to attend to and understand the other's position, she won't be drawn to the "dark side" and he refuses to "see the light." Our couple agrees that in the current climate, and based on current knowledge and circumstances, neither of them is going to change their minds, so further attempts to "convert" the other are going to be wasted and, worse, run the risk of badgering, bullying, or ignoring what one of the two adults in this negotiation wants. So the first path to agreement, where *one person changes their position,* has failed to produce a satisfactory result for our hypothetical

---

[53] Note that swallowing your feelings and needs is not offered as an option. This is because, in the long run, it just doesn't work.

couple and consequently gets taken off the table, so to speak. However, there are still two paths that can be used to work out what needs to be worked out.

The second path to agreement is *the negotiated middle ground*. By specifically agreeing to explore this second path, our couple agrees that trying to change the other person's mind will no longer work, and now both will have to agree to give something up to get some of what they want. For our hypothetical couple, this might be an agreement to set up a budget for household expenses but not for personal ones, or perhaps a once-a-week meeting where both people produce all the receipts for what has been purchased so an accounting, if not a budget, can be assembled. The important point is that there is an expectation that both will be giving up something and getting some of what they want, but neither will get it all their way.

The second path works only when both parties agree that they have a new goal of finding a middle ground. When his desire is black and hers white and neither will be swayed, finding an acceptable shade of grey becomes a viable path to agreement.

Even when the second path fails to resolve a situation, however, and a middle ground can't be found, we still have one more path that might result in an acceptable settlement. When he wants black and she wants white, and it has been determined that there is no agreeable shade of grey, negotiations now become about stripes.

The third path to agreement is about *taking turns*. Here, one person will get what they want for a particular period and then the other will get what they want. Returning to our hypothetical couple, they might agree that for the next two months, they will draw up and apply a budget to their finances. Following that, the budget won't be used for a similar two-month period. At the end of these four months, a new discussion concerning the perceived success and failure of the two different financial approaches will be held, and negotiations as to future budgeting will begin anew. Essentially, our couple agreed to take turns using and not using a budget and at the same time agreed to discuss the outcome of this turn taking. After taking this striped approach, all four paths to agreements are again put on the table.

Of course, it's important that *you both identify which of the paths to agreement are being applied so there is no misunderstanding.* You don't want your partner thinking you've changed your mind when you believe the two of you are taking turns! This is where you start making records of the settlements you have made so that in future conflict situations, previous negotiations or turn taking is taken into consideration.

Of course, the final path to agreement is that you agree that the issue can't be resolved now or in the future *and* is of such magnitude that the viability of the relationship is in jeopardy. Consideration of the fourth path to agreement—that is, *agreeing to the dissolution of the relationship*—often has the quality of making reconsideration of the first three paths to agreement more palatable. Being reminded of what's at stake if nothing useful can be found in the first three paths tends to focus people's attention more acutely on new and different possibilities.

Using the fourth path as a *bargaining threat* is immature and disingenuous. If every disagreement comes down to one person threatening to walk away and end the relationship, then their bluff should be called. Any relationship that is continually maintained by the constant threat of someone leaving is a profoundly unhealthy one and ought to be terminated. This strategy might work in management–union circumstances or military applications, but by their very nature, these relationships are adversarial. And this is a terrible way to live on a day-to-day basis in what is supposed to be an intimate, mature, trusting relationship.

TAKE A BREAK

Perhaps the most common communication problem is letting the intensity of an issue distract you from making progress. When we're feeling intense and we really believe what we're saying, it's hard to remind ourselves that, after we have conveyed how important the issue is to us, we need to move on to solving the problem or finding consensus. Although initially clarifying and motivating, the intensity of the moment now has the potential to derail a productive communication opportunity.

Taking a break from talking about the issue is often the solution to non-productive intensity. If you've found that you're all wound up, some time to unwind might be what keeps the communication watch ticking. You can do this formally using the 30-minutes-of-anger rule (although the need to take a break doesn't have to have anything to do with anger) or the 24-hour rule, or you can be more casual about it and simply suggest a cooling-off period to have a cup of tea. Often calm brings perspective, and "finding calm" has the twofold benefit of settling you and creating the opportunity to see things a bit differently. The principle your mother espoused when she told you to count to ten before you expressed your anger was correct when you were five, and it's still correct today.

Beyond reducing intensity and potentially quelling a "feeling of the moment," the taking-a-break concept also speaks to another relationship truism from which many can benefit. We all know there are "good days" and "bad days," both personally and in relationships. However, there are also good and bad weeks, months, and even years. Life and experience, like so many things in the natural world, has a cyclical quality. The simple recognition that you might be having a bad week or month might just be the answer to why the two of you might not be making the progress you'd like in developing your relationship. Taking a break might not mean just pausing for a few minutes or hours. It might mean that *this is a bad week, month, or even year* to try to tackle a particular problem. Although the phrase is getting overused, recognizing the concept of a "perfect storm" of relationship challenges might be the key to understanding that now might not be the most opportune time to take on a particular issue. Of course, taking this too far means that you constantly put off for tomorrow what needs to be dealt with today. The troubleshooting quality of "take a break" is in its selective use. That is, among the strategies you use to try to work through difficult issues, taking a break is but one alternative course of action, not an answer in and of itself.

And finally, from a take-a-break perspective, we've all experienced circumstances where an issue got beaten to death rather than being dealt with succinctly. Sometimes taking a break also reminds us that quantity does not equal quality. Talking a lot about something might be what's needed, but it might also run the risk of ramping up fatigue and information overload.

ON BEING A RESCUER: DON'T!

We all like to feel useful. Some extend this to a desire to feel needed. It's nice to feel useful, competent, and helpful. But when a line gets crossed and we move toward *taking responsibility* for other people, particularly for another adult's feelings, attitudes, needs, or behaviours, we enter the world of the rescuer, where only certain grown-ups have to assume adult responsibilities while others get coddled, condescended to, infantilized, or absolved of task and duty.

Every captain must chart her own course, every sailor must sail his own race: in case I've been unclear in any other part of this book, let me state here again, unequivocally and for the record that *we all need to take responsibility for our own feelings, attitudes, needs, and behaviours,* and we need to disabuse ourselves of the notion that we are responsible for anyone else's feelings, attitudes, needs, or behaviours. The rescuer chooses to ignore this truth, and in so doing does more to harm than help the mature development of a relationship.

Two really destructive things happen when there is a rescuer in a relationship: one person assumes responsibility for things they can't control and another person gives up responsibility for things they personally have to own. Sadly, what happens is that two people create a tacit agreement concerning behaviour and responsibility that can never succeed.

On our best days, we have *influence* over other people, but we never have *control*. For example, in my professional capacity, I have been helping people solve their problems for two decades. I have trained for this, been exposed to the best ideas on how this might be accomplished, and have had years of experience learning what works well and not so well. Even with this background, experience, and success in helping others to shape their lives positively, I have no illusions about the degree of *control* I have over others: the people who seek my assistance will choose to use my advice or they won't, and that's as far as my degree of control ever goes. What's more, that's as far as it ought to go. As a psychologist, it is never my job or duty to solve someone else's problem or tell them what they should or shouldn't do. Rather, my job is to offer support, ideas, and opinion, all in service of providing my client with the widest range of possible positive options. But of course, at the end of the process, the only person who actually makes a change or tries something different is my client, not me.

The rescuer, however, believes otherwise. The rescuer has the pride that allows them to believe they know what is right for someone else, the illusion of a sense of control, and, sadly, the sense of shame, guilt, and remorse when their Sisyphean task fails to produce the desired outcome.

Rescuing also violates one of the most basic tenets of pre-marital wisdom, and one that has been noted a number of times throughout this book. If you believe that some fundamental aspect of a partner needs to change for your relationship to be healthy, happy, and successful, you're not ready to get married. If you are operating under the illusion that getting married will cause that fundamental change to come about, again, you are indulging in fantasy. People change because they want to and decide they are capable, not because of a partner, a marriage, or any other external source of motivation. Any thinking that resembles, "Once we get married, I'll get that problem of his all straightened out," or "When we're married, she'll be spending more time with me and consequently _____ won't be a problem anymore," needs to be seriously re-examined. Marriage itself doesn't cause people to stop smoking or give up destructive drinking or gambling. Marriage doesn't make people want to upgrade their education, give up other toxic relationships, or resolve longstanding issues with family members. Marriage doesn't cause people to exercise regularly, adopt a healthier diet, or start sorting their recyclable paper and plastic.

I'm not suggesting that the only people who should ever get married are those with no vices, weaknesses, or shortcomings. If that were the case, marriage would be this small, exclusive, Mensa-like club. My point, and I've made it before, is that your belief that a partner could benefit from some kind of substantial change is unlikely to be shared by your partner, and further, that you, as a function of getting married, will be the successful instrument of that change is extremely unlikely.

As a function of socialization both genders come to be rescuers for different reasons. Women are taught to be caring and nurturing, and rescuing is naturally seen as a point just a little bit farther along the supposed "being a good woman" continuum. Men are taught to be leaders and to be decisive, and thus for men rescuing is about assuming control, being superior, and being in charge. Both genders can be forgiven if they fail to recognize that there are times when being nurturing means letting someone make their own mistakes and being a good leader involves allowing others to assume a higher degree of personal responsibility.

If your partner needs some type of assistance with a mental health issue, a substance abuse problem, a financial difficulty, or some other substantial challenge and you think you're doing them a favour by stepping in and trying to solve their problem for them, I suggest you rethink this. As adults, we all need to figure out how to solve our own dilemmas, as difficult as that might be. These issues all have potential solutions, and claims that it's too frightening, threatening, inconvenient, embarrassing, or costly to get on with fixing the problem are all excuses and subterfuge. Any expectations that these issues don't have to be dealt with and consequently must be accepted or tolerated by a partner are ill informed. As I've said before, the primary challenge of the human condition is to seek out and recognize both our strengths and weaknesses and to have the courage and discipline to deal with both. This means that we attempt equally to be all that we can be and to fix, alter, or repair the things we see as personal liabilities. Rescuing often has the unfortunate result of delaying when an adult assumes their own personal responsibilities. Rescuing also fosters an immature sense of dependency. You get married to have an equal partner to spend your life with, not to become a parent to another adult or to have another adult become a parent to you. Sometimes people have individual work to do with a psychologist to understand and meet this challenge before they are ready to be in a relationship.

Younger adults seem to have the biggest problem with stepping away from assuming responsibility for the problems of others. Countless times in my office, when a young person has described how tied up in knots they are about someone else's problem, and I make the observation that in reality the problem belongs to the other person, I'm told how mean or unfeeling I'm being. Similarly, when I offer examples of how to say things frankly and candidly, I'm told, "Yes, that's really what I would like to say, but I could just never be so mean."

Mean is saying something hurtful for no other purpose than to hurt. Mean is being undependable and breaking promises. Being honest isn't mean, being an adult isn't mean, and being clear about personal responsibilities and guarding against others trying to displace their responsibilities onto you isn't being mean either.

As far as the ten conversations go, I'll suggest you give up any illusions you might have about assuming responsibility for your partner's challenges. You're there to help, support, and love, but not to rescue.

ALWAYS BEING RIGHT AND THE HARD OF HEARING

We don't need to waste much space making the case that no one is right all the time. None of the smart people I have had the pleasure to know have ever claimed to always be right, and I have yet to hear of a Nobel Prize winner or respected leader of a modern nation claim never to have made a mistake. Infallibility is an illusion and a mark of immaturity. Always being right actually violates Rule 8 of the communication rules in that it demands the use of an absolute. Nobody likes to be wrong, but this is different than always having to be right. Wanting to be right is natural, but *having to be right* speaks to deep insecurities that are best addressed with a good psychologist. If you're the person who always has to be right, grow up or get help. If you're the person thinking about marrying the person who always has to be right, don't, as they are not ready for a mature, lasting relationship.

With that gratuitous point being made, let's move on to something a little more useful. From a communication perspective, the more common problem is less about someone always being right and more about one person in a partnership not feeling that they're being heard. Not being heard can be the result of a number of issues stemming from either the speaker or the listener, including a failure of personal assertion, poor communication skills, bullying, indifference, fear of losing status or authority, and a variety of other issues too numerous to get into here. However, the point is if you or your partner are not feeling heard because one of you is always winning the argument, getting their way, or talking the other person out of what they want, serious problems are likely to develop.

Reframing the problem is an effective way to ensure that both parties feel heard. So often, couples come into conflict not about the specifics of an issue, but because one or the other feels they have no say in how choices are made or decisions are reached. Reframing the issue with a focus on feelings rather than on facts (Rule 1) can alleviate issues that arise from someone always being right or someone feeling as though they are seldom heard in the relationship.

Reframing means that in conflict situations, a specific effort is made by both parties to refocus the discussion on how each person *feels* about the issue in question, rather than the facts of the issue. Of course, this is not to minimize the need for hard data or reliable information. Rather, this is an expansion of the communication process to make sure that how both people feel about the issue is specifically and methodically taken into consideration as the discussion or decision process unfolds.

To illustrate the process, imagine a physician telling her patient he has two months to live but then leaving no opportunity for him to express his profound fear and anger. The expression and feeling part of this communication will have absolutely no influence on his fatal prognosis, yet we understand instinctively how profoundly lost and hurt someone would feel if denied an opportunity to express their thoughts and feelings. In this imagined circumstance, even though the physician is most probably more informed as far as this medical issue is concerned, the patient continues to have a much bigger stake in what choices are made and how they are implemented. Leaving his thoughts and feelings out of this process would be an obvious error and a missed opportunity for a more humane communication to occur.

Essentially, all we have here is a very specific application of the strength and value of Rule 1, "Focus on feelings, not facts." A focus on facts rather than feelings often puts results in the "winning the battle but losing the war" category. If you want to win both the heart and mind of your partner, you'd better be listening to both.

JEALOUSY

Jealousy is almost always about the person feeling jealous, not their partner. The good news is that if you are the jealous person, it is within your control (and not your partner's) to manage this unpleasant feeling. The bad news is that combatting jealousy means changing how you think about yourself, and this is often a significant and complicated challenge.

Contrary to popular belief, jealousy is actually about personal doubts and insecurities, not the actions of someone else. We feel jealous when we believe we are not being treated the way we deserve. This might be because we are not being given our due, are not being treated with respect, or are being denied something to which we believe we are rightfully entitled to. Most germane to our purposes here, however, is the jealousy that arises as a function of possessiveness for a partner and the fear that we might lose that partner to somebody else.

Let's establish a few basic principles of human interaction. Being in a relationship doesn't mean you own your partner or have the right to tell your partner what to do. Possessiveness can be a very dangerous trait—be wary of it. If you actually want or need to control others, start a business or join the military, as you're likely to have more success in these venues as far as controlling others is concerned. If you need to be in control of your lifelong romantic partner, however, you're not ready to be in a serious adult relationship. And if your partner needs to control you, don't marry them until they get that need worked out of their system.

A relationship is a mutual commitment to care for and trust one another. To the extent that either or both of these characteristics are missing, the viability of the relationship can reasonably be called into question. To be in a relationship, you have to decide how much you feel you can trust the person you're with. If you are unable to trust them, if your doubts about betrayal and your anxiety about being cheated on prevent you from flourishing in your relationship, you need to either attack your doubts and worries or leave the relationship. Every relationship is a gamble, and nothing can guarantee fidelity or loyalty. However, you increase the chances of both through informed up-front choices (i.e., the entire purpose of this book) as well as regular relationship maintenance (i.e., see the fifteen rules of good communication).

As a psychologist, I dearly wish that, by simply telling people to improve their sense of self-worth and by mounting an attack on doubts, worries, and anxieties, clients could accomplish the same. Unfortunately, it's never that simple. Feeling strong and confident about *yourself* is the answer to damaging jealous thoughts and, again unfortunately, there is no quick or easy way to immediately and permanently improve self-esteem. If you find that you are "the jealous type," spending some time with a good psychologist might be a good idea.

Trust me: if there were some really successful, proven self-help methods of getting past the personal insecurity that is always at the root of jealousy, I would offer it to you! For our purposes here, however, it is important to understand that feeling jealous about your partner leaves you with only four alternatives: do nothing and let your jealous feelings damage the relationship and potentially drive your partner away (poor choice); learn to swallow your uncomfortable feelings and pretend they're not there (poor choice); leave the relationship (likely to be a poor choice); or get rid of the jealousy you feel through professional assistance (a much better choice).

Breaking the Rules and Other Signs of Trouble

"Learnin' to talk good" or more correctly, *developing an efficient and emotionally sophisticated way of expressing needs while simultaneously attending to the needs and emotions of others*, can take a bit of time and practice. As the two of you make your way through *The 10 Conversations*, it will be important to cut each other some slack in terms of how closely you both attend to all the communication rules.

That being said, the more closely you both attend to them, the sooner you will see substantial improvements in the clarity and efficiency of what you two talk about. And, as an added bonus, you will find that you fight less but also, when you do, those fights will be over more quickly. In evaluating how well (or poorly) the two of you are doing, ignoring when someone breaks some of the fifteen rules of good communication is poor practice. In fact, you could even consider adherence to the communication rules as a measure of commitment to building a better relationship.

There are lots of ways to break the communication rules, but listed below are some of the more obvious signs of trouble. These particular communication faux pas need to be identified and modified immediately.

• Someone telling YOU what YOUR feelings are or ought to be.

• Someone making statements akin to, "You know what YOUR problem is?"

• Someone saying or acting as if THEIR feelings have greater legitimacy than yours.

• Someone lying.

• As mentioned above, someone who always needs to be right.

When someone consistently breaks or refuses to follow the fifteen rules of good communication, it can fairly be asked, "Do they really want to improve the relationship?" Is their inability to follow the rules simply about lack of experience with a new and challenging set of communication skills, or do they have another agenda? Is their lack of improvement in communication technique about inadequate discipline, or would it be more accurate to question their general level of enthusiasm for the relationship? When someone consistently breaks agreed-upon rules of communication, perhaps that person just wants out of the relationship but doesn't want to take responsibility for saying as much. Although profoundly hurtful, some choose this dishonest approach to relationship management rather than one that is frank and candid.

Another early warning sign of trouble in a relationship is when you are working harder to maintain the relationship than is your partner. If you find that you're doing ninety percent rather than fifty percent of the work to build a happy and healthy relationship, a toxic set of expectations is being created. Similarly, when the behaviour doesn't match the words, there could be trouble on the horizon. When there is little follow-through on commitments or promises, it is fair to ask if this person is ready to make a long-term commitment to another person. And finally, be wary of the "apologizer," those individuals who feel that repeated, over-the-top apologies are sufficient recompense for inappropriate behaviours and broken commitments.

PROFESSIONAL ASSISTANCE

Forgive the shameless promotion of my profession, but there's a large group of people out there who are already familiar with much of what's been described in this book. They've had years of specialized training and are experts in the areas of human relationships, individual needs, positive assertion, empathy, and communication. They have PhDs, which means that after high school they completed an undergraduate degree, followed by at least one and likely two graduate degrees. Typically, this totals somewhere between seven and twenty (!) years of formal university education before they were then allowed to go and work in a hospital or some other setting where people need help sorting out their feelings. This level of education, training, and experience suggests they had to know a thing or two before they were then given permission to complete a series of written and oral exams to prove to other experts that in fact they actually know how to help people. Only when they'd completed all these steps could they call themselves psychologists. Psychologists will always be happy to explain their training and licensing requirements to you, and typically we make sure that we display our credentials for our clients to scrutinize. Psychologists also have licensing and certifying bodies, as well as professional colleges, and these organizations ensure that all members maintain professional standards when they deliver psychological services.

Psychologists, by both inclination and experience, are out there waiting to help the two of you build the life you desire. They know how to listen, they know the useful questions to ask, and on any given day they have only about a thousand different ideas as to how to help make your relationship all you want it to be. Generally, when it comes to premarital therapy, our job is to help a couple determine for themselves where their strengths and weaknesses might be and what courses of action they could take to make desired changes. As specialists in the human mind and personality, we can also identify personality characteristics and mental health issues that might have positive or negative impacts on a relationship.

Just to be clear, many of the people who see a psychologist don't have a diagnosable "mental illness" like clinical depression or a personality disorder (although not a few do, and we offer a lot of excellent help in these areas as well). Rather, many of our clients are simply dealing with everyday challenges, like figuring out how solid a relationship is or how suited to marriage a couple might be. And getting help and advice from someone who has "seen it all," so to speak, and helped hundreds, or even thousands of others with similar issues can be a really efficient use of time and money.

If the two of you are finding that you're not making the progress you want in terms of your communication styles, or perhaps there is a particular issue(s) within *The 10 Conversations* where you can't seem to find common ground, make an appointment with a psychologist to get help.[54] Bring this book with you so you can show them the areas where you have made progress, as well as the areas where you're having trouble.

Final Thoughts on Troubleshooting

Throughout *The 10 Conversations*, I've made the point that *courage and discipline* are two of the key components of making a life together. Both of these are difficult traits to master, but they're well worth the effort, particularly as they apply to all of life's challenges, not just to marriage. Having the courage and discipline to face sad realities with the same aplomb as we face challenges is a necessary part of the maturation process. Learning that you are incompatible is not the end of the world. If such a reality seems to be emerging, better to face it now than years down the road, when you potentially might have a mortgage and children. Painful truths are better than soothing lies, but not everyone has the courage and discipline to honestly face some of life's harder truths.

On the other hand, and as I said at the beginning of the book, the content here is stuff that ought to be put in the water, and if you've reached this point, you've had a good long drink of the elixir of healthy relationship. Regardless of the status of your current relationship, you have now exposed yourself to both the issues and the process that anyone in contemporary Western culture needs to know and undertake if happy, successful, sustaining, and mutually beneficial marriage is going to be part of their future. Trust in what you now know, and feel confident in using what you have learned. Be honest, work hard, and have fun!

---

[54] Not every psychologist deals with premarital or marital issues, in the same way that not every physician is a specialist in infectious diseases and not every mechanic fixes jet airplanes. Usually, psychologists describe their areas of expertise in their ads in the telephone directory or on their websites. However, you can always simply ask them about the type of work they do when you call to inquire about an appointment. And, by the way, you typically don't need a referral from another medical professional to see a psychologist.

FEEDBACK

Think there's room for another important issue in *The 10 Conversations?* Found a particular conversation useful or problematic? Have a specific example that might be useful to others in a future edition? Please let me know! Contact me through my website, **www.drguy.ca.**

FILMOGRAPHY

MOVIES TO SPARK CONVERSATIONS

In case you missed them, here's a recap of the recommendations for movies designed to spark further discussions about each of the ten conversations.

1. Having Kids: *Parenthood* (1989, Steve Martin, Mary Steenburgen)
2. Careers: *Disclosure* (1994, Michael Douglas, Demi Moore)
3. Financial Styles: *Trading Places* (1983, Dan Aykroyd, Eddie Murphy)
4. Sex: *American Pie* (1999, Jason Biggs, Chris Klein)
5. Family: *Fiddler on the Roof* (1971, Topol, Norma Crane)
6. Location: *House of Sand and Fog* (2003, Jennifer Connelly, Ben Kingsley)
7. Division of Labour: *A League of Their Own* (1992, Tom Hanks, Geena Davis)
8. Leisure: *Fever Pitch* (2005, Drew Barrymore, Jimmy Fallon)
9. Spirituality: *Dogma* (1999, Ben Affleck, Matt Damon)
10. (W)rapping Things Up: You each pick your all-time favourite movie

Acknowledgements

I'D LIKE TO THANK MY MOTHER for all her love, interest, kindness, and support, and my father for his enthusiasm and encouragement.

I want to express my gratitude to Lake Muskoka for being such a peaceful and contemplative place, and my parents again for their insight thirty years ago to acquire our particular parcel of windswept rock and tree. I'd also like to thank Celestial Seasoning for Madagascar Vanilla Red Rooibos tea, Bruce Cockburn for *Speechless* (2005), and the discerning individuals who conceived, designed, and brought to fruition the Reading Garden of The Central London Library in London, Ontario, Canada.

I'm very grateful to my agent Linda McKnight, who ushered me through this, my first foray into mainstream publishing. I'd also like to thank Jordan Fenn and Janie Yoon and the team they assembled at Key Porter, all of whom contributed to make this project come to a successful conclusion.

I'd like to thank the spectacular mentors I've have had over the years, particularly Sandi Byers and Bill Fisher. The innumerable ways I have benefited from your wisdom and generosity constantly astonish me.

Many friends and colleagues sat and listened to my endless machinations about the production of this book, and they all deserve my thanks. In particular, Bob and Barb Sandford, Dr.

Christine Rattenbury, and my longtime friends Kevin and Connie Workman all had their ears bent to the point of breaking, and I heretofore take responsibility for any rehabilitation that might be required as a function of their kindness and patience.

I'd like to thank my students and particularly my patients for their bravery and for their willingness to teach me so much.

I'd particularly like to thank my boys, Mitchell and Kenny, for hanging in there while Dad was busy on the weekends writing and too tired in the evening to find more quality time. Specifically, Kenny, thanks for the foot rubs, and Mitch, thanks for solving all our technical problems when I wasn't around.

Most of all, I'd like to thank my wife, Jennie, for bearing the burden of career, home, and family while I attended to the demands of patients, teaching, speaking, and writing. Why don't we take a cruise? I love you.

Index

ABOUT THE AUTHOR

DR. GUY GRENIER is a clinical and counselling psychologist, and has offered service as a psychologist, marital therapist, and sex therapist and educator for over twenty years. He is an Adjunct Professor at the University of Western Ontario and when time allows he teaches Human Sexuality and guest lectures. He has published a number of research articles in scholarly journals and for four years wrote a popular weekly column that appeared in *London This Week*. He lives in London, Ontario, with his wife and two sons.